W9-ADD-069

THE UNITED STATES AND PAKISTAN

STUDIES OF INFLUENCE IN
INTERNATIONAL RELATIONS

Alvin Z. Rubinstein, General Editor

THE UNITED STATES AND PAKISTAN

THE EVOLUTION OF AN INFLUENCE RELATIONSHIP

SHIRIN TAHIR-KHELI

PRAEGER

PRAEGER SPECIAL STUDIES • PRAEGER SCIENTIFIC

Library of Congress Cataloging in Publication Data

Shirin Tahir-Kheli.
  The United States and Pakistan.

  (Studies of influence in international
relations)
  Bibliography: p.
  Includes index.
  1. United States—Foreign relations—
Pakistan. 2. Pakistan—Foreign relations—
United States. I. Title. II. Series.
E183.8.P18S5   327.730549   81-21160
ISBN 0-03-050471-6   AACR2
ISBN 0-03-061663-8 (pbk.)

Published in 1982 by Praeger Publishers
CBS Educational and Professional Publishing
Division of CBS Inc.
521 Fifth Avenue, New York, New York 10175 U.S.A.

3456789   052   98765432

Printed in the United States of America

095501

To Raza

EDITOR'S PREFACE

A perhaps apocryphal curse generally attributed to the Chinese says, "May you live in the most interesting of times." Few relationships in the post-World War II period have experienced such wild fluctuations from friendship and alliance to recrimination and alienation as that of the United States and Pakistan. As we move into the 1980s, each has reason to explore anew the possibility of cooperation; but each is keenly mindful of the serious dilemmas and pitfalls that impede the reestablishment of trust or meaningful ties. For Washington and Islamabad the decade ahead will indeed be an interesting time.

The sweep of revolutionary developments has overtaken the badly battered U.S.-Pakistani relationship and brought about a convergence of concerns: the fear that the upheaval in Iran will spread to the Arabian Peninsula and threaten the flow of oil to heavily dependent non-communist consumers and, with it, Pakistan's security; the perceived threat from Soviet intriguing now that Soviet military forces have moved south of the Hindu Kush mountains to the Khyber Pass and the Pakistani border; and the desire to ensure the survival of Pakistan as a nation-state. At stake is regional stability in an area of vital importance. Yet, notwithstanding the external threats to their mutual interests, Washington and Islamabad have found cooperation surprisingly difficult.

It was not always so.

The Cold War had brought the two countries together. The United States, seeking to extend its military containment of the Soviet Union, had obtained a military base at Peshawar. Pakistan, ostensibly seeking to strengthen itself against a possible Soviet attack, had received large quantities of weapons it intended to use for defense against India—its main enemy— and for its struggle to gain control over the disputed territory of Kashmir. Between 1953 and 1979, Pakistan also benefited handsomely from the approximately 5.7 billion dollars in U.S. economic and military aid. But an asymmetry of motives and objectives plagued the relationship. The United States and Pakistan were unable to agree on the main enemy or on the steps needed to consolidate their friendship; and domestic considerations changed their attitude toward each other.

The disenchantment of Pakistan's foreign policy elite with the United States set in early in the 1960s. Not only was the Pakistani elite's obsessive preoccupation with India regarded unsympathetically in Washington, but with the development of ICBMs, Polaris submarines, and intelligence-gathering satellites in outer space, America's interest in the air facilities in Pakistan waned. When the Sino-Indian border war of October 1962 broke out and the United States rushed military assistance to India, an irate Pakistan began to flirt with China and, to a lesser degree, with the USSR. When Washington clamped an embargo on all arms and spare parts to Pakistan during the Indo-Pakistani war in September 1965 (the embargo also applied to India, which, however, relied mainly on British equipment and thus benefited from Washington's "even-handedness"), the U.S.–Pakistani relationship reached the point of no return. To Pakistan, the United States had become a capricious and unreliable ally. And as the United States pursued détente with the Soviet Union in the early 1970s and directed its attention from South Asia to the Middle East and Africa, the U.S.-Pakistani relationship withered. Once a key member of the United States' network of containment, Pakistan became odd country out.

India's rise to military preeminence on the subcontinent heightened Pakistan's insecurity; their neighbor's detonation of a nuclear explosion in May 1974 intensified the perception of Pakistani leaders that they, too, had to go nuclear, a development that complicates U.S.-Pakistani relations because the United States is strongly opposed to Third World countries crossing the nuclear weapons threshold. Washington appreciates the importance of Pakistani real estate as a buffer against the USSR's expansion to the Arabian Sea and Indian Ocean, but it views uneasily Islamabad's apparent determination, irrespective of the kind of leadership in control at any given time, to acquire a nuclear capability.

All geo-strategic assessments were thrown into turmoil at the end of the 1970s by the suddenly altered conditions in Iran and Afghanistan and by Moscow's growing military intervention in the region. These prompted searching policy reviews in Washington and Islamabad, as both capitals groped for a way of redefining and resuming their former friendship and of promoting their complementary but not necessarily common security goals. But the quest for cooperation is hampered by the divergent priorities and perceptions of threat held by the political-military elites in each country, and any major improvement in relations seems very problematical. For example, the two disagree on how best to respond to the Soviet occupation of Afghanistan and the Soviet military build-up of India. In a word, the roots of discord are deep and make the fruit of cooperation hard to imagine.

Professor Shirin Tahir-Kheli brings a unique background to the study of the U.S.-Pakistani influence relationship. Raised in Pakistan and intimately acquainted in a way that few Western specialists are with the principal political, military, and scientific figures who shaped Pakistan's foreign policy in the 1960s and 1970s, she received her university education in the United States, her adopted country. She knows the political cultures, styles of decision making, and domestic contexts of both countries, and is thus well equipped to assess the actual impact that one side has had on the other, to illumine the perceptions and motivations that impel policies in the two countries, and to identify and analyze the influence that each party has had on the specific and salient problems that have dominated their relationship. Her analysis bridges two very different perceptual and political worlds as few studies of U.S.-Pakistani relations have.

In a study rich in new material and insights, the chapters on the arms relationship and on Pakistan's possible nuclear option command particular attention. They provide us with a basis for better understanding the difficulties that face U.S. and Pakistani leaders trying to repair their relationship; and they add greatly to our understanding of bureaucratic politics in both countries. There are difficult problems and no easy solutions, as Dr. Tahir-Kheli indicates as she guides us through the policy thicket in which a superpower and a Third World country try to influence each other on issues of vital national interest. Her analysis is a timely addition to the series, *Studies of Influence in International Relations*.

Alvin Z. Rubinstein
Bryn Mawr, Pa.

INTRODUCTION

On December 25, 1979, Soviet forces invaded Afghanistan. This action swept away years of U.S. apathy toward Pakistan. One of President Carter's first moves to deal with the situation was his offer of economic and military aid to Pakistan, which Washington presumed would be greatly welcomed in Islamabad. General Zia, however, turned down the $400 million offer, calling it "peanuts." Even more distressing for President Carter was Pakistani wariness toward the reëstablishment of a closely coördinated response. Pakistan, once considered to be the United States' "most allied ally," clearly no longer felt free to embrace openly its long-time friend and one-time benefactor.

How did U.S.-Pakistani relations come to such an impasse? Years of misunderstanding over goals as reflected in the non-proliferation and human rights policies of the Carter administration had done their work. Pakistani desires for greater U.S. assistance—a fairly constant theme in their relations—had found no real response between 1976 and 1980. Pakistani claims of increased Soviet-intervention in Afghanistan after the April 1978 communist takeover and the importance of this development for Pakistan and oil-rich Southwest Asia had fallen on deaf ears. That it took an invasion by 80,000 Soviet troops in Afghanistan before U.S. policymakers suddenly discovered "the threat" raised serious questions in Islamabad regarding both U.S. policymaking process and its policymakers.

The frenzied activity leading to the U.S. offer of aid and Pakistan's rejection of it mirrored the difficulty that has beset other countries in similar positions in the pursuit of international relations: how does a small, weak state, with regional concerns, in an alliance with a large, powerful state having international goals, operate with any range of freedom, and indeed, attempt to maximize its influence?

This study attempts to look at the above problem and illustrate the answer in the case of one such relationship—that of the U.S. and Pakistan. In examining who influenced whom, when, and why, it focuses on the events of the 1970s, although earlier events are briefly analyzed as they provide the backdrop against which later events are assessed. Despite expectations of simpler and smoother relations in less dramatic times, it is nowhere evident that the U.S.-Pakistani relationship was ever smooth sailing.

The course of the relationship between the two countries will be charted to illustrate who influenced whom in certain key areas. Particular attention will be devoted to the dynamics of this fluid U.S.-Pakistani influence relationship. It will be hoped that this approach will lay to rest some of the myths about the nature of influence, and will contribute to greater understanding of the nature of relationships between a superpower and a Third World state in the evolving international system.

A word here with regard to the nature of influence before we proceed to its underlying assumptions and definition. The term "influence" may imply somewhat different things to different people but it is always indicative of power and control for the influencer and dependence (even if it is only temporary) for the influenced. Yet, influence—which may indeed contain elements of power, control, and dependence—is distinctly different from all three and implies something more subtle and therefore more difficult to assess. For example, if power corresponded to influence, we would find that the United States or the Soviet Union would automatically be able to pursue their interests in third states by influencing the latter's policies. If control were influence, then it would exist in perpetuity, because the nation under control—a much stronger concept than influence—would have no option permitting a change. Instead, influence is a more reciprocal and more multi-dimensional concept than control. It is also in today's world more representative of the relationships between nations. Influence may imply dependence but whether or not it actually exists has to be determined in each sample relationship.

Influence is also distinct from force and the physical imposition of will.[1] Where force is involved, influence becomes unnecessary. The nature of influence lies in the diplomatic realm; it is the ability to enhance one's interest in another country so that one does not have to resort to the use of force to carry out one's objectives. It implies the use of different types of instrumentalities, e.g., economic, political, and military. It is an interactive process whereby the results of the exchange accomplish goals making the resort to stronger measures, even if available, unnecessary.

This study draws on some of the assumptions built into a detailed examination of the problem elsewhere.[2] Alvin Z. Rubinstein alerts us to a number of factors: first, that every nation engages in the pursuit of influence, and that a sample relationship (in this case one between a Western superpower and its small Asian ally) can be used as a case study to test various myths that have persisted about the nature and exercise of influence. Second, influence can be assessed through changes in behavior in which the developing country is the target. (Here, U.S. influence will be sought primarily in Pakistan.) Third, the domestic determinants of foreign policy are the underlying bases for analyses. Fourth, influence can be identified through the study of a few key issues. Fifth, there are limits beyond which the stronger power (here the United States) will not push the weaker (here Pakistan) because to do so would undermine the latter's existence—(in this case, certainly not a goal of U.S. policy). On the other hand, Pakistani leaders will not give in to U.S. influence-building attempts and pressures if to do so would undermine their political control. Finally, influence relationships never remain constant, and this study of the U.S.-Pakistani interaction will highlight the shifts and nuances.

The working definition of influence used in this study is the following one, taken from Rubinstein: "influence is manifested when A (in this case the United States) affects, through non-military means, directly or indirectly, the behavior of B (Pakistan's leaders) so that it redounds to the policy advantage of A."[3] We are incorporating into this definition not only the term influence as A getting B to do something B would otherwise not do, but also the broader term implying influence as presence, policy reinforcement, prestige-building; in short, influence is whatever is perceived by A as redounding to its policy advantage.

Some of the specific questions to be raised in this study dealing with the U.S.-Pakistani relationship are as follows. First, is influence *institutionalized?* Here it will be important to examine if the United States and Pakistan have had the capacity to influence the behavior of each other through institutional channels or have they basically acted through key individuals at certain times. The commonly held belief that the United States enjoys influence with "the Pakistani military" has to be tested just as does the theory that the "pro-Pakistani" proclivities of a Richard Nixon or a Henry Kissinger determined U.S. policy. Second, is influence *issue-specific?* Influence is issue-specific when it is of a short duration and is directed toward a limited objective. For example, was the American lifting of the arms embargo the result of direct Pakistani and indirect Saudi influence geared up for this purpose only? Third, is the exercise of influence *incremental?* That is, has U.S. and/or Pakistani influence increased in small amounts based on a series of attempts toward the same, or was there a reasonable amount accruing from a single action with sufficient residual influence to tide the country over through periods when there was no deliberate influence input? For example, did United States' military/economic aid to Pakistan give it influence for a long period or was U.S. influence in Pakistan dependent on a number of aid agreements, increasing proportionately with each new deal? Finally, is influence *interactive?* Has the U.S.-Pakistani influence relationship involved any feedback from the influence attempt of one or the other? It is reasonable to expect that there is interaction between the policy goal that results from successful attempt and the overall objectives of the influencing nation. However, it must be kept in mind that while interaction may bring receptivity, it does not necessarily, of itself, bring influence.

There are additional assumptions which underlie this study. First, there is a difference between joint interests and influence, because what may seem to be the latter may simply turn out to be a case of the former. Discussions of U.S.-Pakistani relations with officials in both countries give the impression that U.S. influence in Pakistan was high in the mid-1950s because they shared joint interests at that time. They cite Pakistani insensitivity to the adverse reactions of much of the Muslim world to Pakistan's entry in the U.S.-sponsored military pacts as indicative of United States' influence. However, in recent months, particularly after the Soviet invasion of Afghanistan, it has become fashionable to cite the opposite, especially as the Pakistani government wanted to change the 1959 Executive Agreement to a formal treaty with the United States. Washington then found that, from the onset, the relationship with Pakistan was based on a false premise and differing perceptions of the nature of "the threat," i.e., for the United States it was the Soviet Union and China; Pakistan, on the other hand, always felt India to be the primary threat.

A second assumption that will be tested in this study deals with the fact that access does not equal influence. While access may be a necessary prelude to influence, it does not itself constitute influence. Notions of U.S. influence in Pakistan have been vastly exaggerated in political and scholarly circles because of the great access its citizens have enjoyed to Pakistani society and its elite. Similarly, while the openness and hospitality of Pakistan did win a few crucial friends in the United States, e.g., Richard Nixon, it did not necessarily add up to Pakistani influence over American policy at a level commensurate with their access.

Third, influence is a relative term, particularly as it applies to U.S.-Pakistani relations. India has loomed large in the calculations of both nations as their bilateral relationship has never managed to separate itself from the regional or international policies of each. Similarly, the present inability of the Pakistani government to subscribe wholeheartedly to U.S. policies in the changing balance in Southwest Asia is largely due to the newly important place Pakistan has acquired in the Islamic world.

Fourth, the problem of spill-over or linkage exists in the pursuit and exercise of influence. Does influence in one aspect of the relationship lead to influence in another? The U.S.-Pakistani relationship has to be examined before any such conclusion can be reached. Fortunately, interaction between these countries has taken place on several fronts (e.g., economic, diplomatic, military), thereby providing data on which to base these judgements.

Fifth, there is asymmetry in the influence relationship and it is not always in favor of the more powerful country. The intertwining nature of dependence today restrains the use of power and permits a range of options for the weaker state. Pakistan has managed to operate within this range even though its post-1971 years have been ones of relative weakness vis-à-vis the United States.

Finally, this study assumes that there is a need to distinguish between the pursuit of broad policy goals and the specific actions and options that are at the heart of government–to–government relationships where it may be more difficult to exercise influence over the target state because issues involving vital interests may be at stake. There is a reasonable data-base in terms of availability and range with which one may study the U.S.-Pakistani influence relationship. However, this compounds problems of distillation to only that information really relevant to the study of influence. Scholars have categorized different types of data into useful clusters—for example: " . . . measures of direct interactions; measures of perceptual and attitudinal change; measures of attributed influence; case studies and impressionistic and idiosyncratic commentary"—but find shortcomings within each category.[4] We will focus on such things as diplomatic exchanges; aid flows; joint communiqués; and impressions of key individuals, all being necessary in examining and evaluating the record.

Records of this exchange of high-level visits provide a useful tool with which to gauge influence. When these visits have been at the head-of-state level, Pakistan has set great stock by them as an index of American commitment. In the Pakistani context, the communiqués issued after these visits have acquired a special importance that may not be universally applicable. In this case, they have been perceived by the Pakistani elite as signalling U.S. policy not only to Pakistan but also to India and the Soviet Union.

Attention to scholarly writings on U.S.-Pakistani relations would, under normal circumstances, be important in gauging the interaction levels between these two countries. However, while there is no dearth of studies on Pakistan, they are generally uneven in focus, and more importantly, they lack any deep understanding of the cultural milieu in which decisions in Pakistan are made. In particular, attitudinal studies of the Pakistani elite by U.S. scholars often display an abysmal poverty of knowledge concerning the background within which the decision maker operates.[5] This difficulty is hopelessly compounded when the very basis of the analysis is not first-hand data (such as is acquired through the cultivation of individuals who actually participated in the relevant decisions) but rather second- and third-hand hearsay. This fact is, indeed, not challenged in some of the relevant studies by Western scholars. For example, we have it from Robert LaPorte that: . . . "since the indirect means of interviewing American nationals had to be used . . . it was impossible to secure interviews with a systematic sample of Pakistan government and private sector leaders ... the testing of these [i.e., his] findings remains incomplete."[6]

In contrast, the work presented here is a distillation of approximately ten years of effort during which key members of the Pakistani armed forces, the civil and foreign service bureaucracies, and, indeed, the political elite (both "in office" and "in the opposition") were interviewed. Many of these people were either known personally to me or to close friends in Pakistan. This is an extensive network—and the process of interviewing was often extended to multiple visits (for cultural reasons it is often difficult to conduct sustained interview sessions). Also, whenever appropriate, interviews with people in power were followed up with interviews after they had lost that power (a detailed comparison of the different versions provided fascinating insights into how the system works).

To study the relationship from the U.S. perspective, a more standard format was followed. In addition to the examination of the relevant materials in the public domain, extensive interviews with officials of the State and Defense Departments and members of the White House staff were conducted over a period of approximately two years.

Additionally, other sources of information such as journalists and researchers in third countries, e.g., India and the United Kingdom, also provided useful information, as indeed did their counterparts in the United States and Pakistan. The final evaluation of the influence relationship, of course, requires careful examination of data from a variety of sources.

The study begins with a survey of U.S.-Pakistani relations in order to set the stage for the changes that followed. The focus is on post-1971 relations when a weaker Pakistan did not come under the United States influence umbrella but instead actively multiplied its options. Two key issues, namely, arms sales and nuclear policy, are examined in detail, since they provide the focal point of relations. The study ends with the Soviet invasion of Afghanistan, which renewed U.S. interest in Pakistan, and a look at the events of 1980–1982 as both nations tried to respond to the changed security picture in Southwest Asia.

The criteria used for identifying influence involved the following: First, isolation of concrete instances when Pakistan or the United States modified its position or behavior in a manner congenial to one or the other. Here influence could be inferred from the degree and frequency of modification. Second, access, i.e., the ability to carry out transactions. The rationale here was that while access may not lead to or equal influence, lack of access makes the acquisition and exercise of influence virtually impossible. Third, marked shifts in the commitments of resources were noted because they can reflect a change in the influence relationship. Fourth, consideration was given to the extent to which the strategic position of the United States or Pakistan improved from their influence relationship: i.e., the regional and global benefits, if any, that each derived from the relationship.

The following hypotheses, which are crucial for assessing who influenced whom, when and why, are to be tested in the U.S.-Pakistani relationship:

1. Increase in access leads to increase in influence.
2. The greater A's presence in B, the greater A's influence.
3. The greater B's economic dependence, the greater A's influence.
4. The greater A's aid to B, the greater A's influence.
5. Military aid is more effective than economic aid in providing A with influence over B.
6. The political use of economic aid diminishes over time.
7. The more sophisticated the weaponry sent to B, the greater the likelihood of A's influence.

Before commencing this study of the U.S.-Pakistani influence relationship, we would do well to take note of the frustration inherent in the remarks of former Secretary of State, Cyrus Vance:

> We would like beneficially to influence the affairs of people living in adverse circumstances all over the world but our power to do so is so goddam limited. We're beginning to understand that whatever influence we're going to exert . . . is going to have to be of a different kind . . . a lot wiser and more sophisticated.[7]

NOTES

1. Barry M. Blechman and Stephen S. Kaplan, eds., *Force Without War: U.S. Armed Forces as a Political Instrument*, Washington, D.C., The Brookings Institution, 1978, p. 13.
2. Alvin Z. Rubinstein, *Red Star on the Nile: The Soviet-Egyptian Influence Relationship Since the June War*, Princeton, N.J.: Princeton University Press, 1977, pp. xii–xiv.
3. *Ibid.*, p. xiv.
4. *Ibid.*
5. Robert LaPorte, *Power and Privilege: Influence and Decision-Making in Pakistan*, Berkeley: University of California Press, 1975, exemplifies this sort of oversimplification as it projects Pakistani decision makers through the eyes of untrained U.S. observers with varying degrees of exposure to the elites.
6. *Ibid.*, p. 9.
7. Quoted in *The New York Times*, April 30, 1980, editorial.

CONTENTS

EDITOR'S PREFACE   vii
INTRODUCTION   xi
   Notes   xvii
LIST OF ACRONYMS   xxi

1   THE U.S.–PAKISTANI RELATIONSHIP IN PERSPECTIVE: 1
    1947–1965
   Arms Assistance: Prize and Punishment   4
   Kashmir: The Litmus Test   12
   The 1965 Indo-Pakistani War   19
   Observations: The First Decade   24

2   BIRTH OF BANGLADESH   29
   The Grand Deception   31
   Mounting Crisis   35
   The Reaction   36
   The Indo-Soviet Treaty   38
   The Deluge: War and the "Tilt"   41
   Task Force 74: Influencing the Outcome   44
   Observations   47

3   BHUTTO AND BEYOND   53
   U.S. Support: Bhutto's Perceptions   54
   U.S. Arms and Pakistani Needs   57
   Bhutto and the Bomb: Confrontation With the United States   62
   The Islamic Connection   63
   The Fall of Bhutto and Charges of U.S. Involvement 66
   General Zia and U.S. Policy   72
   Observations   76

4   ARMS AND INFLUENCE   81
   The Road Back   82
   State Visits, Regional Pressures, and Arms   85
   1975-1976 Arms Sales: A Limited Promise   90
   The Arms Export Control Act: New Restraints   91
   Crisis in Afghanistan: A U.S. Shift?   97

The Reagan Administration's Aid Package   104
Observations   106

5 NUCLEAR POWER AND POLITICAL FALLOUT   115
The Pakistan Atomic Energy Commission   115
The Rationale   116
The Ayub Years   118
The Security Framework of a Changed Nuclear Policy   119
The Reprocessing Plant and U.S. Pressure Under Ford   123
Carter and Nuclear Policy: A Major Quarrel   127
Congressional Legislation and Restrictions   131
The Uranium Enrichment Plant: U.S. Response   133
Security Perceptions and the Utility of Nuclear Weapons   136
The Impact of Afghanistan on U.S. Nonproliferation Policy   138
Observations   143

6 THE EVOLUTION AND INTENSITY OF INFLUENCE   151
Nature of Alliance   151
How Do We Know?   152
The Unworking of Influence   154
Two Instances of U.S. Success   156
The Domestic Factor   157
Whither U.S.-Pakistan?   158

BIBLIOGRAPHY   163
INDEX   165
ABOUT THE AUTHOR   169

LIST OF ACRONYMS

ACDA	Arms Control and Disarmament Agency
AECB	Arms Export Control Board
AID	Agency for International Development
APC	Armored Personnel Carrier
CENTO	Central Treaty Organization
CIA	Central Intelligence Agency
DOD	Department of Defense
FLIR	Forward-Looking Infrared System
FMS	Foreign Military Sales
FSF	Federal Security Force
IAEA	International Atomic Energy Agency
IMET	International Military Education and Training Program
MAAG	Military Assistance Advisory Group
MAP	Military Assistance Program
MDA	Mutual Defense Agreement—first signed in October 1959
MDE	Major Defense Equipment
MLA	Martial Law Administration
NEA	Bureau of Near Eastern and South Asian Affairs
NPT	Non-Proliferation Treaty
NSC	National Security Council
PAEC	Pakistan Atomic Energy Commission
Pak	Pakistan
PNA	Pakistan National Alliance
PPP	Pakistan People's Party
PRC	People's Republic of China
RDF	Rapid Deployment Force
SEATO	South East Treaty Organization
US	United States of America
USIS	United States Information Service
USSR	Union of Soviet Socialist Republics
WSAG	Washington Special Action Group

THE U.S.–PAKISTANI RELATIONSHIP IN PERSPECTIVE: 1947–1965

The study of U.S. relations with Pakistan must begin with the earliest contacts between the two countries so that the framework for their interaction and evolving influence relationship can be established. This chapter examines the context of the relationship, its expectations and benefits, and the key issues that helped to establish the dynamics of who influenced whom.

Much like today, the importance of Pakistan to American policy-makers in the early 1950s derived from the fear of communism and a perceived threat of a shift in the global balance of power in favor of the Soviet Union and the People's Republic of China (PRC). Conditioned by Soviet moves in Iran, threats to Turkey and Greece, and the Berlin crisis, U.S. leaders embarked on a policy of containment. This policy actively sought to confine the communist contagion by establishing a "cordon sanitaire" around the periphery of the Soviet Union, the PRC, and Eastern Europe. The objective of this doctrine was not only to contain physically the Soviet and Chinese military expansion, but also to restrict their political and cultural intercourse with states outside their sphere of control lest the pestilence spread.

Pakistan's strategic location, on the boundary of both the USSR and the PRC, greatly commended itself to the United States for use in its containment policy. Indeed, Pakistan was seen as directly augmenting U.S. capability. The military might of Pakistan was taken to be "the measure of America's military power on that continent...."[1] Increase in Pakistan's military capability was seen as a natural corollary of the U.S. global power equation. Being a country in the right location at the right time, Pakistan thus emerged to have utility for U.S. policy. It was a marriage of convenience but one that both partners sought quite eagerly, at first.

President Truman initiated the "Point Four" technical assistance agreement with Pakistan in December 1950. This was an extension of his doctrine providing similar assistance to Greece and Turkey.

Receptivity to Pakistani overtures on the part of the U.S. was no doubt further enhanced by the beginning of the Korean War. For the Pakistanis, military support was an urgent requirement in the aftermath of their own 1948 war with India over Kashmir. Against this backdrop, whereby each country needed the other, albeit for its own reasons, the development of close relations was seen as natural and inevitable. Thus, Prime Minister Liaquat Ali Khan's first official state visit to the United States commenced just as the Truman administration began wrestling with the management of the Korean War. Liaquat was warmly received in Washington. And he wasted no time in declaring Pakistan's alignment with the United States.[2]

When in February 1952 the United States provided economic assistance to Pakistan as "defense support," the possibility of larger and more fruitful cooperation between the two countries was already being discussed in Pakistan at the highest levels. The personalities included the prime minister, Liaquat Ali Khan; his foreign minister, Sir Zafrullah Khan; and last, but not the least, the newly appointed commander in chief (c. in c.) of the army, General Mohammad Ayub Khan. Thus, there is little evidence to support the contention that not until late 1953 did the United States consider Pakistan separately from India in the subcontinent and that prior to this time "no interest was shown in developing Pakistan's strength."[3]

The election of General Dwight D. Eisenhower to the presidency inaugurated an era of even closer U.S.-Pakistani ties. The U.S. policy toward Pakistan became even more positive in its tone as the establishment of a "Northern Tier of defense" became an early goal of the Eisenhower administration. The Northern Tier concept was, in some ways, the precursor of the Nixon Doctrine of 1969 (Nixon was, after all, vice president in 1952). Basically, the aim of President Eisenhower, his secretary of state, John Foster Dulles, and his chief military advisor, Admiral Arthur W. Radford (appointed chairman of the Joint Chiefs of Staff [JCS] in 1953) was to reduce U.S. involvement in other Korea-type operations and build up instead the indigenous fighting capability of countries such as Pakistan, Iran, Turkey, and Iraq—the front-line states.

In search of ways to turn the concept into reality, Admiral Radford journeyed to Karachi barely a week after the election to assess the possibility of Pakistani participation in defense arrangements aimed against the USSR and the PRC, including the use of Pakistani military personnel against either or both U.S. adversaries. It is in this sense that a buildup of the Pakistani military capability was seen as an extension of the U.S. fighting power in Asia.

The first major initiative from the Pakistani side for the specific purpose of securing military assistance came during General Ayub Khan's visit to Washington in September-October 1953, prior to the visit in October of Ghulam Mohammad, who by then was the governor general, and his foreign minister Zafrullah Khan. Ayub came at his own volition seeking a deal whereby Pakistan could—for the right price—serve as the West's eastern anchor in an Asian alliance structure. He made a favorable impression on both Dulles and Radford. Indeed, by this time the mystique of the martial Pathans with their splendid warrior traditions was beginning to take firm hold in Washington. Ayub, himself a Pathan and in person an impressive man, was readily seen as epitomizing the best of these traditions. Better still, he was in a position to deliver the goods and seemed willing to do so.

Speculation abounds as to why Ayub was so keen to seek U.S. assistance. Various theories have emerged. For example, it has been conjectured that Ayub had a grandiose plan to propel himself to power. The army was his base. He needed to develop that base in order to capture the prize. In other words, the 1958 coup was preplanned as early as 1953 and was not occasioned, as Ayub later stated, by the rapidly deteriorating political situation in Pakistan between 1955 and 1958. Others have argued that Ayub was a true nationalist who felt that keeping Pakistan weak was courting disaster and who saw the United States as the only logical source of help. Yet others have speculated that Ayub was simply a victim of his early socialization, i.e., he was a product of the West. As such he looked to the West to provide succor and sustain Pakistan by strengthening its military capability. The truth would seem to incorporate some of all these views, though one is hard put to agree with the theory that he preplanned his later takeover. Whatever the case, his hand was certainly strengthened when President Eisenhower announced in February 1954 that the United States would provide military assistance to Pakistan.

In pursuit of this new policy, General Harry Meyers visited Pakistan in March 1954 to survey Pakistani needs. Ayub pressed the point to Meyers that he had made earlier in Washington: that U.S. aid would have to be substantial enough to underwrite the costs of economic development. The interaction of this period, which set the tone for later relations, can be traced through a discussion of two key issues: namely, U.S. military assistance and the Kashmir question. Both were critical tests for U.S.-Pakistani relations. Each merits discussion.

ARMS ASSISTANCE: PRIZE AND PUNISHMENT

There was a quid pro quo built into the U.S.-Pakistani relationship, i.e., arms for Pakistan and alliance membership for the United States. Accordingly, as negotiations regarding the nature of the military assistance progressed toward a successful conclusion, discussions were already underway for Pakistan to join a suitable alliance. Thus the signing of the U.S.-Pakistan Mutual Defense Agreement on May 19, 1954 was soon followed, on September 8, 1954, by Pakistan joining the South East Treaty Organization (SEATO).[4]

Given the weakness of the Pakistani defense establishment and the country's faltering economy, the scenario of its partnership with the military-industrial giant would perforce imply a unidirectional influence flow. The logical conclusion, it appears, would have been the placing of Pakistani based facilities and manpower at the disposal of the United States, to be used as the latter deemed fit. After all, Pakistan was worth cultivating only because it offered a "centrally positioned landing site" for possible operations against the USSR and China.[5] Needless to say that the simplicity and the linearity of such a "cause and effect" logic was violated in actual practice.

Despite the overwhelming disparity in the power equation, Washington was not able to convince Ayub—who as commander in chief of the army was the key relevant figure—to grant full access rights. Ayub tantalized Washington with possible offers of such facilities and manpower only "if the price was right." There were three main reasons for his demanding the maximum price.

First, Ayub fully recognized the enormous costs of Pakistan's military expansion program, which could not be borne indigenously. Second, he was aware of the resentment the cost of military expansion would engender in the civilian sector if the funds were abstracted from the civilian budget and allocated for defense. Washington represented a possible way out of the dilemma because it could become the source not only for military assistance but also for other economic aid. Ayub could thus become a national hero for bringing home both guns and butter, so to speak. Third, Ayub was keenly aware that Pakistan needed its military for defense against India and could not deplete its rank in pursuit of U.S. options. The only way Pakistan could play this proxy role, in his view, was if Washington guaranteed Pakistan's security against India.

This was a tall order. In particular, demand for security guarantees exceeded any price that the U.S. leaders could comfortably pay. Openly acknowledging that India posed a threat to Pakistani security would have annoyed India and Indian supporters in the United States. But, at the same time, Washington could not state that India was not a threat because this would be quite unacceptable to the Pakistanis. Moreover, it would make it very difficult, if not impossible, for the Pakistani elite to enter into any meaningful mutual defense agreement with the United States. So the United States came up with an ambiguous settlement that left the nature of the threat *deliberately* vague. This vagueness has plagued U.S.-Pakistani relations ever since 1954 and has led to much misunderstanding with regard to the nature of the relationship in later years.

While the Pakistanis, both at the official and private levels, have consistently viewed this settlement to have been fairly explicit, there are reasons to believe that the Pakistani rulers were cognizant of its studied imprecision. Accordingly, their response to Secretary of State Dulles, when he visited Pakistan and other "front-line" states, displayed appropriately circumscribed elation. Concluding his visit, Secretary Dulles stated, "We are not in general in a position to demand specific return for our investment at this stage. The only chance is to proceed with an indication of trust and friendship and hope to obtain results."[6] Dulles clearly understood that both parties had got less than they wanted. He did not, however, wish to jeopardize the chance of establishing a strong base in Pakistan. He was, for the time being, satisfied with a presence and hoped in future years to acquire the influence "to obtain results."

Dulles was not alone in this view. Admiral Radford seemingly shared it. He was much impressed with Pakistan's position, in general, and with Ayub's, in particular. In fact, Ayub was able to use this fact to Pakistan's advantage as he sought to increase Washington's defense allocation for Pakistan. In addition, U.S. ambassador to Pakistan, Horace Hildreth, had established close relations with Iskander Mirza, who was the defense minister in 1953, and with Mohammad Ali Bogra, who had taken over as prime minister in 1953 after having served as Pakistan's ambassador to Washington. Hildreth's daughter had married Mirza's son in October 1954, and he continued to represent the United States until 1957.

Thus, despite the preponderance of U.S. power, Pakistan played a good game. The United States applied pressure through its secretary of state and the chairman of the Joint Chiefs of Staff for Pakistani membership in SEATO and the Baghdad Pact (renamed in 1959 the Central Treaty Organization—CENTO). Pakistan bowed to the first part of this demand, but countered with one of its own: for greatly increased military assistance.

With Prime Minister Bogra, Ayub again journeyed to Washington in October 1954 and pressured U.S. officials in the State and Defense Departments into increasing their original allocation of $29.5 million for military aid in the first year to $50 million, with a four-year program for modernizing and equipping five Pakistani divisions. The total program cost the United States nearly $175 million. Upon his return from Washington, Ayub assumed the portfolio of Defense in the cabinet reshuffle that followed Governor General Ghulam Mohammad's dismissal of the Constituent Assembly. Iskander Mirza became the minister of interior, in charge of Pakistan's paramilitary forces.

The stage was now set for Pakistan's membership in the Baghdad Pact. This came into being in September 1955, following earlier accession to it by Turkey, Iraq, Britain, and then by Iran (in October). Curiously, the United States did not join the Baghdad Pact. Its absence meant that U.S.-Pakistani relations were kept largely on a bilateral basis that, in turn, resulted in the continued absence of any multilateral institutional basis for the relationship. Dulles was pleased at obtaining the base at Peshawar, a valuable piece of real estate for U.S. use and a U.S. goal since 1952.

However, the vagueness of the American commitment to Pakistan began to raise serious problems by mid-1956, when Hussain Shaheed Suhrawardy took over as prime minister. It sowed divisiveness amongst the leadership. For example, while the foreign minister continued to say that "Americans at the highest level" had given assurances of assistance against an Indian attack, others felt that the pace of U.S. deliveries did not match the earlier promise. Meanwhile, Ayub began to be dissatisfied with the state of the U.S.-Pakistani relationship.

Suhrawardy's view of the United States was greatly colored by his American political adviser, Charles Burton Marshall, who also enjoyed close relations with Mirza, then Pakistan's president. Marshall himself has admitted to the breadth and depth of his contacts and the variety of domestic and international issues on which he advised Suhrawardy.[7] This resulted in keeping Pakistani diplomacy in tune with U.S. requirements of support: that is, on issues such as Hungary, Suez, and matters related to the PRC.

At the same time that Suhrawardy was supporting U.S. policy, Ayub was expressing great disappointment and constantly trying to get the level of the American aid package raised.[8] Often this was effected directly through Ayub's Washington contacts rather than the Pakistani-based office on the Military Assistance Advisory Group (MAAG). Ayub also questioned as early as 1956 the reliability of the U.S. commitment to Pakistan's military modernization—a theme to which he frequently returned.

Questions began to be raised in Washington, in 1957, about the advisability of large-scale U.S. assistance to Pakistan and the latter's reliability as a Northern Tier state in meeting any anti-Soviet contingency on behalf of the United States. Although this debate was conducted in low key, it had substantial and farreaching effect. While no decisions were announced, in retrospect it is clear that at this juncture U.S. policy underwent a subtle but important modification. The changing international scene had once again broken the reverie of Pakistani wishful thinking—and the parameters for U.S.-Pakistani relationship had once again to be tuned to resonate with reality.

In this new climate the United States began to ask, with tangibly greater assertiveness, for concrete steps to demonstrate Pakistan's usefulness. The Pakistani leadership, already divided between the acquiescent Mirza position and the militant posture personalized by Ayub, began to be further polarized. Because of Ayub's persevering struggle to strike an ever more improved bargain with the United States on behalf of the Pakistan military, his popularity within the armed forces, which was already quite substantial, began to rise rapidly. This, combined with other local factors, gave Ayub considerable advantage over his rival, Mirza, when the two declared martial law and dismissed the civilian government in October 1958. Accordingly, Mirza was soon bundled off to London to live out his last years in quiet retirement as Pakistan settled down under its first of a series of martial law rules.

Once Pakistan was securely under Ayub's "benevolent martial law dictatorship," Ayub turned his attention to striking an acceptable settlement with the United States. However, now that Ayub had the ultimate responsibility for the welfare of the country and the armed forces, his militancy was suitably toned down. His first major foreign policy act was the conclusion of the Bilateral Agreement of Cooperation with the United States in March 1959. This was a marvelously balanced agreement that fully responded to the new assertiveness on the part of the United States, but gave ample room to Ayub to declare it to be a supremely successful settlement for Pakistan—one that explicitly stated in its preamble that the "Government of the United States of America regards as vital to its national interest and to world peace, the preservation of the indpendence and integrity of Pakistan." The United States, in return, received a written promise of unfettered access to the Peshawar base for ten years.

Thus, the admission of Pakistan's place in the U.S. scheme of things was taken in Pakistan—along with other concurrent and past assurances—as being virtually tantamount to guaranteeing an effective U.S. role in the preservation of Pakistan's independence and security. There were no denials from Washington on the above score, but United States policy, nonetheless, moved in new directions.

For the U.S.-Pakistani relationship, 1959 had begun auspiciously enough. The conclusion of the historic defense agreement, MDA, had given a firm reciprocal basis to the relationship. However, as spring wore on, events turned dramatically sour. First came the death of John Foster Dulles in May 1959. He had been the main architect of the relationship. Also, his vision of a "cordon sanitaire" had provided the major *raison d'etre* for the relationship. The watershed, however, was reached with the

Eisenhower-Khruschev get-together at the Maryland retreat whence emerged the "Spirit of Camp David," which was an attempt to move U.S.-Soviet relations from a posture of cold-war confrontation to one of peaceful coexistence.

In perspective, these events can be seen as wiping out whatever advantages may have accrued to Pakistan from the 1959 treaty. With Dulles gone and the rationale for the Northern Tier under review, Ayub complained of the "lost opportunities" and "broken promises" in Pakistan's relations with the United States.

Congressional review of U.S. commitments to Pakistan in 1959 was received unfavorably by Ayub. It was a harbinger of changes to come. Hearings on Capitol Hill questioned the wisdom of Pakistani forces being kept in excess of the requirements for external defense. Given Ayub's close identification with the growth of the military in Pakistan, he could be counted upon to respond negatively to such sentiments, which he described as being: "totally erroneous and based on an incorrect appreciation of the military requirements of Pakistan, which has 1400 miles of common frontier with India and with 80 percent of the Indian forces poised at Pakistan and capable of launching an offensive attack at ten days' notice."[9]

To make matters worse, the United States tried to reduce the rent it paid for the Peshawar base and decrease the Military Assistance Program (MAP). Characteristically, however, Ayub pressed for more military aid, advancing the argument that the United States still needed Pakistan and could count on it to be a dependable ally but could not expect "to lead [it] into confused thinking against the hard facts of life."[10]

Matters came to a head when in early fall (1959) the U.S. Senate cut the foreign aid bill authorization for 1960 by a whopping $383 million. In response, Ayub pointedly noted that the Pakistani commitment to the United States was predicated on continued aid. He also overcame his natural reluctance to look for aid from other quarters and put out feelers to the effect that Pakistan had not foreclosed its diplomatic option. This led to a dramatic turnabout when, in late 1959, after years of rejecting Soviet offers, the foreign minister announced that: "Pakistan would welcome aid from any quarter provided it did not affect the ideology, integrity, and solidarity of Pakistan."[11]

At this time, when Pakistani leaders began openly differentiating between communist doctrine and relations with countries where the doctrine prevailed, Ayub nonetheless continued to view U.S. aid as the only means of guaranteeing the independence of Third World countries against communist encroachment. Ayub and other members of the Pakistani military and civilian elite were, after all, products of Western education and their natural tendencies were toward the maintenance of close relations with the West, so long as the utility of the relationship was not entirely one-sided in the West's favor. Ayub, however, was to be further disabused of this ambivalence by events that were soon to unfold.

Francis Gary Powers was shot down while flying high across the Soviet Union in a United States U-2 plane in May 1960. This event had major international repercussions, including the cancellation of an impending Eisenhower-Khrushchev summit meeting. What made the event especially fateful for Pakistan, however, was the fact that a few hours before he hurtled down on Soviet soil, Mr. Powers had taken off from the U.S. base in Pakistan near Peshawar.

The ensuing uproar particularly galled Ayub. Here he was, a devoted friend of the United States, whose favors were fetching ever decreasing returns and who was now publicly humiliated and embarrassed for having allowed his soil to be used for shenanigans over which he had absolutely no control. He was subjected to considerable internal pressure—which he would undoubtedly have withstood in better times—to alter the arrangements which, thus mishandled, could profoundly influence the country's fate.[12] What really stiffened Ayub's resolve, however, had an external origin. Khrushchev, in his characteristically blunt and plebeian fashion, threatened horrific retaliation against Pakistan if the U.S. military activities in Peshawar did not cease. Also, he spelled out the long-term danger to Pakistan inherent in its pro-U.S. policy.

The U.S. presidential election later that year further aggravated these misgivings. Richard Nixon, who did not wield any real power as vice president, was nonetheless perceived to be a friend of Pakistan. Therefore, despite the doleful state of U.S.-Pakistani relations at the time, Pakistanis wistfully awaited Nixon's election victory in the forlorn hope that this would turn things around. A certain degree of ignorance about the American democratic process, coupled with a modicum of what is euphemistically called "positive thinking," had enabled Pakistanis to take the vice president's election victory for granted. Accordingly, the election of John Fitzgerald Kennedy in November 1960 came as something of a shock. Still, it was not because the Pakistanis had completely written off Kennedy, but rather because Nixon was a known, friendly figure.

Bad things tend to get worse is not literally an Urdu proverb, but it might just as well have been one because once Kennedy took office it became clear to the Pakistanis that he had a "soft spot" for India. And this automatically translated into a "hard spot" for Pakistan!

The meeting point in the declining utility curves for both the United States and Pakistan for each other came early in 1961 when the policy review by the Kennedy administration downgraded Pakistan's importance. This occurred not only because of Kennedy's political affinity for India, but also because of the not unreasonable extrapolation that the dawning era of spy satellites would render bases such as Peshawar obsolete.° Pakistan took the U.S. attitude to signal the demise of the special relationship that had existed between the two countries. Given the U-2 incident, close alliance had demonstrated itself as a particularly heavy liability, and Pakistan was now ready to embark on a search for alternatives.[13]

Thus, the marriage of convenience began to break down. When Ayub visited Kennedy in July 1961 and addressed the U.S. Congress about the need to stand by allies or be faced with the prospect of alliances ending in animosities, there was an edge to his message. Yet, hoping against hope, Pakistanis persisted in making much of the characteristically confusing signals that the great U.S. democracy often sends to the foreigners. The signal being referred to here was the show of genuine enthusiasm with which Ayub's address to the Congress was received![14]

The public annulment of the marriage, however, did not come until autumn, 1962, when, in the aftermath of the Sino-Indian border war, the United States offered military supplies to the Indian government.[15]

During his 1961 visit, Ayub had made clear that, in the absence of a solution to the Kashmir problem, Pakistan would find U.S. arms for India "a tremendous strain on our friendship with the United States."[16] In response, he had been promised consultation by Kennedy *prior* to any arms agreement with India and was consoled with the grant of one squadron of F-104 jet fighters. However, when the military supplies for India were decided upon, it received help with the raising of fifteen additional squadrons and six additional army divisions. Such massive military aid to India caused major trauma for Pakistan, particularly for its pro-Western elite who were hard put to explain their failure to read correctly the signals from Washington. Despite Ayub's efforts to strike an advantageous deal for Pakistan, he was personally subjected to criticism because of his role in formulating Pakistan's pro-American policy. This was particularly ironic because by 1962 Ayub had already begun to initiate shifts toward a more balanced foreign policy.[17] The difficulty of the elite in 1962 stemmed from their decision in early 1950 to avoid an open discussion on the basic divergence of aims between the United States and Pakistan. Never having explained that Washington was looking at Pakistan as an "anchor" in defense against the Soviet Union and China rather than cooperating in Pakistan's goal of defense against India, Ayub and the

---

°Peshawar is perched amidst a shallow bowl, surrounded by rugged foothills of the mighty Hindu Kush range of mountains. From here, only a short sixty-odd mile hop carries one into the southern stretches of the Soviet territory. While this is an attractive spot for launching spy planes into Soviet territory, it is not much use for stationing a long-range radar facility because of the height of the intervening mountains.

others were hard put to explain a move that was seen in Pakistan as being tantamount to "American treachery."

Over the years, no debate had occurred in Pakistani forums to indicate that the United States did not support *all* aspects of Pakistani foreign policy. The general consensus, even amongst the elite, was that the United States understood that India was the major threat to Pakistani security and that this fact was subsumed under U.S. concern over regional security issues. The elite, including Ayub, clung to what they have repeated in interviews as "the assurances at the highest level" that the United States understood Pakistan's needs against India and would stand by Pakistan. It was never quite understood by Pakistani leaders that the United States was just as concerned with "communist aggression" in 1962 as it had been a decade earlier when the Northern Tier policy was launched.[18] In 1962, Washington saw the possibility of reaching a goal that had eluded it in 1952: namely, drawing India close to the United States and, if possible, wiping out all traces of Indian nonalignment.

It was, perhaps ironically, left up to Pakistani Foreign · Minister Mohammad Ali Bogra—who had served as a critical link to the United States in 1953 and become prime minister in time to sign the first Mutual Defense Agreement with the United States in 1954—to admit "the failure," in Pakistani terms, of its pro-Western foreign policy. Bogra spoke of his "anguish" as he admitted that President Kennedy was putting pressure on Pakistan not to take advantage of Indian vulnerability while at the same time rushing in military equipment and supplies to India. Bogra concluded his remarks with the first public explanation from a key policymaker of the basis for Pakistan's entry in defense arrangements with the United States:

> When we entered into these pacts . . . we did so purely for defensive purposes . . . . We were in desperate need of arms and equipment and while we are interested in the defense of our region, we were no less interested in boosting the morale of our people. Now with a change in military strategy, the military importance of these pacts has necessarily diminished . . . . Friends that let us down will no longer be considered our friends.[19]

Any assurance by the United States that the arms supplied to India would not be used against Pakistan were dismissed by Bogra and Ayub as an indication of U.S. naiveté and ignorance regarding Indian intentions and the nature of the Indo-Pakistani conflict.[20]

The issue of military assistance highlights the basic difficulty that has haunted the U.S.-Pakistani relationship. From the outset, the relationship was based on predilections of a few key individuals who determined both its direction as well as its intensity. Pakistani leaders needed a personal equation with their U.S. counterparts in order to put across their needs. When this occurred, they were very successful. For example, Ghulam Mohammad, Mirza, Ayub, and Bogra had all been able to influence Eisenhower, Dulles, Radford, and Hildreth in supporting Pakistan's military development to a greater extent than they were initially willing to undertake. When they lost that contact with the Kennedy administration, they felt frustrated and misunderstood; worse still, deliberately deceived.

For the United States, military support was rationalized on the basis of establishing a presence in Pakistan and building U.S. prestige in a critical area, even though the United States could not, for the time being, get Pakistan to do something it would otherwise not do—for example, get Pakistani military personnel to serve for U.S. contingencies, as Dulles and Radford had originally envisioned. But for a time there was adequate payoff for U.S. policy, as in the use of the base at Peshawar, and Eisenhower, Dulles, or Radford never really questioned the pro forma nature of Pakistan's participation in SEATO and CENTO nor did they push hard to use aid as leverage to enlist greater Pakistani cooperation in the military sense. Their reasons were fairly simple. They were unwilling to jeopardize the use of the Peshawar base. Equally importantly, they were unwilling to force the issue to the point where, in order to free Pakistani personnel for use elsewhere, admission of the Indian threat, and the guaranteeing of Pakistani security against it, would be needed.

KASHMIR: THE LITMUS TEST

Kashmir was an issue of great importance to Pakistan from 1947 to 1965. Two wars, one in 1948 and another in 1965, were fought between Pakistan and India over the state. Pakistan used support of its diplomatic position, namely for an independent referendum to be held by the people of Kashmir to decide whether they wanted to join India or Pakistan, as the litmus test for its friends. The 1948 war had given Pakistan control over only the least desirable one-third of the state. This failure continued to rankle Pakistani politicians and the public alike. It was as though, by the loss of Kashmir, their success in establishing an Islamic state had been considerably mitigated. Furthermore, members of the Pakistani elite felt that it was only due to the preponderance of military material that India had captured the much more desirable vales of Jammu and Kashmir. Given an opportunity to correct this imbalance, the martial Muslims of Pakistan would surely march to victory.

While military assistance from the United States was one arm of a policy that sought to regain control over Kashmir, diplomatic support for the cause was the other. The United States could, in Pakistani opinion, deliver diplomatically the support necessary to force the Indians to hold a plebiscite in Kashmir. Much as the military elite had invested time and energy into developing a military equation with the U.S., the political leaders spent considerable effort in pursuit of this diplomatic goal.

Liaquat, Mirza, Bogra, and others were fully aware of the negative impact Pakistan's membership in SEATO and CENTO alliances had had on its relations with states such as the Soviet Union, People's Republic of China, and members of the nonaligned movement. Nevertheless, they felt confident that this price was worth paying since on Kashmir the United States alone counted for more than all these countries put together. Moreover, their perceptions of U.S. revolutionary-democratic history had led them to believe that its people would be the natural supporters of the freedom of choice that the concept of plebiscite embodied.

Needless to say, this was a gross overestimate of the U.S. capacity to shape events around the world. Worse still, it was a disastrous presumption to equate Washington's priorities with their own. The saddest part of it all, however, was its fallout on Pakistan's relations with key Islamic countries. Here, Pakistani alliances with the United States had a devastatingly negative impact. This was graphically demonstrated in Nasser's public cold-shouldering of Pakistan—which hurt because of Nasser's international stature—and in his lashing out, during the Suez crisis, when he called Pakistan a "stooge of Western imperialism." The ultimate insult was hurled, however, when Nasser declared: "Suez is as dear to Egypt as Kashmir is to India."[21] Nasser was not unique in pronouncing such condemnations. Even Saudi Arabia bitterly attacked Pakistani membership in alliances, calling it a case of "having joined hands with those who had bad intentions toward the Arabs."[22]

Pakistan's U.S. connection may also have impinged on its relations with India and provided the Kashmir-born Indian prime minister, Jawahar Lal Nehru, with a convenient excuse to back away from his earlier pledge to hold a plebiscite in Kashmir. Claiming that U.S. military aid to Pakistan was creating a "grave situation for India," Nehru refused to go ahead and implement his earlier promises.[23] Some Indians claim that the plebiscite issue was indeed open until April 1954, but after that because of "Pakistan's endeavors to introduce the cold war into the region," the matter was closed.[24]

To get a feeling for how tenuous the Pakistani leadership's grasp of the complexities of international politics really was, one needs only to look at the manner in which opportunities were missed. Indeed, viewing this against the background of accumulated evidence suggesting considerably less than total devotion on the part of the United States towards Pakistan's position on the Kashmir dispute, their lack of perceptiveness becomes even more obvious.

When the Soviet Union backed away from its 1948 UN vote favoring a general plebiscite in Kashmir, it did not spark a political debate in Pakistan. Indeed, Pakistan appeared quite unconcerned! Expectations of strong U.S. support were considered sufficient to implement the UN's promise of a plebiscite. This view was further reinforced when, in 1950, the United Nations adopted its Korean resolution entailing a strong military response for its enforcement. Accordingly, Liaquat Ali Khan perceived his forceful support for the UN action in Korea to serve as the basis for a similarly strong stand on Kashmir.

Periodic consideration of Kashmir in the United Nations brought perfunctory U.S. support for previous resolutions calling for a plebiscite. A UN commission to inquire into the problems of organizing such a plebiscite in Kashmir was also supported by Washington.

The lack of progress, however, did not go unnoticed in Pakistan. Indeed, Liaquat complained that the "United States is not really giving consideration to Pakistan's case" on Kashmir.[25] Nonetheless, the expectations continued to be entertained that once Pakistan fully aligned itself with the United States, support on Kashmir would be forthcoming.

Around the mid-fifties, it had become clear that, short of deliberate pressure, such as the withholding of economic aid by the United States, India would not be persuaded to abide by its earlier promise to hold a plebiscite. The United States, however, was loath to apply this kind of pressure. This fact was interpreted by the Pakistani public, and presumably also its leadership, to mean that the United States was not sincere in its support on Kashmir.

This interpretation was indirectly corroborated by a memorable event that took place in December 1955 when Nikita Khrushchev, who was then the secretary general of the Communist Party of the Soviet Union, and Marshal Nikolai Bulganin, the premier of the USSR, visited India. In Srinagar, the capital of Kashmir, they declared that Kashmir was an "integral part of India," a statement which, although not totally unexpected, nonetheless stunned the Pakistanis. In response, the Pakistani public and the leadership fully expected the United States to express strong sentiments countering this statement—especially since, according to the Pakistani view, their cause was just and it had all to do with morality and the sanctity of solemn promises. When no such response was forthcoming, there was tangible disappointment. At this juncture, various lower-level political leaders urged the government to revise its foreign policy because "declarations of sham friendship are likely to drive us into a sense of false security which is very dangerous."[26] In their view, U.S. failure to respond to a direct attack against the integrity of the country had made the Washington connection irrelevent. Dissatisfaction was also voiced with the slow pace of economic assistance ($100 million in 1955).

General feeling amongst the middle and lower echelons of the political leadership (which didn't include such stalwarts at the top as Ghulam Mohammad, Suhrawardy, Bogra, and Mirza) was that U.S. support was not commensurate with the commitments undertaken by Pakistan. Ayub, who was perhaps the strongest of the top leadership at the time, did not disagree with these sentiments. However, he still had use for the American alliance and felt that so long as military assistance was forthcoming and alternative sources of aid were not available, Washington's weaknesses had to be put up with. At the same time, Ayub was not averse to exerting periodic pressure on the United States in the form of public statements to the effect that unless the United States put less of a premium on neutrality, even "the staunchest believers in ideological friendships" would be forced to make room for others.[27]

Pakistani charges of a deliberately slow rate of aid delivery, and unhappiness over the lack of a response countering Soviet statements of support to India and Afghanistan against Pakistan, prompted Ambassador Hildreth to note that, on a per capita basis, Pakistan and other countries with mutual assistance agreements with the United States were doing very well. They were receiving seven times as much aid as the "neutral" countries. Furthermore, Hildreth stated that Pakistan and three other countries were scheduled to receive more than one-half of the $4.3 billion in U.S. military aid earmarked for 1956–57. Dulles, who was not insensitive to Pakistan's position on Kashmir, also took note of Pakistani frustrations. At a SEATO ministerial council meeting in Karachi on March 7, 1956, he persuaded the group to agree that all SEATO powers supported Pakistan in (1) securing a peaceful settlement of the Kashmir dispute in accordance with UN resolutions (an indirect reference to a plebiscite); (2) guaranteeing the Durand Line against possible aggression by Afghanistan, and (3) recognizing that the sovereignty of Pakistan extended up to the Durand Line, which was the international boundary between Pakistan and Afghanistan.[28]

However, U.S. economic aid to India continued unabated because Washington could not afford to alienate India by acquiescing to Pakistani desires. Quite apart from Pakistan's wishes, there were strong supporters of Nehru in Washington who saw him as one of the undisputed leaders of the nonaligned movement. Nonalignment itself had become increasingly palatable to U.S. tastes; and as it became respectable, alignment was questioned in Pakistan as a luxury the country could ill afford.

In 1959–60, U.S. leaders were also questioning Pakistan's value to the United States. For example, in the Senate, then Senator John F. Kennedy urged the United States to give massive aid to India, stating that the "U.S. treaty relationship (with Pakistan) should not stand in its way."[29] Other Kennedy influentials such as Chester Bowles put it this way:

Some nations who agree with us do not really agree with us. They agree with us only out of necessity. They are so very close to the margin of survival that they have wrapped their arms around our neck in desperate effort to be saved. Other nations, more proud perhaps, but more sure of themselves, more confident of what they have, are less likely to do that.[30]

While it was well known that Bowles was a leading member of the pro-India lobby, Pakistani leaders worried that he was representative of an influential constituency that belittled the alliances with Pakistan.

These thoughts were uppermost in Ayub's mind as he prepared to visit Kennedy in July 1961. Several questions were raised by him in his pretrip discussions with advisers. First, was it worthwhile for Pakistan to continue to rely on alliances that had brought no more economic and military aid than was given to such neutral countries as India by the same sources (the subtlety that India was not just *any* neutral country had escaped Ayub). Second, should Pakistan continue to side with the West in its quarrels when reciprocity did not extend to similar support for Pakistan on Kashmir. Third, should Pakistan continue to play the role of an anticommunist nation at all times or should Pakistan normalize its relations with the USSR and the PRC?

On the eve of his departure for Washington, Ayub spoke of SEATO and CENTO, saying that they were entered into for the express purpose of enhancing Pakistani security. Hence, continued membership was dependent on the extent to which the alliances satisfied this criterion and, if nonalignment was a better guarantee of Pakistani security, the country would move in that direction. Ayub's public statement also displayed his nervousness at the new direction that U.S. policy was taking in South Asia. Regarding this he said: "Smaller Asian countries are apprehensive. If India became overwhelmingly strong militarily or economically, these countries would look for protection elsewhere."[31] In particular, Ayub was chafing at Vice President Lyndon B. Johnson's statement that: "At President Kennedy's request, I have urged Mr. Nehru to extend his leadership."[32] Once in the United States, Ayub did not succeed in getting any greater cooperation. Kennedy pleaded his inability to become directly and actively involved with the Kashmir dispute.

Given this background of discontent, the events that followed the Sino-Indian border clash, including the rapid shipment of U.S. arms and equipment to India, were seen as constituting the final blow. Pakistani attempts to influence Washington into forcing India to a settlement of Kashmir were not appreciated by the Kennedy administration. In no uncertain terms, Kennedy characterized this as a "totally wrong response to the threat facing India" and pressed Pakistan to make a "no-war" pledge to India instead. Both the U.S. ambassador to Pakistan, Mr. Walter

McConaughy, and the assistant secretary of state for Far Eastern Affairs, Averell Harriman, stressed to Pakistani leaders the importance of cooling their passions against India on Kashmir.

Kennedy was worried that Pakistan might use the opportunity presented by India's chaotic response to the Chinese thrust to wipe out years of frustration at the negotiating table. A military response by Pakistan could make things even more difficult for India by opening up a second front. Ayub and his senior advisers were not unaware of the opportunity, and the soul-searching that took place in October-November 1962 with regard to this option has not been recorded in the United States. The Chinese would probably have welcomed such a move and the Soviet Union had not yet decided that its split with China was a permanent fact of life.

Despite the resentment that Pakistani leaders felt at U.S. pressure, they refrained from using force in Kashmir *at this time.* Ayub, in particular, felt that India was using the border clash—for which, in his view, India had only itself to blame°—as a "camouflage for getting more Western weapons." For example, Ayub stated that: "taking advantage of the favorable response for arms, India is planning to raise two armies, one with which to face China and the other to use against Pakistan."[33] According to this view, if Kennedy was really serious about peace in the area, he should have pressed India to settle the Kashmir dispute immediately and thus remove the underlying threat. Kennedy's proposal for Indo-Pakistani talks on Kashmir (which got underway in December 1962 but soon bogged down) was seen as merely a cosmetic attempt since it did not provide a permanent solution.

Bogra died in 1963 and was replaced as foreign minister by youthful Zulfikar Ali Bhutto, then a protégé of Ayub. Even prior to the October 1962 border clash, Bhutto had stated to the National Assembly that Pakistan would be forced to consider "a fundamental decision to withdraw from Western Alliances if long-term aid to India was not coupled with a settlement of the Kashmir dispute."[34] In response to questions from the Assembly, Bogra, in his last public appearance as foreign minister—it was said in Pakistan at the time that he had died of a broken heart because the United States, which had promised him much in 1953, had changed its mind!—categorically stated that any massive military aid to India would disturb the precarious balance of power in the subcontinent and would therefore be considered an "unfriendly act" by Pakistan. Asked publicly how Pakistan would react to American aid for India, Bogra replied: "We

---

°Ayub claimed that he had warned Nehru about "danger from the north" and proposed a joint defense agreement between India and Pakistan to deal with any such contingency. Nehru had replied to the offer with a sarcastic "defense against whom?"

expect all those who have helped us in the past to maintain that balance pending the settlement of the Kashmir dispute."[35]

The failure of the United States to play a constructive role in a resolution of the Kashmir dispute in late 1962 was perceived in Pakistan as a classic case of American bias in India's favor and a missed opportunity for the subcontinent. In a sense, it was the nervousness of Kennedy and men like Harriman and Bowles who feared a Pakistani military solution to the Kashmir problem in 1962 that put the idea in Ayub's mind to try for it in 1965, under far less promising circumstances. Having pledged no-war in Kashmir in 1962 at Kennedy's behest, Ayub gave the United States the benefit of the doubt and a last chance to mediate on Kashmir. When that failed, the U.S. was seen as having failed the test of reliable friendship and effective leadership.

Ayub's response was a recourse to *realpolitik*. He normalizd relations with the PRC. Specifically in March 1963, he signed a border agreement with China that had the effect of making China a party to the Kashmir problem. He also moved to improve cultural, scientific, and economic relations. In 1964, he refused to comply with President Johnson's request for a show of support in Vietnam through even a token Pakistani military participation. Johnson was annoyed at Pakistan's "opening a window for the communist world," as the civil aviation agreement with China was portrayed in Washington, with the State Department saying that it would have an adverse affect on efforts to strengthen the security and solidarity of the subcontinent and also that it was "an unfortunate breach of free-world solidarity."[36]

There were other concrete dissonances. Johnson cancelled Ayub's Washington visit scheduled for April 1965. Also, the 1965 meeting of the aid-to-Pakistan consortium, which was to pledge $500 million toward Pakistan's Third Five-Year Plan, was cancelled. This sort of economic and political pressure did not alter Pakistan's behavior. Instead, it merely reinforced the opinion that dependence on a single country was no longer desirable or even necessary. So long as the United States refrained from supporting India in a direct fashion—in this context the previous $10.5 billion in aid to India was seen as indirect—then Pakistan, too, would stay away from developing other options; but once the United States changed the status quo in 1962, then Pakistan considered itself free to follow suit.

This line of thinking was ill-received by Johnson, and the Pakistanis were told as much. Johnson' argument was as follows. First, what was good for the goose was not necessarily good for the gander. The United States, a superpower, had global responsibilities and a commitment to a larger view that necessitated a variety of options. On the other hand, Pakistan, as a small and dependent country, a recipient of U.S. largesse, was not free to exercise other options. Second, the United States had made a commitment to Pakistan and that should be seen as a sufficient guarantee of Pakistani security. There was no further need for Pakistan to make friends with its communist neighbors since that action would destroy—from the U.S. point of view—the *raison d'etre* of the alliances that underwrote the security guarantee. (From the Pakistani perspective, the *raison d'etre* had already been destroyed in 1962.) Third, the 1962 arming of India had been a particularly personal act of President Kennedy, who had always seen India as the bastion of democracy with special rights and privileges. Johnson was not similarly committed, though he did consider the Sino-Indian clash as typical of the same aggressive communist tendencies that were being played out in Vietnam.

By the end of 1964 anti-Americanism in Pakistan reached a peak of intensity, and Pakistan's stock stood at an all-time low in Washington. Accusations of CIA involvement (because of Washington's unhappiness with the new direction of Pakistan's policy) with anti-Ayub demonstrations in major Pakistani cities were a commentary on what had transpired in fifteen years. A man who had worked so hard to establish a special relationship with the United States was seen in Washington as symbolizing anti-Americanism.

In any case, according to Pakistani perceptions, by this time the United States had failed the test of friendship in Kashmir. Thereafter, while Pakistan remained in the alliance, it sought a type of disengagement *à la de Gaulle* through nonparticipation in military exercises and restrictions on the use of its territory by alliance members. The remarks of the Iranian secretary-general of CENTO that the alliance was "like insuring your house against fire; the policy does not cover damages by earthquake or theft" echoed the mood in Islamabad![37]

THE 1965 INDO-PAKISTANI WAR

The examination of the 1965 war is important, because it brought together elements of both the arms policy and the Kashmir problem. The differing expectations Pakistan and the United States had for their relationship came a cropper in 1965. The divergence in perceptions could no longer be ignored. Instead, both the United States and Pakistan were confronted with each other's demands and were forced by events into responding.

The deterioration in U.S.-Pakistani relations, mentioned earlier, gave Ayub to understand that there was no hope of arriving at a solution of Kashmir via Washington. When Johnson cancelled Ayub's visit in April 1965, it was obvious that relations had reached an impasse. The same month Ayub visited Moscow and received a surprisingly warm welcome.

He was left with the feeling that there no longer existed the "strategic symmetry" that had led parallel Soviet and American interests to build up India in the early 1960s.[38] The Soviets were willing to be somewhat more neutral in their support of India, having become quite nervous about friendly relations between China and Pakistan.[39]

Johnson's displeasure with Pakistan was keenly felt in Islamabad in July 1965, when the aid-to-Pakistan consortium meeting was cancelled. Pakistani leadership reacted swiftly. They proudly announced that under no circumstances would they allow their need for economic aid to be used as an instrument of political pressure.[40] Less than a week later, it was disclosed that concrete proposals were under discussion between Moscow and Islamabad in connection with "offers of economic and other assistance by the Soviet Union following the United States aid freeze."[41] Ayub, Bhutto, and Shoaib (the finance minister) all spoke of the "new look" in Pakistan's foreign policy that would enable Pakistan to solve the economic crisis by increasing revenues from indigenous sources and supplementing these with assistance from other countries, in particular the socialist-bloc nations and China. Ayub reiterated Pakistan's right to normalize relations with its neighbors, irrespective of differing ideologies, stating that this "right we shall never allow to be compromised."[42]

While this public reaction of the Pakistani leadership to the withholding of U.S. aid displayed a dramatic departure from the halcyon days of the U.S.-Pakistan relationship, it paled in comparison with what was being wrought behind the scenes. Indeed, this affair catalyzed a chain reaction that rapidly culminated in sparking a full-scale war between India and Pakistan in September of that year. Already, in April, there had been some limited warfare in the Rann of Kutch—a marshy wasteland astride the border. In August, Ayub decided he no longer had much to lose in search of the option that had suggested itself at the time of the Sino-Indian border war in 1962, namely, the use of force in Kashmir.

Ayub reckoned that Washington would be unhappy, but the special relationship with the United States had already ebbed. Furthermore, Washington's attention was riveted at the other end of Asia, in Vietnam.

Among the other factors that figured in Ayub's calculations were that India was rapidly developing an indigenous arms manufacturing capacity. Moreover, because Pakistan was almost totally dependent upon the United States for arms, the developing strains in their relationship did not augur well for future improvement in Pakistani military capability. A logical deduction, therefore, was that while the optimal time for military action against India had been in the past, when India was engaged in a border war with China on its northeastern frontier, any opportunity for exercising this option was, nevertheless, slipping away forever. Another major factor, often overlooked, was the impassioned counsel of the foreign minister, Zulfikar Ali Bhutto. His contacts with the Soviets had led him to believe that, as long as the United States was not assisting Pakistan, the USSR would stay neutral. Of equal importance, according to Bhutto's thesis, was that the Chinese would provide *matériel* and, if needed, even come to Pakistan's rescue.

These were convincing arguments, but Ayub was not fully swayed. Being a military man, he worried about the ability of the Pakistani forces to engage the much larger Indian army across such a long, meandering frontier. Once again, Bhutto came to the fore. In a brilliant tactical analysis he proposed a method whereby the encounter with the Indians could be strictly localized to Kashmir. His proposal was to infiltrate suitably trained politico-military cadres across the UN armistice line in Kashmir, with orders to establish cells to assist the local population in the making of a "national rebellion." This was to be supplemented by scattered acts of violence to be carried out by the Pakistani commandos. The crux of Bhutto's argument was that under international law Indians would be restricted to their response only to the "disputed territory" of Kashmir. Ayub saw the logic of the argument. He further rationalized it by his own analysis that, given the difficult logistics of Indian access to Kashmir, Pakistani armies would prevail in the Kashmir sector.

Shortly thereafter, Pakistani infiltration of Indian Kashmir began. It is important to remember that this was largely a political decision, made by the political elite. The military, an effective and disciplined force in 1965, complied with the decision to wrest control of more of Kashmir through an admixture of military subversion and covert assistance. The local population, predominantly Muslim, was expected to see this as the golden opportunity they had long awaited to gain independence from India.

When serious fighting got underway in Kashmir by late August 1965, the failure of the Kashmiris to rise up in revolt was a bitter disappointment to both Ayub and Bhutto. This was, however, not the worst of it. When Indian leaders realized the difficulty of fighting the Pakistani army in a restricted fight in Kashmir, they did the unthinkable. They attacked across the international frontier in West Pakistan and began to thrust ominously toward Lahore. This action stunned the Pakistanis. Outwardly elegant, the Ayub-Bhutto scenario had been shattered and instead the wolf was now at the door!

The United States and the Soviet Union both reacted with alarm at the outbreak of hostilities in South Asia. The war forced the Johnson administration to refocus on Pakistan, as it and the Kremlin worried about the possibility of Chinese intervention in the subcontinent. Both superpowers urged an early end to the fighting.[43] The United States clamped a total suspension on all military and economic aid to India and Pakistan on September 8, 1965. This way, it hoped to force an end to the hostilities and was encouraged by a similar action undertaken by Moscow. However, the Soviets withdrew their ban on arms shipments to India on September 17, 1965, in recognition of Chinese support to Pakistan.

The U.S. arms embargo further embittered U.S.-Pakistani relations. Although affecting India as well as Pakistan, it was perceived as being particularly devastating for Pakistan because of Pakistan's total dependence on the United States for supplies in artillery, tanks, aircrafts, and logistical support systems. India relied on the United States for less than 10 percent of is equipment. Through the arms embargo, Washington hoped to influence Pakistan to agree to an early termination of hostilities, and also to punish it for its resort to force in Kashmir. This was quite evident when, in response to the Pakistani ambassador's request for U.S. assistance, Secretary of State Dean Rusk firmly stated on September 20, 1965, that while the United States had looked into the bilateral agreement it really felt that it was "being invited in on the crash landing without being in on the take-off."[44] Rusk referred here to the absence of Pakistani consultation prior to the infiltration in Kashmir.

Washington preferred an end to the war without having to choose sides. It felt this was "even-handed" and eminently sensible. On the other hand, Pakistan viewed this behavior as betrayal by an ally whom it had served well. As Bhutto recalled several years later: "Whenever we said we were not being given assistance, or that the treaties were not complied with, we were told that we were passive members of the organizations, so how could they (U.S. leaders) fulfill their part of the commitment."[45]

While U.S. pressure on Pakistan to terminate the war through the denial of supplies destroyed whatever little was left of the public relationship after 1962,[46] the private relationship on the government level had already reached its nadir in the first six months of 1965. In fact, it can be said that the anti-Americanism and general hysteria that led to the burning down of the U.S. Information Service (USIS) library in Karachi (and almost led to similar action against the U.S. Embassy itself) was a useful public release for the Ayub government to camouflage the real sense of deep frustration. The anger and resentment directed toward Washington for its failure to support Pakistan in its hour of need enabled Ayub to avoid the domestic consequences of his failure in Kashmir. Thus, while the United States did succeed in influencing Ayub into terminating the war in seventeen days, Ayub's use of the United States as a scapegoat enabled him to hang on as head of state.

Ayub went to Tashkent[47] and in January 1966 signed a declaration with India to formally end the 1965 war. Bhutto resigned as foreign minister in protest, saying: "We are fully aware of the treacherous nature of India and we do not want to endanger the existence of Pakistan in the name of cooperation" (with the Soviet Union).[48] Bhutto repeatedly accused Ayub of having "sold the advantages won in battle for dubious gains at Tashkent," to which Ayub retorted: "How could I have got Kashmir at the diplomatic table when it was not won on the battlefield!" Bhutto found himself a *cause célèbre*, which he exploited with tremendous adroitness as he developed a separate constituency and prepared himself for replacing Ayub.

Ayub felt that the Soviet leadership was particularly solicitous of him, in sharp contrast to what he perceived as his shabby treatment by Lyndon Johnson. He accepted the Soviet offer the second time around because diplomatic as well as military solutions were wanting. The Soviet offer of good offices (the actual role was closer to mediation) provided an opportunity to break the stalemate and return to the *status quo ante*. And "inherent in the Soviet diplomatic initiative was the claim that South Asia, being geographically close to the USSR, was a natural sphere of Russian interest."[49]

Ayub's sense of betrayal, first at Kennedy's arming of India without the promised consultation with Pakistan, then at Johnson's postponement of his visit to Washington closely followed by the cancellation of the aid-to-Pakistan meeting and, finally, the arms cutoff, was genuine and deep, even though he had been the major motivating force behind Pakistan's pro-U.S. policy in the early 1950s. Equally painful was the ingratitude shown by his own protégé, Bhutto, whose rash counsel had caused Ayub so much harm; worse still, perhaps, was the ignorance displayed by the Pakistani masses, who accepted Bhutto's characterization of the 1965 war as a "victory" when all that the Pakistani forces had really achieved was a temporary stalemate that prevented a total rout by the Indians.

After 1965, U.S. policy toward Pakistan entered a period of benign neglect. Washington seized the opportunity offered by the Soviet initiative to disengage itself from the squabbling neighbors on the subcontinent, though such a move had repercussions on other U.S. allies. For example, the shah of Iran criticized U.S. policy, saying, "You forced the Pakistanis to buy arms from the Chinese. Since you and the British dropped Pakistan in the war with India, even though it was a member of CENTO and even though India violated its national integrity, I figure it can happen to me . . . ."[50] What did the 1965 war demonstrate in the way of who influenced whom? In order to arrive at any conclusions in this regard, we have to examine first the policy goals of each side. The United States clearly did not wish to see India and Pakistan parties to a war. The specter of two impoverished countries whom Washington had nourished by expending much energy and treasure, destroying each other with American-supplied weapons and support systems, haunted U.S. policy-makers. Once the war began, the U.S. leadership wanted an expeditious termination of the conflict. Here it could be argued that Washington instituted the arms embargo because it lacked influence over Pakistani policymakers. The only resort available was to deny Pakistan the necessary weapons to continue the war and thus force it into a ceasefire. U.S. attempts to bring about a ceasefire through the United Nations were not effective until the arms embargo cut deeply into the availability of war matériel. Once the war was over, it was the Soviet Union and not the United States that took the initiative in restoring Indo-Pakistani relations to their normal level of hostility! Washington's frustration was evident in the desires of Johnson, Rusk, and others not to get involved with the perpetual hassles of the subcontinent at a time when U.S. involvement in Vietnam was escalating. The arms embargo hurt Pakistan, and it remained unmodified until April 12, 1967, when the United States announced it would resume the sale of spare parts to Pakistan, but would close its MAAG offices because it expected no further weapons sales.

Pakistan's goals in 1965 were two-fold. It primarily wanted to resolve the Kashmir problem through infiltration into Kashmir, thereby nucleating a public uprising against Indian control. Secondarily, Pakistan wished to wean the Soviet Union away from its exclusive support of India. U.S. policy goals figured low in Pakistani priorities, even though after the war there was much public condemnation of the U.S. failure to support Pakistan. The public was even more bewildered by the U.S. arms embargo because it had never really been told that the United States did not subscribe to the Indian threat theory that had been used in Pakistan as the *raison d'etre* of the alliances with the United States. Pakistan did succeed in bringing the Soviets into a mediating role that required receptivity to Pakistan as well as India—and the Tashkent agreement was indicative of Soviet influence with Ayub and reflected negative U.S. influence. However, the key goal of a Pakistani-inspired Kashmir uprising went unfulfilled.

OBSERVATIONS: THE FIRST DECADE

The U.S.-Pakistani influence relationship began under the classic conditions: perceived need for each other. As it progressed, difficulties arose stemming from ethno-cultural, historical, and political differences between the two nations. These difficulties were aggravated by the communications gap that was occasioned by the mutual irreconcilability of the U.S. and Pakistani concepts of the source of the threat. This gap grew wider with the passage of time.

The United States saw itself as the leader of the free world threatened by world communism and sought global allies whose geographical location and political proclivities were suitable for a joint enterprise in defense. The first concrete objective for U.S. policymakers in Pakistan was the establishment of a presence. They did this in Peshawar, which provided facilities for spying on the Soviet Union and China. Eisenhower, Dulles, and Radford were willing to supply the military and give economic assistance because the price seemed reasonable and because a defensible Pakistan was consistent with their policy goals. Moreover, they hoped that trained Pakistani personnel would be available for use in future contingencies in Southwest Asia and the Middle East.

Pakistan was keen on the relationship because its leaders saw a golden opportunity to buttress military strength against their primary threat, India. There were no other real sources of immediate aid available to Pakistan and, in any case, the Pakistani elite's political outlook was oriented toward the West. Another factor that figured in the Pakistani calculations was the usefulness of the American diplomatic support for their cause in Kashmir.

Difficulties arose early in the relationship. The fundamental dichotomy between the U.S. and Pakistani perceptions of the source of threat was irreconcilable. Diplomatic niceties of studied imprecision, though temporarily useful, sowed the seeds of serious discord in the future. The issue of the availability of Pakistani military personnel for fulfilling U.S. needs in Southwest Asia was handled even more ambiguously. Its treatment in unarticulated, hushed tones seemed to satisfy Dulles and Radford in the early stages of the relationship. However, the absence of concrete Pakistani guarantees on this score, and its lack of fulfillment in actuality, contributed significantly to the later disenchantment of the United States with Pakistan.

The pattern of personalized diplomacy was established early on. There was no institutionalized framework for cooperation, such as active U.S. membership in CENTO might have provided. Key decisions, on either side, were made by a few personalities. Thus devoid of middle-level contacts in the U.S. bureaucracies, Pakistan was ever at the mercy of changes in administrations in Washington. While contacts between MAAG and the Pakistani military fostered some receptivity on both sides and gave Pakistan entrée to the military in the Pentagon, there were few such opportunities for interaction with the professional staff in the State Department or in Congress. This was amply illustrated at the very beginning. Ayub and Mirza had contacts with Dulles and Radford. When they, particularly Ayub, found a difference of opinion at the junior ranks, they went above these groups directly to the bosses. This worked so long as the bosses were as friendly as Eisenhower, Dulles, and Radford. However, when the bosses were less forthcoming, as in the case of Kennedy and Rusk, there was no other constituency within key U.S. agencies that could put forward Pakistan's views or influence the decision makers.

Pakistan missed the opportunity for building up friendship on Capitol Hill. Being used to ignoring their own legislative leaders, Ghulam Mohammad, Mirza, and Ayub set a similar pattern in Washington, leaving behind an unfortunate legacy for others who came after them. There was little recognition or appreciation of the semiautonomous centers of foreign policymaking implicit in the separation of powers doctrine. Little more attention on this score might have made Pakistan's dealings with Congress on such crucial matters as aid a little easier.

Aid clearly gave the United States access and furthered its strategic aims in Pakistan. However, it is worth noting that economic assistance was simply a corollary of military aid. The latter was crucial. Furthermore, there were no donors for military aid who could have substituted for the United States during the period between 1948 and 1965. Thus, it was natural that the termination of military sales would considerably reduce, if not totally end, the U.S. influence with Pakistan.

The fervor with which Pakistan was courted by Dulles and Radford in the early fifties cooled with the passage of time. Furthermore, with the passing of these ardent suitors, and the ambiguous articulation of Pakistani usefulness to the United States, the relationship became dispensable under Kennedy and Rusk. Pakistan reacted to the ebbing relationship in a manner typical of a superceded first wife who, past her voluptuous prime, nevertheless continues to bemoan the ingratitude of her fickle husband whom she gave her all in her youth.

NOTES

1. Hans Morgenthau, *The Impasse of American Foreign Policy*, Chicago: University of Chicago Press, 1962, pp. 13–14.
2. Liaquat was generally applauded for aligning Pakistan with the cause of freedom and democracy. He was perfectly willing to go along with the theme of "Communist menace," as he pledged Pakistani support of U.S. actions in Korea, which were, he said, aimed at "saving Asia from the dangers of world communism." Liaquat Ali Khan, *Pakistan: The Heart of Asia*, Cambridge: Harvard University Press, 1950, p. 28.
3. J. W. Spain, "Military Assistance," *American Political Science Review*, Vol. XLVIII (September 1954), p. 748.
4. For text and papers dealing with it see: Council on Foreign Relations, *Documents on American Foreign Relations, 1954*, New York: Harper and Bros., 1955, pp. 373–383.
5. R. D. Campbell, *Pakistan: Emerging Democracy*, Princeton, NJ: Van Nostrand Co., Inc., 1963, p. 116.
6. Part 9, *John Foster Dulles Papers*, Princeton University Library, Princeton, NJ.
7. For example, a speech to the Philadelphia Chapter of the International Studies Association, 1976.
8. Mohammed Ahsen Chaudhri, "Foundation of Pakistan's Foreign Policy," in L. A. Sherwani, *Pakistan: An Analysis*, Karachi: Allies Book Corp., 1964, p. 20.
9. *Dawn*, Karachi, June 22, 1959.

10. *Ibid.*
11. *Pakistan Times*, Lahore, March 18, 1959.
12. Hafeez-ur Rahman, "Pakistan's Relations with the USSR," *Pakistan Horizon*, Vol. XIX, No. 1, 1961.
13. To multiply its options, Pakistan entered into discussions with both the Soviet Union and the PRC. It signed a $30 million agreement with the USSR for assistance in oil exploration in Pakistan in 1960 and began discussions toward a border agreement with China in 1961. Herbert Feldman, *Revolution in Pakistan: A Study of the Martial Law Administration*, London: Oxford University Press, 1967, p. 191.
14. *Dawn*, July 7, 1961. Also, television interview with ABC (Washington), July 10, 1961.
15. *The New York Times*, October 22, 1962.
16. Mohammad Ayub Khan, *Friends Not Masters: A Political Autobiography*, Lahore: Oxford University Press, 1967, pp. 136–37.
17. Lawrence Ziring, *The Ayub Khan Era: Politics in Pakistan 1958–69*, Syracuse, NY: Syracuse University Press, 1971, p. 44.
18. Herbert Feldman, *From Crisis to Crisis: Pakistan 1962–1969*, London: Oxford University Press, 1972, p. 86.
19. *National Assembly of Pakistan: Debates*, Official Report, Karachi: Government Printing Office, November 21, 1962, p. 10.
20. Ziring, *op. cit.*, p. 52.
21. G. W. Choudhury, *Pakistan's Relations with India, 1947–1966*, London: Pall Mall Press, 1968, p. 245.
22. K. Sarwar Hassan, *Pakistan and the United Nations*, New York: Manhattan Publishing Co., 1960, p. 76.
23. *Keesing's Contemporary Archives*, 1954, p. 13462.
24. See, for example, Sangat Singh, *Pakistan's Foreign Policy: An Appraisal*, London: Asia Publishing House, 1970, p. 55.
25. *Pakistan Times*, January 4, 1951.
26. Statement by Sardar Mohammad Zafrullah, president of the Lahore Muslim League, *Pakistan Times*, December 20, 1955.
27. *Dawn*, January 23, 1956.
28. Arif Hussain, *Pakistan: Its Ideology and Foreign Policy*, London: Frank Cass and Co., 1965, p. 115.
29. John F. Kennedy, *The Strategy for Peace*, New York: Harper & Row, 1960, pp. 157–58.
30. Selig S. Harrison, "India, Pakistan, and the U.S., Cost of a Mistake," *New Republic*, August 24, 1959.
31. *Dawn*, July 7, 1961.
32. *Round Table*, 1960–61, p. 409.
33. Mohammad Ayub Khan, "The Pakistan-American Alliance: Stresses and Strains," *Foreign Affairs*, Volume 42, No. 2, January 1964, pp. 195–209.
34. *Pakistan: National Assembly Debates*, April-May, 1962, 1st Session, No. 1–15.
35. *Pakistan Times*, October 29, 1962.
36. Cited in G. S. Bhargava, *Pakistan in Crisis*, New Delhi: Vikas Publishing, 1969, p. 127.
37. *New York Times*, February 19, 1967.
38. Bhabani Sen Gupta, *Soviet-Asian Relations in the 1970s and Beyond: An Interperceptional Study*, New York: Praeger Special Studies, 1976, p. 139.
39. Donald S. Zagoria, *The Sino-Soviet Conflict: 1956–61*, New York: Anthenum, 1964, pp. 350–51.
40. *Pakistan Times*, July 25, 1965.
41. *Dawn*, July 30, 1965.
42. *Dawn*, August 2, 1965.

43. G. W. Choudhury, *Pakistan's Relations with India: 1947–66*, New York: Praeger, 1968, p. 297.
44. G. W. Choudhury, *India, Pakistan, Bangladesh, and the Major Powers: Politics of a Divided Subcontinent*, New York: The Free Press, 1975, p. 121.
45. For text of the statement, see Government of Pakistan Document E. No. 2597 R.
46. Hugh Tinker, *India and Pakistan: A Political Analysis*, 2nd ed., London: Pall Mall Press, 1967, p. 208.
47. For a discussion of the agreement, see M.S. Rajan, "Tashkent Declaration, Retrospect and Prospect," *International Studies*, July-October 1966, p. 8, and Mushtaq Ahmad, *Pakistan's Foreign Policy*, Karachi, 1968, pp. 53–54.
48. *Times of India*, New Delhi, June 6, 1966.
49. Bhabani Sen Gupta, *op. cit.*, p. 140. For text, see "The Tashkent Declaration," *International Studies*, July-October 1966, pp. 27–28.
50. Interview with the *Washington Post*, July 9, 1966.

2

BIRTH OF BANGLADESH

The 1965 war marked the end of the Johnson administration's concern with Pakistan. Despite suspicion of Pakistan's growing friendship with the PRC and the increasing Soviet stake in affairs of the subcontinent after the Tashkent Conference, Washington became less interested in South Asian concerns. Pakistani attempts to rebuild its war-shattered military strength were basically ignored by the United States. The PRC became the major source for arms supplies. Requests to the Soviets for similar help met with a straightforward reply that the USSR found such assistance impossible in the face of U.S. base facilities in Pakistan.

On the domestic front, the quiet calm that had characterized the Ayub years was broken. First, the economic dislocations occasioned by the war started to work themselves through the system. Inflation, which had been in check since Ayub's takeover seven years ealier, once again became rampant. Secondly, the implicit respect with which the populace had viewed the armed forces began to crumble. Despite Bhutto's catchy rhetoric that "Kashmir had not been lost at the battlefield," the public nevertheless started to doubt the invincibility of the Pakistani Army. Along with it came the realization that, under Ayub, the armed forces were indeed in charge and that Ayub's "basic democracy" was not much more than an apology for one.

What inflamed the masses, however, was the latter half of Bhutto's charge that Ayub's acquiescence to the Tashkent agreement was nothing short of a "surrender" and a national "sell-out." Bhutto cleverly manipulated this feeling when in mass gatherings in Lahore and Karachi he graphically contrasted the "massive frame" and the "puny brains" of Ayub with the "cunning" of his ailing and physically diminutive adversary, Lal Bahadur Shastri. Mr. Shastri was the Indian prime minister who signed the Tashkent agreement on India's behalf.[°]

Bhutto formed his own political party (the Pakistan People's Party— PPP) and rallied opposition elements to a renewed call for participatory government that could guarantee the nation's independence, as well as its security. He used the issue of Pakistani dependence on the United States to illustrate how Ayub had always bet on the wrong horse. Citing the president's role in aligning Pakistan to the United States as a guarantee against the Indian threat, Bhutto pointed to the U.S. arming of India in 1962 without the accompanying pressure on India to settle the Kashmir dispute, the absence of U.S. help to Pakistan in the 1965 war with India, and, indeed, the U.S. arms embargo that Washington knew would hurt Pakistan more than it would India as ample proof of the failure of Pakistan's U.S. option. Ayub, the chief architect of that failed policy, was, according to Bhutto, now relying on Soviet goodwill! This policy, Bhutto warned, would also end disastrously. China was Pakistan's only real friend. As Bhutto said, " . . . it is worth emphasizing that the policy of close relations with China . . . is indispensable to Pakistan; that in dealing with Great Powers one might resist their pressure by all means available, when they offend against the nation's welfare."[1]

The PPP became the first cohesive movement to work toward ousting the military regime and to question the very *raison d'etre* of the military rule. Heretofore, the military had been assumed to be the one truly patriotic group that was above politics. The Pakistan Army, born out of the trauma of independence, had been projected as the only institution that lay between Pakistan's existence and its destruction at Indian hands. But after Tashkent the integrity and even the loyalty of the military rulers (and thus the military) came under suspicion.

Protest against Ayub grew rapidly into widespread agitation. Demand for political participation was the blanket issue under which various political groups from different provinces in West Pakistan, as well as the populous East Pakistan, could comfortably unite.[2]

Civil unrest began also to take its toll on the allegiance of the senior military officers to the continued leadership of Marshal Mohammad Ayub Khan. Once indispensable, he was seen as a liability to the military. Moreover, his recent espousal of the pro-Soviet line was viewed with a

---

[°]According to Pakistani public lore, he was so overjoyed at befooling mighty Ayub that he promptly died of a heart attack. His body was flown from Tashkent to India for a hero's funeral.

certain skepticism. Yet, being unable to gauge the true extent of his lingering popularity among the rank and file of the army, senior officers remained hesitant. Their hand, however, was strengthened by events in the United States.

In November 1968, Richard Nixon was elected thirty-seventh President of the United States. His presidency augured well for Pakistan. Relations that had worsened under Democratic presidents were expected to improve under one who had befriended the country in 1952 during the halcyon days of the U.S.-Pakistani relationship. Nixon had visited Pakistan four times, in official as well as private capacities. He had recognized U.S. interests in Pakistan early and, as president, the military leadership expected him to renew the old ties and reestablish some of the old relationships.

As Ayub's position grew more tenuous, Moscow watched the events in Pakistan with a certain bewilderment. On personally witnessing the mounting anti-Ayub feeling during his trip to Pakistan early in 1969, Premier Kosygin is said to have remarked, "How can the Pakistanis not appreciate such a good man who has done so much to improve Pak-Soviet relations?" Had Kosygin been less wistful, he would have realized that Ayub's pro-Tashkent policy had become a veritable millstone around his neck!

THE GRAND DECEPTION

Despite long-standing personal friendship between Ayub and Nixon, the displacement of Ayub by General Agha Mohammed Yahya Khan on March 25, 1969 was not unwelcome in Washington. Unbeknownst to the world at large, Nixon and Kissinger were writing a secret play with a large act for Pakistan. And Ayub, who had so recently played a title role in Tashkent, was ill-suited to star in it.

Nixon's fifth visit to Pakistan in July 1969 came amidst a temporary domestic lull, as the country prepared for elections. It was a brief visit, but momentous. Nixon asked General Yahya Khan to act as a conduit between Washington and Peking and explore the possibility of normalization of relations between the two countries. Yahya agreed and promised to carry out the task in utmost secrecy. In return, Nixon assured Yahya of his goodwill and a place for Pakistan in his emerging strategy.[3] To Ayub, as a gesture of his regard for the man he remembered as the principal architect of the Pakistani alliance with the United States, Nixon sent a private note through an unofficial but secret channel. The note was personally delivered to Ayub in Swat[4] where he was living quietly, convalescing from a heart ailment.

The military leadership, despite their lack of trust in Soviet friendship, was nevertheless curious to see how far Ayub's Soviet option would be helpful. This created a dichotomous situation. The Soviets, as a prerequisite to their military and economic assistance, were demanding a formal end to the Peshawar base lease agreement with the United States. On the other hand, because the miliary leadership had started to dream that under Nixon the United States would reestablish the old pipeline of assistance, they were hesitant to jeopardize it in favor of what might turn out to be no more than empty promises of Soviet aid. The mutual inconsistency of these options was, however, inexplicably overcome. This owed itself to the special situation that Nixon's request to Yahya had created. To Nixon, the continued availability of the Peshawar base was of no particular concern. On the other hand, Nixon had just developed a vital interest in Yahya's survival.

Through personal contacts with people in a position to know, a partial but plausible picture has emerged of what transpired during Nixon's contact with Yahya in Lahore during his brief visit to Pakistan. Yahya's need to test the Soviet intentions with regard to developing an even-handed approach toward the subcontinent was noted by Nixon as something he could live with, at first with certain reluctance. It soon became apparent, however, that Yahya's outward display of sincerity at seeking and developing such a Soviet option, while at the same time pursuing the sensitive and secret mission to the PRC on behalf of Nixon, had considerable merit as a diversionary tactic.

The secret nature of this understanding created a totally anomalous situation. Accordingly, in contrast with the warmth of the relationship between Nixon-Kissinger and Yahya, the government-to-government-level relations rapidly degenerated. The abrupt Pakistani order for closing the Peshawar base, on the occasion of the tenth anniversary of the 1959 bilateral agreement, caused considerable resentment among the U.S. embassy personnel in Islamabad—particularly because the Pakistan government wanted the matter to be carried out expeditiously. Moreover, the worst fears of the State Department that Pakistan was playing favorites with the Russians were soon confirmed in August 1969, when Pakistan received an offer of $30 million in Soviet military supplies. The sum was small, but it caused great excitement in Pakistan, where it was wishfully seen as only the "tip of the iceberg."

The Soviet option continued to be nursed. Yahya went to Moscow in June 1970. He signed an agreement for a steel mill to be built in Karachi. The Soviets agreed to provide an equivalent of about $500 million in credits for this purpose. Yahya also informed Soviet leaders of "unsolved controversial issues" between India and Pakistan. The USSR favored their solution[5] through "bilateral negotiations in the spirit of the Tashkent

Declaration." However, behind the scenes Yahya continued the pursuit of Nixon's closely guarded secret mission to Peking.

Following his seemingly successful Moscow trip, Yahya prepared noisily for his China visit to be held five months later. The ostensible purpose was to reassure the Chinese leadership that Pakistan's emerging relationship with the Soviet Union was not meant to be to their detriment.

Three weeks prior to his departure for Peking, Yahya journeyed to New York to attend and address the meeting of the UN General Assembly. With animated generosity, he declared that enmity between India and Pakistan was "tragic for both of us." His suggestion that India and Pakistan withdraw their troops from the disputed territory of Kashmir was rejected disdainfully by the Indian defense minister, Jagjivan Ram, as "amounting to asking India to withdraw from her own territory."[6]

Two days after Yahya's arrival in Peking, the annual China debate in the General Assembly was getting under way. That all was not as usual would have struck a very careful observer had he pondered the import of the rather momentous words of the U.S. deputy permanent representative, Christopher H. Phillips, who declared, "The United States is as interested as any to see the PRC play a constructive role."[7] This public signal heralded a dramatic shift in the U.S. policy on the admission of China to the United Nations. Presumably, while in New York, Yahya had been apprised of this pronouncement in advance, so that he could personally convey the message of its imminence to the leadership in Peking.

Yahya's real purpose for the China trip was further camouflaged, and his labors rewarded, when the Chinese publicized, on November 14, the offer of an additional package of $200 million in economic aid to Pakistan. As an aside, China also gave its unqualified support to Yahya's call for the demilitarization of Kashmir, which had already been rejected by India.

In the meantime, the gathering storm in East Pakistan loomed ominously over the horizon. Yahya Kahn, whose achievements even as a military leader were questionable, was ill-equipped to deal with the complexity of the issues that were being raised. His circle of advisers was narrowing and the caliber of advice was uneven. His taxing personal life of drunkenness and debauchery, which was widely talked about in Pakistan, added further fuel to the anxiety the Pakistani elites felt about his ability to cope. Typical of Yahya's responses during the period were his categoric rejection of the political demands, as they first appeared, and of his piecemeal, spasmodic acceptance of some of them at a later occasion. For instance, his agreement to the demands for a promise of free elections based on the principle of universal franchise and the reconstitution of West Pakistan from "one unit" into separate provinces, as was the case prior to August 1955, was for him a major concession. Also, of course, it was a constructive act. This, coupled with Yahya's public statement that he would work toward the evolution of a constitution that would ease the political, economic, and social tensions facing the nation, sounded eminently reasonable. Certainly, it was seen by the White House as a promising move indicating political awareness on the part of Yahya and the beginning of the process for making restitution of East Pakistani claims against the Western Wing of the country. Nevertheless, the East Pakistani politicians and, indeed, the U.S. personnel on the scene were less sanguine about the prospects. There was a growing feeling among the U.S. Agency for International Development (AID) and the State Department that East Pakistan was still not receiving its fair share. Statements to this effect by State Department officials in Pakistan led to a feeling that functionaries of the U.S. government were "interfering" and that "Washington was actively backing the secessionists in Dacca."[8] For example, both the U.S. ambassador to Pakistan, Joseph Farland, the U.S. consul-general to Dacca, Archer Blood, were accused of acting in a fashion inimical to the Pakistani national interest.

The saga of the escalating domestic crisis facing Yahya Khan and the events leading to the Indo-Pakistani War of 1971 has been detailed elsewhere.[9] However, it must be mentioned that the Legal Framework Order (LFO) promulgated by Yahya on March 30, 1970, set the stage for the elections promised for October 1970. LFO provided for a federal structure for Pakistan with maximum provincial autonomy, established election rules for the National Assembly, set the political stage for popular participation, and called formally for ending the disparity between the two wings of Pakistan.[10] These acts, combined with the earlier acceptance of universal franchise and the dissolution of the One Unit in the Western Wing had left no doubt in the minds of both the political and the military elite, including Yahya's advisers, that the Eastern Wing will produce the next prime minister of Pakistan.

Scholarly analyses suggesting Yahya was suprised by the size and the completeness of the Awami League victory in East Pakistan can therefore not be given too much credence, especially since the emergence of Mujib as the undisputed leader was treated as a foregone conclusion in West Pakistan.[11] What did, however, occasion surprise in the ruling military-bureaucratic circles was Mujib's total lack of interest in becoming the leader of the united Pakistan. This stance coincidently paralleled Bhutto's equally unexpected insistence not to settle for the second highest position in Pakistani leadership. To understand the rationale behind these seemingly curious stands on the part of the two leading politicians (who were both overwhelmingly elected by the electorates in their own wings of the country in the fairest election ever held in the history of Pakistan, but who had little, if any, following in the other wing of the country), would require a psychological portrait of Bhutto and Mujib that would take us far afield. Suffice it to mention here that the impasse subsequent to this grand election was created as much by Mujib, who used his electoral mandate to make his "six points" totally nonnegotiable, as by Bhutto, who invoked the authority of his electoral majority in the West to equally adamantly oppose any accommodation with Mujib.[12]

MOUNTING CRISIS

Nixon's sympathy for Yahya stemmed as much from the fact of the latter's usefulness in the establishment of the China connection as from the seemingly genuine belief on Nixon's part that Yahya was sincere in seeking a political solution. For Nixon, the fairness of the general election held in December 1970 was evidence par excellence of Yahya's sincerity, as was the fact of Yahya's begrudging but nevertheless correct acquiescence to the modalities of the election process. Thus, the White House followed the search for a political consensus, subsequent to the elections, with especial keenness in early 1971. The disappointment in Washington mounted as the fabric of the negotiations for a consensus came apart when on February 16, 1971 Bhutto announced that his party, the PPP, would boycott the National Assembly scheduled to convene on March 3, 1971.[13] Mujib also held his ground, talks broke down, and the whole process of "negotiation" came to an end.

Up to this juncture, Yahya had escaped any serious consequences from his habit of misguided first responses. There had been time enough for wiser counsel to prevail. This time, however, he embarked on an inhumane and a despicable course of action that he found totally irreversible; he ordered the military to move against civilians in East Pakistan. The crackdown came on March 25, 1971. Henceforth, sane advice did not seem to reach Yahya in any substantial measure. Or, if it did arrive in his vicinity, it clearly failed to sway him from the disastrous course he was holding.

Stories about the bizarre character of his court during the subsequent sad days were legend and were told as nightmarishly bad jokes at parties attended by the bureaucratic and military elite. Perhaps the most pathetic of these tells how once Yahya's bacchanalian revelry was interrrupted by an official of the foreign office who brought a Soviet letter urging compassion in East Pakistan. In response, Yahya demanded the dispatch of a rejection letter along with the gratuitous insult that it was strange, indeed, that the Soviets were preaching compassion, considering what they had done in the past to the people of Hungary and Czechoslovakia! Apparently, Yahya continued to befool himself with the thought that this was just a funny joke and that he still enjoyed good relations with the

"Russians." The Soviets, on the other hand, treated this as anything but a laughing matter. They saw this as the last straw in their relationship with Pakistan and it entailed profound consequences for South Asian political geography.

THE REACTION

Once the crackdown in East Pakistan became established policy, President Richard Nixon and his national security adviser, Henry Kissinger, began to see the writing on the wall. Kissinger's analytical mind focused narrowly on the inevitable, logical outcome of the process: the eventual breakup of United Pakistan. As the train of events unfolded, Nixon and Kissinger tailored their reactions toward a set of central objectives: to buy more time, to reduce the accompanying damage, and to guard against any possible derailment of their own behind-the-scenes initiative to the PRC. They decided that the events in Pakistan were proceeding as a result of the internal dynamics of Pakistani politics rather than from any action of the United States, and that any U.S. efforts, short of an unwarranted, major intervention, would not completely prevent their tragic culmination. As such, they felt the best they could do under the circumstances was to reduce the pain—at least for their friends in West Pakistan.

This hopelessness engendered a certain preordained futility to the Nixon-Kissinger efforts and caused their actions to look erratic and unreasonable. Unaware of the Nixon-Kissinger secret relationship with Yahya, the U.S. Abassador Kenneth Keating in New Delhi, U.S. Consul-General Archer Blood in Dacca, and various foreign policy bureaucrats in the State Department all advocated tough measures against Pakistan. These included a prompt public condemnation of Yahya by the United States, the stoppage of all economic assistance including that which was then in the "pipeline" and, perhaps somewhat symbolically, the cutoff of whatever little military assistance program still remained in effect. While Nixon and Kissinger gave a half-hearted approval to these plans, Nixon's overriding proviso, according to Kissinger, was more accurately expressed in the following order: "To all hands. Don't squeeze Yahya at this time."[14] Nixon's frustration at the fundamental split between the White House and the State and Defense Departments is also recorded by Kissinger: "On no other problem was there such flagrant disregard of unambiguous presidential directives. The State Department controlled the machinery"[15] and through small shifts was able to interpret presidential directives in a manner that actually "vitiated the course Nixon had set."[16]

As the repression in East Pakistan mounted, the U.S. Congress gradually involved itself with the issue. By June 1971, the Congress had become an important factor in U.S. policy affecting events in East Pakistan. In particular, Senator Edward Kennedy soundly condemned Pakistani actions and Nixon's reactions, and called upon the United States to reject Pakistani policy in words and in deeds. Both the Senate and the House passed resolutions calling for an end to all U.S. economic and military aid to Pakistan, an act which the House amended only to permit food and medical assistance to continue.

Nixon did not see this as a bipartisan effort motivated solely by humanitarian considerations. Aware of the "Catch-22" dilemma that Indian policy presented him with, he saw an Indian move to arm guerrillas and create instability as feeding the refugee influx into India and circumventing any settlement. By mid-July 1971, Mrs. Gandhi had begun to speak of the birth of Bangladesh. There was mounting recognition that this was India's golden opportunity to cripple and dismember Pakistan. Nixon viewed Kennedy's espousal of pressure on Pakistan as a deliberate attempt to embarrass him and gain support in his quest for the presidency.[17]

Recognizing the limitations that Congressional displeasure imposed on his ability to buy off Pakistan with infusions of aid large enough to be able to make a difference, Nixon felt his best recourse was to press Yahya to take a number of steps that cumulatively could still defuse the crisis. These steps were, first, to internationalize the crisis by making the relief effort multilateral (an Indian demand); second, to replace the military governor of East Pakistan by a civilian (a Bengali demand); third, to grant general amnesty to all persons not accused of specific criminal acts. (Yahya did, in fact, announce a general amnesty, but most of the relevant individuals stayed on in India.)

When Kissinger left for his Asian tour on June 28, 1971, he sought to avert a war that was fast becoming inevitable in the face of Yahya's bumbling inability to move expeditiously and Mrs. Gandhi's shrewd assessment, shared by the Soviets, that a golden opportunity, of Pakistan's own making, had arisen that ought not to be passed up. Kissinger, unlike the State Department or Congress, was aware of "the need for Yahya as a channel to Peking," as he was to reiterate in his 1979 interview with David Frost.[18] He was also aware that the Soviet Union—well before the July 15 disclosure of his secret trip to China—had promised India support for guerrilla operations in East Pakistan as well as protection against any Chinese reprisals. Kissinger fully expected these assurances to alleviate any anxieties that Mrs. Gandhi may have felt in this regard.

Kissinger's meeting with Mrs. Gandhi was a strained affair. He gave her no inkling that he was heading for Peking from Islamabad. She gave him no indication of the impending Indo-Soviet treaty. Instead, they talked of Pakistani policy and U.S. support. The Indian prime minister complained that all aid to Pakistan had not stopped, pointing out that even though the value of the aid was minuscule the symbolism of any U.S. support at all was a significant factor in Pakistani intransigence. This drew the following response from Kissinger:

> Indian leaders evidently did not think it strange that a country which had distanced itself from most of our foreign policy objectives in the name of nonalignment was asking us to break ties with an ally over what was in international law a domestic conflict.[19]

During the course of Kissinger's visit to Islamabad, he pressed on Yahya the necessity for a political resolution of the refugee and autonomy problems. Yahya promised to consider these questions, but could not be pressed to follow U.S. wishes; nor was he convinced that India would launch a war, or that it could win, if it did. Kissinger's main preoccupation remained his trip to China, although he noted Yahya's total lack of ability to recognize the reality of the situation and the impending disaster. In China, Kissinger found approval of the Pakistani position. He responded that U.S. friendship and gratitude (for the China opening) did not, however, include military aid or military support for Pakistan.

Kissinger had foreseen that India would move militarily into East Pakistan, yet he persisted behind the scenes to get Yahya to compromise in the vain hope of defusing the crisis. For example, this pressure resulted in July in Yahya's acceptance of two of the basic U.S. proposals: UN supervision of refugee resettlement efforts and the appointment of a civilian governor. But India refused to go along because "the very reasons that made the strategy of concentrating on refugees attractive to us [the U.S.] caused India to obstruct it."[20]

THE INDO-SOVIET TREATY

The announcement that a twenty-year "friendship" treaty between the USSR and India had been signed on August 9. 1971, struck Islamabad like a bolt of lightning. It came at the conclusion of Soviet Foreign Minister Andrei Gromyko's two-day visit to India. The joint communiqué issued at the end of Gromyko's visit stated that both sides believed the treaty to be an outstanding historic event, and that it was the logical culmination of a long history of "sincere friendship, respect, mutual trust, and comprehensive relations which have been established between the Soviet Union and India over many years and which have stood the test of time."[21] While explaining the framework it provided for regular contacts and mutual consultations aimed at "safeguarding the peace and security" of both countries, the treaty asserted that it was not directed against anyone and trusted that it would meet with "full approval from all who are genuinely interested in the preservation of peace in Asia and the entire world."[22]

Despite protestations that the treaty was not a military alliance and did not affect India's nonaligned status, the most important clauses in the treaty had military-strategic significance. Article VIII stated that "each of the High Contracting Parties solemnly declares that it will not enter into or participate in any military alliance directed against the other side."[23] This foreclosed the possibility of any Soviet military help to Pakistan. India was fully cognizant of this facet of the treaty in that the "treaty prohibits the Soviet Union from giving any assistance to Pakistan which militates against Indian interests."[24] This also amounted to a belated public admission on the part of the Soviets that they had abandoned all attempts to balance their policy in South Asia between India and Pakistan, thus shedding the last vestige of what they in the past had proclaimed as the "Spirit of Tashkent." Another, less well-appreciated aspect of this clause was the limitation it placed on any future rapprochement between India and China or the United States.

Article IX of the treaty pledged that each side will "refrain from giving any assistance to any third party in an armed conflict with the other side" and provided that in the event that either side is attacked or threatened the signatories would immediately engage in consultation and take steps that are appropriate in eliminating the threat.[25] Taken in the context of the Nixon visit to China and the rapidly deteriorating situation in East Pakistan, this article pledged help to India, neutralized the fledgling 1969 arms transfer agreement between Moscow and Islamabad, and precluded the possibility of Chinese intervention on Pakistan's behalf because it would constitute a "threat" to India.

A number of advantages accrued to the USSR from the treaty. Moscow succeeded in aligning India—a major feat by the standard of U.S. foreign policy successes. The treaty also guaranteed a future role for the Soviets in South Asian affairs. Furthermore, the treaty enabled Moscow to deal with a number of its concerns, notably, fear of China and the incipient Sino-American rapprochement.

The treaty provided a classic example of a "non-zero sum" game: both contracting parties won concrete benefits. For India, the treaty explicitly provided for Soviet diplomatic support and implicitly laid the basis for the continuing flow of military hardware that had already started to arrive on a massive scale in the months preceding the treaty. The signing of the treaty, coupled with the presence of a million-man Soviet army on the

Chinese border, served as a crucial guarantee to India against any overt Chinese action to help Pakistan in India's forthcoming action against Pakistan.[26] The Indian middle classes understood well the neutralization of the Sino-Pak relationship that the treaty entailed. Furthermore, they took pride in the realization that the treaty would force other nations to take India "more seriously" and to help it "achieve and sustain the role which should (rightly) belong to a country of this size, these resources, and such strategic location."[27] Accordingly, unlike in Egypt after 1973, the treaty occasioned little backlash against the Soviet Union.[28]

Washington's initial reaction to the treaty was, in Kissinger's words: "astonishingly sanguine."[29] It was based on the mistaken impression that the Soviet connection would provide a restraining hand on India, "a fatuous estimate" according to former Secretary of State Kissinger, as well as others.[30] Instead, the treaty ensured war because it promised a Soviet veto in the United Nations and also removed any fears the Indian leaders previously had of a drying up of Soviet military supplies. For the Soviets, the treaty was a great prize, a veritable victory, one in which

> The Soviet Union had seized a strategic opportunity. To demonstrate Chinese impotence and to humiliate a friend of both China and the United States proved too tempting. If China did nothing, it stood revealed as impotent; if China raised the ante, it risked Soviet reprisal. With the treaty, Moscow threw a lighted match into a powder keg.[31]

However, despite its great value, the prize was hard won. It had come after months of planning and behind the scenes wooing of the Indian leader Mrs. Gandhi. As such, it is interesting to examine how and why much of this came about.

With the worsening of the civil unrest, after the Pakistani Army began its infamous crackdown in East Pakistan, came the realization that Yahya and his court were not tuned into receiving and analyzing the full import of the signals abroad in the land. Rumors regarding this state of suspended reality at the top were rife in the capital, Islamabad, particularly among the diplomatic circles. The puerile and insulting note sent by General Yahya Khan in response to a Soviet diplomatic message was a case in point. Despite the extreme seriousness with which Yahya viewed his delicate mission to Peking on behalf of Nixon and Kissinger, his alcoholic and sexual intemperence militated weightily against his ability to guard his secrets. His heavy dependence on General Pirzada, who was perhaps his closest adviser, and a far less discrete paramour, mischievously dubbed as "General Raani" by the rumor mill in the capital, was well known. Moreover, as the difficulties in East Pakistan mounted, Yahya's lucid moments in the course of his "working" day tended to contract further.

Given this background, it stands to reason that, besides Nixon-Kissinger, Yahya, and the Chinese leadership, others in Pakistan became aware of the Nixon initiative on China. As such, the Soviet intelligence network in the subcontinent, being widespread and not grossly inefficient, may well in the course of time have acquired more than an inkling of the plans afoot. Certainly, this assumption would offer a possible explanation for the mystery that has surrounded the inexplicable change of course in the fledging Soviet move to establish a more positive military-economic relationship with Pakistan. The move had been the product of considerable prior negotiation between Pakistan and the Soviet Union. Moreover, when it finally became public in August 1969, it had come at the heels of a complete severence of the Peshawar base tenancy relationship, coupled with certain well-publicized friction between the Pakistani and U.S. governments. These happenings would under normal circumstances have further cemented the emerging Pak-Soviet ties. However, it will be recalled that just prior to the official launching of the Soviet friendship move toward Pakistan there had occurred a brief and outwardly insignificant visit of President Nixon to Lahore where his secret initiative to China through Yahya was first mooted. Therefore, as the Soviet Union began to get wind of the behind-the-scenes U.S.-China rapprochement effort via Pakistan, its feelings toward Yahya's Pakistan chilled rapidly. In the emerging chaos in East Pakistan, the Soviets saw an opportunity not only to return Yahya's favor, but also to checkmate the possible strategy of its two superpower rivals. In executing their move, the Soviets displayed not only military agility, but also diplomatic dexterity. They kept their motives suitably camouflaged. Thus, when on a later occasion both the Soviet ambassador, Anatoly Dobrynin, and the Indian ambassador to Washington, Mr. L. K. Jha, freely admitted to Kissinger that the Indo-Soviet Friendship Treaty had been in the making for nearly a year, they were stating a factual truth.[32]

THE DELUGE: WAR AND THE "TILT"

Enmeshed in ineptitude and inertia, Yahya turned a deaf ear to Nixon's warnings not to try Mujib for treason and to adopt a political solution that would gain support from the international community. The United States made direct contacts with the Bangladesh government-in-exile in Calcutta. These were undertaken without Islamabad's knowledge. The hope was to mediate the crisis short of independence so that war could be averted. Even though Yahya finally approved of these contacts, the Indians and their supporters in Moscow did not wish to lose this opportunity of dealing a decisive blow to Pakistan. Nixon received Mrs. Gandhi in Washington in November 1971 and was unable to stop her showdown with Pakistan. She refused to accept Yahya's offer for a unilateral withdrawal and a return to civilian government in East Pakistan, both offers having been made through the United States. As recorded by Dr. Kissinger, in her conversations Mrs. Gandhi challenged not only the very concept of Pakistan, but also its right to include the provinces of Baluchistan and the Northwest Frontier in its territory because they "did not properly belong to Pakistan . . . and should never have been part of the original settlement."[34]

The Indian leader's return from her tour of Europe and the United States was followed by a steady increase in Soviet military aid, airlifted to assist in the impending war, which came with the Indian putsch into East Pakistan on November 22, 1971. The official U.S. view is reflected in Kissinger's memoirs. It held that, despite the obfuscation, India could not realistically state that its 200,000 troops had been attacked by 70,000 Pakistani soldiers or that one squadron (12 planes) of the aging, Korean vintage saber jets of the Pakistan air force had been launched at the approximately 200 planes (a majority of which were the more modern MIG 21) that the Indian air force had available for action over East Pakistan. India was merely using the war "to establish its preeminence on the subcontinent."[35] And the Soviets were helping because they were eager to deliver a blow to the U.S. alliance system and to demonstrate China's impotence. In response came Nixon's erratic policy of diplomatic support to Pakistan. This support derived in part from the sense that an ally that had been instrumental in the opening to China could not be totally abandoned; also, there was concern that the China policy could quickly collapse—a possibility if the Chinese were humiliated or felt that the United States had stood by and merely watched as an ally was destroyed. Normalization with China was the finest hour of the Nixon presidency and the president felt that on no account should it be jeopardized. In addition, Nixon subscribed to the theory that even though the 1959 bilateral agreement was specifically aimed at communist threats, subsequent U.S. assurances (e.g., that from Kennedy to Ayub during the 1962 arms shipments to India) covered some measure of support against India.[36] In addition, there was a sense of betrayal that Nixon seemed to feel against Mrs. Gandhi, summed up in the following passage from his report to the Congress: " . . . it is clear that a political process was in train, which could have been supported and facilitated by all parties involved if they had wished. This is the basis for the profound disappointment we felt and expressed when war erupted."[37]

Yahya Khan's pathetic presidency,° well known to the ruling elite in
Islamabad, became publicly exposed once the Indian army began its
march into East Pakistan. The day-to-day running of the government had
already been entrusted to the senior civil servants. However, Yahya felt
that the management of the war was a different matter since he himself
was the most illustrious army commander at hand. Consequently, the
execution of the war was in total disarray: new, ill-considered field actions
were ordered; others, in the process of execution, were halted without
reason. Indeed, Yahya personally ordered the December 3rd Pakistan air
force attack on Indian airfields in the west, with the expectation that such
an action would surely help relieve Indian pressure on the Pakistani Army
in the east. This provided Mrs. Gandhi with a needed pretext to extend the
war in West Pakistan, a move that she was actively considering and one
that might have ended disastrously for Pakistan if Nixon had not intervened.[38]

The deteriorating situation was noted in Washington, and both Nixon
and Kissinger were busy with multiple tasks between November 23, when
India moved into East Pakistan, and December 3, when the war spread to
West Pakistan. The key to understanding the Nixon-Kissinger policy, as
gleaned from interviews with U.S. officials who were involved in this
event, lies in the global view taken by the U.S. president of the unfolding
crisis in South Asia.[39] Thus, quite apart from the commitment to a U.S. ally,
it became a case of demonstrating U.S. resolve vis-à-vis the Soviets and the
Chinese.

Kissinger journeyed to New York for a secret meeting with Huang
Hua, the new PRC permanent representative to the United Nations,
impressing upon him the seriousness of Washington's concern as well as
coordinating a common strategy at the UN where George Bush was the
U.S. permanent representative. He also met with Bhutto, who had come to
plead the Pakistani case before the UN Security Council. On December 5,
1971, the United States proposed a cease-fire resolution in the Council.
But Moscow twice vetoed all attempts to stop the fighting. It was waiting
for New Delhi's green light, and Mrs. Gandhi wanted Indian troops to
secure their objective, namely, the capture of Dacca. The Indians
extended recognition to Bangladesh as early as December 6, 1971, upon
which Pakistan promptly severed diplomatic ties with India. Sometime
between December 5 and December 8, when the UN General Assembly

°Yahya, after all, had made it to the top on the basis of his loyalty to Ayub and not
because of any demonstrated qualities of leadership.

was debating a call for a cessation of the fighting.[40] Yahya's lucidity returned long enough for him to agree with his advisers that the government should now be willing to accept any settlement short of a total rout in East Pakistan. In this connection, all that Yahya's military advisers were seeking was the safe return of the 70,000 West Pakistani troops who, after being hopelessly encircled and defeated, were in the process of surrendering to the advancing Indian army.

In the meantime, Bhutto, acting as Yahya's special representative, put on a star performance at the United Nations. Instead of reading his prepared speech, in an emotion-charged delivery he accused the delegates of superficiality and insensitivity to the plight of the Pakistani soldiers and civilians undergoing untold miseries as the UN machinery observed its diplomatic niceties and nursed its onerous inertia. After this he dramatically tore up the paper containing the text of his speech and stormed out of the chamber. He also carefully arranged to make himself unavailable to any further instructions from Islamabad. Knowing that Bangladesh was about to become an internationally accepted reality, Bhutto's studied action ensured that the Pakistani military would not be spared any humiliation, including total defeat and imprisonment. After all, it was necessary to emasculate the military if Bhutto's imminent ascendancy to the leadership of Pakistan was to be immune from any further challenge from the military.

TASK FORCE 74: INFLUENCING THE OUTCOME

A ten-ship naval task force was dispatched on December 10 from the U.S. Seventh Fleet off South Vietnam toward the Bay of Bengal in order to signal the U.S. commitment to the continued territorial integrity of West Pakistan. This move, ordered by Nixon, coupled with Kissinger's "background" briefing to the press that Moscow's inability to restrain the Indians could jeopardize the entire fabric of East-West relations, was meant to ensure that both New Delhi and Moscow understood the seriousness of any Indian move into West Pakistan.

Critics of the above decision explain in great detail that by the time the task force, led by the aircraft carrier *Enterprise*, entered the Bay of Bengal on December 15, India had already secured its objective in ensuring the birth of Bangladesh and "unilaterally chosen to confine its attention in the West to the long disputed territory of Kashmir."[41] Further, to emphasize that the Indians did not dispute the integrity of West Pakistan, they cite statements from the Indian leadership that New Delhi coveted no Pakistani territory with the caveat that, of course, any augmentation of the Indian-held portion of Kashmir was, if not quite fair game, at least understandable.[42] Carrying this argument to its logical conclusion, Mrs. Gandhi was seen to have no designs on Pakistan, she was therefore not subject to any Soviet and, in turn, through them, to any U.S. pressure. That the Indian leadership did make the relevant statements is not in doubt, given the authoritativeness of the source these critics cite.[43] Rather, it is the acceptance of public statements by national leadership at face value that is debatable.

In other words, did the United States, by sending a strong military signal to both Moscow and New Delhi, influence India's acceptance of the cease-fire on December 16, 1971, a day after Task Force 74 entered the Bay of Bengal and the same day that the CIA reported PRC's military deployment along the common border with India? The problem lies in various scholars treating the presence of the task force as signaling a U.S. commitment to the point of possible military action rather than as an attempt by the United States to influence India to maintain a hands-off policy toward West Pakistan, including Kashmir—a preventive diplomatic action that made diplomacy more credible through a U.S. presence.[44] With a long-standing tradition of independence and pride, Indian leaders cannot but be expected to state that the U.S. action was of no consequence, that Moscow did not lean on India, and that, "despite provocation," India in its magnanimity decided to spare West Pakistan.

Unquestionably, the Soviets possessed the capability to meet the United States militarily in the Indian Ocean. In this connection, a list of Soviet ships dispatched from Vladivostok toward the Bay of Bengal makes an instructive reading: two combat ships, a cruiser armed with surface-to-surface cruise missiles (SSM) and an antiship missle-armed submarine, dispatched on December 7, 1971 to join the mine sweeper and two destroyers already in the Indian Ocean on December 5. Three additional armed Soviet ships, a cruiser, a destroyer, and a submarine, were organized at Vladivostok and sailed for the Bay of Bengal on December 13, 1971.[45]

The point is that the charge leveled against Nixon's decision to send in Task Force 74 into the Indian Ocean as having had no impact on the Indians and in fact forcing the Soviets to react is unsupportable.[46] As the list above shows, the Soviets had dispatched two armed ships on December 7 for the Bay of Bengal four days prior to the sailing of the Task Force 74. In fact, one can say that Nixon, after reviewing the Soviet naval moves and learning through the CIA contact within the Gandhi Cabinet of the sentiment "to teach Pakistan a final lesson" by moving into West Pakistan, decided to send a clear signal to forestall the Indian invasion in the west.[47] Only the December 13 dispatch of Soviet ships can be said to have been reactive.

Once Nixon made the decision, the U.S. task force entered the Bay of Bengal ahead of the Soviet ships, given the approximate sailing time of seventeen days from Vladivostok for the Soviets. Both Yahya as well as the Chinese leadership (Chou En-lai, in particular) were counting on some demonstration of U.S. commitment to the territorial integrity of West Pakistan and, at least as far as these two parties were concerned, the U.S. move was eminently successful. It has to be remembered that Nixon was not using Task Force 74 as a military instrument (although naval experts believe that the United States could always get to the Indian Ocean faster than could the Soviets from their more distant bases), but rather as a visible political instrument when verbal communication had failed to have the necessary impact. Washington did not need to attack New Delhi or Moscow to nudge the Indians into a cease-fire, which came on December 16, 1971, only one day after the naval task force appeared in the area and two days after Kissinger's warning to the Soviets on East-West relations. Thus, the United States succeeded in obtaining a cease-fire in the subcontinent. By raising the ante it risked escalation, but it was a calculated move that prevented rather than risked great power in- volvement by shortening the crisis. Had events gone the other way, the onus would have been on the Soviets, who were the first to dispatch ships—which were already en route when Nixon gave his orders. Just as it happened in Cuba in 1962, the Soviets backed away from this particular involvement. While India cannot be classified as being a typical client state of the Soviet Union, it is also unrealistic to accept at face value Mrs. Gandhi's protestations that India is too independent to be affected by any external pressures or constraints. Indeed, neither the decision to start the conflict nor to terminate it was entirely India's alone.

In a similar vein, Chinese public pronouncements in the *Peking Review* to the effect that "no domination or carving up of the area by U.S. imperialism and Soviet revisionism will be tolerated,"[48] cannot be taken at their face value. Indeed, to look for consistency between these public declarations and behind-the-scenes Chinese efforts to coax the United States into actively assisting Pakistan is to miss the whole point. Thus, construing the public Chinese posture as "warning" the United States against intervention and as displaying Peking's anger with regard to the U.S. naval presence, as has been suggested, is fallacious.[49]

Nixon's dispatch of the task force was generally welcomed in Pakistan, as the first concrete steps taken by an ally to signal its resolve.[50] Pakistani leaders were not ashamed of Nixon's personal preference for Pakistan over India, although unlike the Indians they did not subscribe to the prejudice theory.[51] They felt more that both Nixon and Kissinger understood power diplomacy (not a bad word in the Pakistani lexicon) and exercised a legitimate U.S. option when all diplomatic signals had failed to convey the seriousness of the situation. Islamabad was desparately aware that since December 5, 1971 all UN attempts to achieve a cease-fire were led by the United States and had foundered due to Soviet vetoes and Indian unwillingness. Mrs. Gandhi's statements that the time had come to settle the score in Kashmir, coupled with her earlier statements in Washington that even the NWFP and Baluchistan were questionable as Pakistani territory, had frightened Pakistani officials.[52] In this connection, it has to be noted that the Indian view about the Indian-held part of Kashmir has a close parallel in Pakistani perceptions about the Pakistani held part of Kashmir. Much like the Indians, the Pakistanis do not consider their part of Kashmir to be at all disputed, in any manner or form. Rather, they consider it an integral and inviolable part of their country. Thus, any military threats to Pakistani Kashmir were viewed as threats to West Pakistan itself. Furthermore, severance of Kashmir was considered additionally unacceptable because it would have cut off Pakistan's physical contact with its ally China. Pakistanis were, therefore, very grateful for Nixon's use of the Hot Line to convey warnings to New Delhi through Moscow not to encroach on West Pakistan, including Kashmir. Islamabad also viewed Moscow's dispatch of Deputy Foreign Minister Kuznetsov to New Delhi as a positive sign that would not have occurred without U.S. pressure.[53] By mid-December, Pakistan was clutching at straws and Nixon had offered a life-line. Pakistani leadership and the knowledgeable elite were profoundly appreciative of Nixon's actions as far as the outcome was concerned, namely, the sparing of West Pakistan and the securing of a cease-fire.

OBSERVATIONS

The 1971 Indo-Pakistan War and U.S. involvement illustrate the possibilities as well as the contraints inherent in the exercise of influence. Washington preferred that Islamabad seek a political solution to the East Pakistan crisis. It did not condone the military crackdown of March 25, 1971. But neither did it publicly condemn the Yahya regime for the brutal suppression in East Pakistan. This is where policy was divided between the White House and the bureaucracy. The State Department, AID and, on occasion, individuals in the Defense Department all felt that the United States should strongly condemn the actions of the Yahya regime, pressure it to accede to Mujib's demands in East Pakistan, and side with India as it sought to return the refugees to their homes. They felt the objective of U.S. policy in this case was to look at the Bangladesh crisis in the regional perspective to which it belonged and to recognize the primary role of India in South Asia, a role that it deserved by virtue of its size and form of government.

Nixon and Kissinger, on the other hand, looked at the unfolding of events in South Asia as part of a larger global framework where the triangular relationship between the United States, the USSR, and the PRC had to be balanced. South Asia was regarded simply as the first test of this relationship.[54] Indian actions thus had a larger meaning, since they were assumed to represent a Soviet decision—signaled through the Indo-Soviet treaty—not to exercise restraint. These sentiments were reflected in the following notes from a WSAG meeting: "Dr. Kissinger states that we may be witnessing a situation wherein a country [India] equipped and supported by the Soviets may be turning half of Pakistan into an impotent state and the other half into a vassal."[55]

There was also the imperative of the China connection. Having created a stake in Yahya's survival, Nixon and Kissinger could not push too far toward the settlement of the dispute with Mujib's Awami League in East Pakistan. They hoped to influence Yahya gradually in the direction of a political solution and they believed that if Mrs. Gandhi, supported and encouraged by the Soviets, had not intervened, Yahya would have moved toward an accommodation with the Awami League. Nixon was able to influence Yahya to agree to the repatriation of refugees through an award of amnesty, the appointment of a civilian governor, and the internationalization of the relief efforts. However, the importance of Yahya's role as an intermediary in providing an opening to the PRC and making possible the "first serious, nonsparing exchange" with them constrained Nixon's ability to influence Yahya further.[56] Thus, Nixon was only partially successful in that he could not influence the disastrous Pakistani policy to accommodate quickly enough to the changing situation in East Pakistan and to escape the predatory net being laid by the Indians in alliance with the Soviet Union. Yet, Nixon's success was not altogether insignificant since, in the judgment of many of the senior Pakistani officials involved, Nixon's intervention was crucial in saving West Pakistan.[57]

From the Pakistani perspective, the possibility of influencing the United States was limited, given the horrific mistake of military action on civilians in East Pakistan. Yahya and his advisers were aware of pressures within the U.S. Congress and the government bureaucracy to punish Pakistan. They also knew that not only were State Department representatives unhappy with the White House, but also that Melvin Laird, the secretary of defense, was "dragging his feet" on weapons to Pakistan and arms supplies through third countries, such as Turkey, Iran, Saudi Arabia, and Jordan.[58] Yahya and his close advisers were also cognizant of Nixon's need for Pakistan because of Nixon's commitment to a rapprochement with China. Although this policy gave Yahya some claim over Nixon, it was recognized in Islamabad that any leverage was limited because Nixon had serious domestic constraints.

The dispatch by Nixon of Task Force 74 to the Bay of Bengal and its presence in the area until the crisis had passed were perceived by Yahya, Bhutto, and civil and military leaders as being an unequivocal signal to India not to attack West Pakistan—a view shared by the Chinese leadership.[59] Pakistan's leaders fully subscribed to CIA reports that the Indian Cabinet was discussing an attack on West Pakistan, and they believed that it was only pressure from the United States that prevented the fruition of the plan. Yahya's confidence in Nixon stemmed from his contacts over China. Bhutto accepted the contention that the United States had prevented India from attacking West Pakistan. However, he was peeved that Yahya, a military man, had stolen the thunder on Bhutto's China connection by acting as the liaison in Sino-American relations.

While the United States received a measure of thanks for dispatching the task force and providing diplomatic support, the absence of concrete military assistance was nonetheless noted. Even though Kissinger and other high officials of the Nixon staff have spoken of the U.S. military assistance to Pakistan through third countries as being a decisive factor in saving Pakistan, in Pakistan this support was seen as being pitifully inadequate.[60] Moreover, it was contrasted with the huge transfer of Soviet weaponry to India during most of 1971 and, in particular, with the massive airlift of weapons just prior to, and during, the war. The immense size of this assistance, and the directness of its transfer, were compared with the "meagerness" of the U.S. contribution to Pakistan and the clandestine, indirect maner in which it had to be transferred. Therefore, on balance, it has to be concluded that because the ultimate measure of another country's support and friendship has always been weighed in Pakistan in terms of concrete military assistance, the United States once again fell short as an ally. Consequently, U.S. influence post-1971 was not commensurate with the crucial role Nixon played in preventing a widening of the war and saving West Pakistan from Indian military occupation.

NOTES

1. Zulfikar Ali Bhutto, *The Myth of Independence*, Lahore: Oxford University Press, 1969, p. VIII.
2. W. Norman Brown, *The United States and India, Pakistan, Bangladesh*, Cambridge, Mass.: Harvard University Press, 1972, pp. 211–12.
3. Richard Nixon, *U.S. Foreign Policy for the 1970s: A New Strategy for Peace*, A Report to the Congress, February 18, 1970, USGPO, February 9, 1972, pp. 145–46.
4. Ayub's eldest daughter was married to the former ruler of this northern state, which had been incorporated into Pakistan.
5. *Facts on File*, Vol. XXX, No. 1549 (July 2–8, 1970), p. 489.
6. *Facts on File*, Vol. XXX, No. 1568 (November 12–18, 1970), p. 838.
7. *Ibid.*, p. 827.

8. Wayne Wilcox, *The Emergence of Bangladesh: Problems and Opportunities for a Redefined American Policy in South Asia*, Washington, DC: American Enterprise Institute, 1973, p. 18.
9. Two such studies are: G. W. Choudhury, *The Last Days of United Pakistan*, Bloomington: Indiana University Press, 1974; and Richard Sisson, "Escalation and Crisis Decision-Making: Pakistan's First War of 1971," a paper presented at the Annual Meeting of the Association for Asian Studies, 1980, Washington, D.C.
10. Wilcox, *op. cit.*, p. 15.
11. For example, Donald Watt, "Pakistan from Within," *Commonwealth Journal of International Affairs*, (January 1972), p. 16.
12. The Awami League's six points briefly were: (1) a federal structure; (2) the federal government to be responsible for only defense and foreign affairs; (3) two separate currencies; (4) a fiscal and tax policy to be the responsibility of each federating unit; (5) separate foreign exchange accounts and (6) a militia and paramilitary force to be allowed in each federating unit.
13. These negotiations are documented in Rahman Sobhan, "Negotiations for Bangladesh," *South Asian Review*, July 9, 1971.
14. Henry Kissinger, *White House Years*, Boston: Little, Brown & Co., 1979, p. 856.
15. *Ibid.*, p. 864.
16. *Ibid.*
17. Dan Haendel, *The Process of Priority Formulation: U.S. Foreign Policy in the Indo-Pakistan War of 1971*, Boulder: Westview Press, 1977, p. 100.
18. Kissinger, *op. cit.*, p. 857.
19. Kissinger, *op. cit.*, p. 861.
20. Kissinger, *op. cit.*, p. 863.
21. "Joint Soviet-Indian Statement," *Pravda*, August 12, 1971, *CDSP*, Vol. XXIII, No. 32.
22. *Ibid.*
23. "Friendship Treaty with India," *Izvestia*, August 10, 1971, *CDSP*, Vol. XXIII, No. 32.
24. Pran Chopra, *Before and After the Indo-Soviet Treaty*, New Delhi: C. Chand & Co., LTD., 1971, p. 16.
25. For an appraisal of the Indo-Soviet Treaty, see Ashok Kapur, "Indo-Soviet Treaty and the Emerging Asian Balance," *Asian Survey*, Vol. XII, No. 6 (June 1972), pp. 463–74.
26. A high-level Pakistani delegation led by Mr. Bhutto (who was out of office but had good relations with the Chinese leaders) visited Peking in early November 1971. While the Chinese promised diplomatic support, they failed to provide Pakistan with the necessary military aid that would have been crucial against the better equipped India.
27. Chopra, *op. cit.*, pp. 18–19.
28. Stephen S. Kaplan, *Diplomacy of Power: Soviet Armed Forces as a Political Instrument*, Washington, D.C.: The Brookings Institution, 1981, p. 185.
29. Kissinger, *op. cit.*, p. 866.
30. Kissinger, *op. cit.*, p. 867; and Barry M. Blechman and Stephen S. Kaplan, *Force Without War: U.S. Armed Forces as a Political Instrument*, Washington, D.C.: The Brookings Institution, 1978, p. 219. The authors note the limited nature of Moscow's leverage over an aspect of the Indian policy that New Delhi considered to be vital to its interests.
31. Kissinger, *op cit.*, p. 867.
32. *Ibid.*
33. This celebrated word was applied to the 1971 war in the following passage from Kissinger to WSAG on 3 December 1971: "I am getting hell every half hour from the President that we are not being tough enough on India. He has just called me again. He does not believe we are carrying out his wishes. He wants to tilt in favor of Pakistan. He feels everything we do comes out otherwise." Document 1-29643/73, Marta R. Nicholas

and Philip Oldenburg, *Bangladesh: The Birth of a Nation*, Madras, M. Seshachalam and Co., 1972, p. 115.
34. Kissinger, *op. cit.*, p. 881.
35. *Ibid.*, p. 885.
36. That these assurances exist is an article of faith in Pakistan.
37. Richard Nixon, *U.S. Foreign Policy for the 1970s: A report to Congress*, pp. 145–46.
38. Richard Nixon, *RN: The Memoirs of Richard Nixon*, New York: Grosset and Dunlap, 1978, pp. 525–26.
39. Haendel, *op. cit.*, p. 180.
40. Robert Jackson, *South Asian Crisis: India, Pakistan and Bangladesh*, New York; Praeger, 1975, pp. 55–105.
41. In Blechman and Kaplan, *op. cit.*, p. 178.
42. *Ibid.*, p. 191. Also, Christopher Van Hollen (deputy secretary of state for Near East and South Asia, 1969–72), "The Tilt Revisited," *Asian Survey*, Vol. XX, No. 4 (April 1980), p. 356 and Haendel, *op. cit.*, p. 180.
43. Pran Chopra, *India's Second Liberation*, Cambridge, Mass.: The MIT Press, 1974, pp. 212–13.
44. For example, David Hall in Blechman and Kaplan (*op. cit.*, p. 201) cites the presence of various Soviet vessels to counter those of the United States.
45. James M. McConnell and Anne M. Kelley, "Super-Power Naval Diplomacy: Lessons of the Indo-Pakistani Crisis 1971," *Survival*, Vol. XV, No. 6, (November-December 1973), p. 289.
46. Van Hollen, *op. cit.*; Haendel, *op. cit.*; and Chopra, *op. cit.*
47. Admiral Moorer, chairman, Joint Chiefs of Staff (1970–74), recalled recently in a speech that Nixon told him at a fully assembled National Security Council meeting to "sail the *Enterprise* into the Indian Ocean." Moorer replied "aye-aye, sir" and the meeting ("the shortest ever") was adjourned, according to Admiral Moorer.
48. January 14, 1972.
49. In Blechman and Kaplan, *op. cit.*, p. 205.
50. Dan Haendel, *op. cit.*, p. 264.
51. For example, as implied by the following: "In a fit of petulance, the President (Nixon) sent a naval task, force. . . . " Vinod Gupta, *Anderson Papers: A Study of Nixon's Blackmail of India*, Delhi, 1550, 1972, pp. 163–64.
52. Kissinger, *op. cit.*, p. 881.
53. L.F. Rushbrook Williams, *Pakistan Under Challenge*, London: Stacey International, 1975, pp. 214–15.
54. Interview with U.S. Government official in Haendel, *op. cit.*, pp. 130–31.
55. Anderson Papers, in Nicholas and Oldenburg, *op. cit.*, pp. 130–31.
56. Quote from Kissinger in Marvin Kalb and Bernard Kalb, *Kissinger*, Boston: Little, Brown & Co., p. 234.
57. Interviews in Pakistan, 1977, 1979.
58. Interview, former U.S. government official, 1980.
59. See Bhutto interview with Sulzberger in *New York Times*, February 13, 1972.
60. Khurshid Haider as cited in Blechman and Kaplan, *op. cit.*, p. 210.

3

BHUTTO AND BEYOND

As 1971 drew to a close, Pakistan's truncation had become a reality. Bhutto returned from New York to a hero's welcome. He was personalized, at once, as the champion of the defeated Pakistan—for having put on a defiant show at the United Nations—and as its redeemer. The future of Pakistan, and its salvation, now rested solely in the hands of Zulfikar Ali Bhutto.

Bhutto's background and exposure to the United States made him a possible friend but his reputation as a self-styled socialist raised doubts in Washington about his reliability.[1] His personality was responsible for abrupt policy shifts, and the Nixon administration was never quite sure which Bhutto would prevail. A consummate politician, Bhutto played all sides as he sought to expand Pakistan's options through the cultivation of countervailing sources of friendship in order to avoid the one-sided pro-U.S. dependence, which he saw as an inherent weakness in his country's foreign policy.[2]

From Washington's point of view, 1972 augured well for U.S.-Pakistan relations. Pakistan had survived without much loss to India on its Western front because of timely American actions. The Sino-American rapprochement ensured continuing recognition of Pakistan's role in bringing it about. Indeed, the 1971 war had accelerated cooperation between these two former antagonists. Nixon did not quite trust Bhutto, but Kissinger was impressed and recognized him as having been the "architect of Pakistan's friendship with China," a policy that was valued by Washington in 1972.[3] Even though the U.S. arms embargo was still in effect, there were few, if any, other outstanding issues between Washington and Islamabad when Bhutto took office in January 1972. Rehabilitation of Pakistan's international image was in the White House's interest, as it still suffered from domestic and international criticism for its failure to condemn Yahya's brutal policies in 1971. Bhutto's energetic pursuit of just such a rehabilitation was therefore all the more welcome.

On the other hand, Bhutto had at least two issues on which he wished to influence the U.S. president: support for Pakistan to shore it up through appropriate economic and diplomatic moves, and renewal of U.S. arms sales. In addition, discord developed after the clash in 1976 over the nuclear issue and Pakistan's role in the Third World.

U.S. SUPPORT: BHUTTO'S PERCEPTIONS

A fundamental change had occurred between 1969 and 1972 in Bhutto's views of the value of the U.S. connection. Whereas in 1969, when he was out of power, he had argued the futility of relying on the United States for support, because Washington always hoped for a change in Indian policy and was loath to annoy Indian leaders,[4] in 1972 Bhutto recognized the role played by the United States in saving West Pakistan in the 1971 war. Even though Bhutto had built his reputation on being staunchly anti-Indian,[5] once in office, he modified his views, maintaining that the changed circumstances and altered character of Pakistan's national interest required peace with India—hence in July 1972 the Simla Accord, which Bhutto called a "triumph."[6] Indeed, it was creditable that Bhutto convinced Mrs. Gandhi to release the 90,000 prisoners (comprising West Pakistani military personnel who surrendered in East Pakistan and many civilians who were also taken into custody) and to vacate some West Pakistani territory taken by the Indian troops in the closing days of the 1971 hostilities, in exchange for a comparatively tiny group of Indian troops taken prisoner and a somewhat smaller tract of land captured by the Pakistanis.

Bhutto was a great public orator and crowd swayer. His flamboyance attracted mammoth gatherings of people whom he kept agog by adding ever new twists to his utterances. Occasionally, his old public pronouncements and policies got in the way. As, for instance, happened when after the Simla Accords he mooted the idea of "thousand years of peace with India" at one of these gatherings that had been orchestrated to win public support for the agreement. Knowing his oft-repeated stand that "Pakistan can maintain her vital interests only by confronting India,"[7] the crowd demanded what about "thousand years of war?" Taken aback, Bhutto needed a few moments to recover. He beckoned the gathering to quiet and thanked them for always seeing the wisdom and the logic of his decisions.

Normalization of relations with India was not only dictated by the incarceration of 90,000 Pakistani prisoners at Indian hands; it was also an imperative for sustaining good relations with Washington. Bhutto was aware of Nixon's discomfiture at the hands of the India lobby, both within the U.S. Congress and without, and the accusations that he (Nixon) had ordered a "tilt" in favor of Pakistan during the course of the war over East Pakistan. He therefore concluded that adjusting Pakistani posture to give recognition to New Delhi's dominant role within the subcontinent was acting in Pakistan's enlightened self-interest. Touting the "Spirit-of-Simla," for which Bhutto took credit as the agreement's architect, was not only good policy in the subcontinent; it was also a masterful public relations move designed for influencing the United States.

A measure of Bhutto's flexibility of belief is provided by noting the distance he had traveled since he declared his moral aversion to Pakistani ties to the SEATO and the CENTO alliances and its "subservience to a great power on whose help it depended."[8] Indeed, while out of office and campaigning for elections the previous year, Bhutto had reiterated his distaste for alignment with the United States:

> You know how harmful and incorrect a foreign policy Pakistan had before I became foreign minister. We had been completely isolated from the rest of the world. Pakistan's foreign policy had chained the people. We had no free will to go anywhere. We had to obey what the United States ordered us to do.... Our policies were those of SEATO and CENTO. The U.S. ambassador could keep Pakistan's policy in line with Washington's. If he wished Pakistan's foreign policy to be a particular line ... Pakistan obliged him.[9]

Bhutto's posturing can be somewhat attributed to his penchant for the grandstand play. However, his anti-Americanism had served him well in his election campaign as he sought to link the military rulers and the economic elite with U.S. "imperialist" interests and predicted that the fall of one inexorably meant the fall of the other.

Yet, when Bhutto witnessed the measure of cooperation between the United States and China in achieving a cease-fire in the United Nations, which he had always referred to as an empty organization, he seemed to have undergone a change of heart. Furthermore, Bhutto had observed, with considerable pain, the inability of China to move in any concrete way to help Pakistan out of its 1971 dilemma. The truth was that Pakistan's China connection—of which Bhutto claimed proud parentage—had been effectively neutralized by the Indo-Soviet treaty. The Chinese also counseled patience with Washington. They did not wish so soon after having used Pakistan as a link with the U.S. to have to choose between the two.

As Bhutto explored his options, he decided to see if his erstwhile whipping boy CENTO could somehow be revived. He recognized that only military assistance could breathe any life into this alliance. For a weak, truncated, and sobered Pakistan in 1972, this aid had to come primarily from the United States. In the aftermath of a shattering war and humiliating defeat, Bhutto was keenly aware of the need to shore up Pakistani defense. While he talked "peace" with India, he did not altogether believe that, given another political opening à la Bangladesh and a demoralized, unequipped Pakistan, India would not move once again to dismantle whatever remained of Pakistan. He also recognized that in order to keep the military out of domestic politics he would have to satisfy at least some of their demands for arms. In addition, there was the feeling that the Nixon administration would not be averse to helping, especially in view of the Guam Doctrine, which offered assistance to allies who would be able to use it to help themselves.

Bhutto began to talk of the importance of CENTO as an anchor in U.S.-Pakistani relations. As proof of his seriousness, he went a step further and offered the United States a naval base at Gwadar on the Baluchistan coast. He felt that the base facility at this natural port would be greatly advantageous to U.S. policy because of its close proximity to the Persian Gulf and at the same time would enhance Pakistani security, since the lesson of the *Enterprise* in 1971 was not lost on anyone. U.S. policymakers were quite taken aback at this offer and did not take it seriously. Officials in the State Department were suspicious of Bhutto's motives in view of "his known dislike of the American alliance network."[10] They felt that Bhutto's real purpose was to use the U.S. commitment, technology, and know-how to develop the port into a full-fledged naval facility at a cost they estimated to be in the region of $2.5 billion. Once this was accomplished, Bhutto, they argued, would throw the U.S. out in favor of the next "highest bidder." The shah of Iran, slightly to the West, seemed a better bet to ensure the security interests of the United States in the area.

The U.S. presence in the area was to be augmented by the use of naval facilities at Diego Garcia in the Indian Ocean. Over a thousand miles to the south of the Persian Gulf, Diego Garcia had the dual advantage of being far from the troubled areas of South and Southwest Asia (which meant that the United States need not get directly embroiled in local conflicts) and yet close enough to reach there "in time" when the need arose. The opposition from India to this U.S. base was considered in keeping with Indian hostility toward Washington's policy in the area, especially in the aftermath of the 1971 "tilt" in favor of Pakistan.

The commitment to use Diego Garcia was not an easy policy for the Republican administrations of Nixon and Ford to sell to Congress. After much arguing they were able to secure the $30 million needed to upgrade the facility and lengthen its runway. In keeping with post-Vietnam skepticism in Washington, any expansion of U.S. commitments abroad was unpopular until the Soviet invasion of Afghanistan in late 1979 and, certainly, Diego Garcia was considered to be of little or no use except as a means of engaging the Soviet Union in a discussion of a general reduction of their naval presence in the Indian Ocean. Since the Soviets had established a base in Somalia, at Berbera (which they lost, however, in October 1977), and had port facilities at Aden, the United States hoped to engage them in such a general discussion by offering to reduce its presence in Diego Garcia in return for comparable Soviet moves. Talks between Moscow and Washington finally broke down when the Soviet Union aided Ethiopia against Somalia in 1977–78.

Bhutto was not averse to a U.S. presence because it served as a thorn in the side of the Indians and was a potential restraint on their future policy. He was also aware that China approved of a continued U.S. presence in Asia to counter the Soviet search for "hegemony." Somehow, toleration of U.S. policy had become more respectable simply because Peking no longer shied away from it. And since, according to this view, no one could accuse the Chinese of being a stooge of anyone, following such a policy in itself did not detract from the country's independence. It was in this mold that Bhutto fashioned his policy toward Washington. His perceptions of the Pakistani national interest required a U.S. role. He was fortunate that there was residual goodwill for Pakistan with Nixon and Kissinger. To influence U.S. policy further into closer collaboration, Bhutto not only used the indirect approach by improving relations with India (which precluded any further need for a "tilt"), but also involved the PRC directly as a conduit for making a plea for Pakistan (e.g., the Shanghai communiqué). Only this way, he felt, could the stage be set for influencing the next phase in U.S.-Pakistani relations: namely, the resumption of military sales.

U.S. ARMS AND PAKISTANI NEEDS

Bhutto came to the United States in September 1973 aware that the embargo that had been reimposed in 1971 had hurt Pakistan. While the details of the arms issue are the subject of a subsequent chapter, some of the background will be provided here as it was an issue of primary importance in U.S.-Pakistani relations under Bhutto.

The 1971 war had cost Pakistan some $200 million in military equipment. To replace some of the lost equipment, Pakistan's military purchases amounted to almost $115 million in 1972. In addition, defense spending accounted for almost one-third of the government's budget. Even though Pakistan's export earnings rose appreciably in 1972 as a result of the discovery of export markets in the Persian Gulf countries, Pakistan had a rough year in 1971, which forced it to request an extraordinary moratorium on its aid repayments in May. After the war, some 20 percent of Pakistani export earnings were earmarked for military purchases.

In Washington, the case was made by the State Department that in view of Pakistan's open purchases from other countries, and the military equipment valued at $65 million given by China, there was no real need for additional weapons from Washington and therefore the lifting of the arms embargo was not necessary. Bhutto, on the other hand, pleaded for a resumption of U.S. military aid on the ground that Pakistan was hurting economically and that, given substantial Indo-Soviet cooperation in both military and economic spheres, the United States should support an old ally, at the very least by selling it needed arms and spares.

In order to persuade Washington with this line of reasoning, Bhutto used his contacts with the shah of Iran to press Pakistan's case. He reportedly convinced the shah to support not only Pakistan but himself (Bhutto) personally, saying: "If I go, it will be all over for you within two years!"[11] This approach was clearly successful because, despite a number of moves that Bhutto had to make—owing largely to his friendship with the PRC—which the United States firmly opposed (such as the recognition of North Korea, North Vietnam, and the Sihanouk government-in-exile, withdrawal from SEATO, etc.), Bhutto did manage to have the total arms embargo lifted in February 1975. Although Washington agreed to the sale of only nonlethal (end) items and military spare parts, Bhutto saw this as a necessary prelude to the resumption of full-scale military sales.

Several factors had contributed to this favorable turn of events. First, and perhaps foremost, was Nixon's personal interest in the viability and survival of Pakistan, coupled with his desire not to let down his new-found friends in China, who had continued pleading Pakistan's case to the United States. Secondly, Bhutto's warm personal equation with the shah, and the latter's access to Nixon's ear, must also be given some credit for bringing it about.

Despite Bhutto's success at lobbying the White House through the PRC and the shah, he lacked the kind of direct interaction with the top echelons of the U.S. bureaucracy that Ayub had enjoyed in the fifties when he had succeeded in obtaining military aid. Bhutto's access, on the other hand, was indirect and in any case it was limited exclusively to the White House, where journalist Jack Anderson's disclosures of WSAG meetings in 1971 and the pro-Pakistan "tilt" had resulted in a more cautious stand toward Pakistan. Nor did Bhutto profit from the lower-level interaction that MAAG personnel used to have with their Pakistani counterparts in the 1955–65 period, when Pakistan had important access to the Pentagon.

Institutional channels of access were still missing when Bhutto took office. There was no Pakistani lobby in Washington. Moreover, ever since the East Pakistan debacle, the media had been very unfavorable toward Islamabad. Bhutto recognized the importance of public relations and its usefulness in creating the right image. He was the first Pakistani head of state to embark on a deliberate policy of "wining and dining" representatives of the Western media accredited to Pakistan and talking to them about his vision for Pakistan and the West's role in its future. While the image of the urbane, articulate, and impeccably dressed Bhutto, in his "pinstripes, Sulka ties, and Gucci loafers," flashed across Western televisions and was reinforced by descriptions in newspapers of his suavity of manner and culture of thought, his coterie of advisers in the Cabinet had begun to move Pakistan along new, socialist directions.[12] Prominent among these were Mubashir Hasan (Finance), Sheikh Rashid (Health), J.A. Rahim (Industrial Production), and Khurshid Hassan Meer with the portfolio of "Establishment." While this important segment of the Cabinet was steering the country leftward, Bhutto was busy nurturing his rightist connections. His U.S. policy was an important element in this strategy. The dichotomy, nevertheless, began to be felt in the summer of 1972, when Bhutto experienced difficulties with riots in Sind, labor alienation, strikes, and a recognition of the need for private-sector industrialists, while the PPP manifesto firmly committed Bhutto to the nationalization of all industries and financial institutions. Some influential members of the Cabinet, Abdul Hafeez Pirzada (who replaced Kasuri as law minister) and senior bureaucrats (the deputy chairman of the Planning Commission and the governor of the State Bank foremost amongst them) began counseling Bhutto to go slow on socialism.[13] The finance minister stated that no interference in the government's plans for a new (socialist) order would be tolerated, but Bhutto continued to cultivate a nonsocialist option, and he wanted the lifting of the arms embargo to reflect the ultimate success of such a policy.[14]

Bhutto needed the United States to permit military sales for yet another domestic reason. He had set up the Federal Security Force (FSF) in 1973 as a 20,000-man strong paramilitary force to be used by the prime minister in domestic situations as he personally saw fit. (Bhutto had sorely missed such a tool during the unrest of 1972–73.) In order to ensure its effectiveness, Bhutto wanted to give the best equipment to the FSF since they were to be his private army. His move in this direction made the military unhappy. While maneuvering to neutralize the military by reforming its command structure to reflect greater civilian control in substance as well as in style (as an example of the latter, he abolished the title of commander-in-chief for the head of each branch of service, naming them instead chief-of-staff), he also hoped to win their allegiance through such actions as posting senior military officers abroad as ambassadors, his decision not to try Yahya Khan, and his ability to acquire sophisticated weaponry. Moreover, even though Bhutto had succeeded in procuring some weapons from China and France, he was aware of the U.S. superiority in technology, in general, and of the Pakistani military lore, in particular, that only U.S. supplied armaments stood up to the modern Soviet weaponry recently acquired by the Indians. As such, he viewed the lifting of the U.S. arms embargo as an important goal to achieve.

When Bhutto came to Washington in Setember 1973, Hafeez Pirzada figured prominently in the entourage that accompanied him. Bhutto's success in obtaining a U.S. commitment to the "independence and territorial integrity of Pakistan as a cornerstone of American foreign policy" was perceived by the Pakistanis as being a necessary precursor to the resumption of military sales.[15] The visit was considered by both sides to have been a success: it created a favorable climate and reaffirmed the importance of the relationship. Bhutto was aware that Nixon's domestic difficulties militated against the lifting of the arms embargo. He recognized that Nixon preferred not to irritate further the critics of his "tilt" policy because he needed their goodwill in the unfolding drama of Watergate. Yet, Bhutto felt that the lifting of the embargo was only a matter of time. His hunch was proved correct when the embargo was finally lifted after he paid a second state visit to Washington in March 1975. It was, however, left to a different Republican president—Gerald Ford—to authorize its lifting. The details of that action follow in a subsequent chapter, but it must be pointed out here that by 1974 Bhutto had moved the PPP out from under the control that the left had exercised over its affairs during the 1971–74 period. He threw out the most committed of the leftists from his Cabinet. Rana Hanif replaced Mubashir Hasan in the Ministry of Finance (which eventually went to Hafeez Pirzada); Rafi Raza (with no political base—a conservative lawyer with an English wife) took over J.A. Rahim's post as minister of production (and along with Yusuf Buch wrote the 1977 PPP election manifesto); Yusuf Khattak (an NWFP landlord industrialist and a member of the "old guard") became minister of fuel, power, and natural resources. Feroze Kaiser (who had been Bhutto's Special Adviser) took charge of the Industries Ministry.

The purge of the leftists was an astounding affair. Mubashir Hasan, J.A. Rahim, and Khurshid Hassan Meer, the founding members of the People's Party, were also the most dedicated believers of its catchy, socialist slogans. With their departure, Bhutto lost his direct access to the disciplined grass roots of the PPP, namely, the industrial laborers in the urban centers and the landless peasantry in Sind and Panjab. These were the groups that had provided the bulk of the votes for the PPP, ensuring Bhutto's sweeping victory in the December 1970 elections. This action shocked the leftist forces and estranged many of Bhutto's erstwhile supporters in the movement. They bitterly complained of "Bhutto's total lack of gratitude to those who had helped him when he was out of power and of his ruthlessness in destroying them."[16]

The ouster of the leftists was motivated by circumstances beyond Bhutto's immediate control. His policy of double politics, whereby he simultaneously supported both the "left" and the "right," had become untenable. There were audible rumblings of dissatisfaction arising from both the groups. Bhutto was thus left with the option of either choosing between the two groups, or else losing his credibility with both. That he chose to break with the left was natural in view of the fact that Bhutto was a "socialist-of-convenience" rather than one of "conviction." He hailed from one of the richest landed families in the country. Steeped in Western upper-class traditions, with his Oxford education and University of California background, he spoke articulately and easily in support of socialistic ideals, only, he had great difficulty actually living with them. In particular, Bhutto had become painfully aware that the policies espoused by the left, e.g., nationalization of key industries, had been disastrous failures. Thus, the direction of future policy had to be changed. Moreover, having witnessed the lack of soundness of politically motivated decisions, especially in the economic realm where discipline was acutely needed, Bhutto wanted to depoliticize the decisionmaking process and move it back into bureaucratic hands.

Another important factor in Bhutto's calculations favoring a break with the left was his perception of the growing need for solidifying Pakistan's ties to the conservative Arab regimes. It was well-known in the inner circles that Saudi Arabia's King Faisal was unhappy with the "socialist" programs of the PPP, as championed by its left.[17] Bhutto concluded that he had to jettison this wing of the party, if his vision of flying high among the ranks of the influential Islamic leaders was ever to be realized.

Equally important in this equation was also the role played by the United States. Now that the Chinese rapprochement with the United States had made pro-Americanism respectable again, there were few if any rewards for an anti-American policy, which would be a corollary to supporting the leftist movement within the PPP. Besides, Bhutto needed the U.S. arms embargo to be lifted for the reasons outlined earlier.

Last, and perhaps most important, there was also a personal twist to this strategy. The prominent leftists within Bhutto's Cabinet legitimately claimed the leadership of the PPP, in view of their efforts at founding and nurturing it through its difficult initial period. This implied that Bhutto's leadership of the party and his election owed itself to the largesse of others rather than to his own charisma, vision, and leadership qualities. Bhutto resented these implications and wished to rid himself of their instigators.

BHUTTO AND THE BOMB: CONFRONTATION WITH THE UNITED STATES

When it came, Bhutto's clash with the United States was based not on his self-proclaimed status as a socialist, but rather as the result of his views as a national leader on the desirability of the pursuit of a nuclear option for Pakistan. As he ran into difficulties on this score, Bhutto tried to mobilize support from other quarters in order to influence Washington to back away from policies aimed at curbing Pakistan's nuclear program. Pakistan's standing in the Islamic world and its role in Third World forums offered an opportunity to counter the United States, and this route was exploited adroitly by Bhutto, even while at the same time he sought to improve his direct access to Washington.

Bhutto had been head of state for scarcely over two years when the Indian Atomic Energy Commission burrowed deep under the Rajasthan desert and shook its vast sandy scape with a massive nuclear blast. India's explosive entry into the restricted ranks of the nuclear club, in May 1974, sent shivers down the Pakistani spine. Despite Bhutto's friendly overtures to India, largely to free the 90,000 Pakistani prisoners it held after the capture of East Pakistan, he had never been fully disabused of his much publicized earlier belief in the Indian desire for the domination of the subcontinent.[18] Bhutto announced at first that Pakistan would eschew a nuclear option of its own and would rely instead on guarantees from the major nuclear powers against nuclear blackmail.[19] However, Bhutto gave up this stand when his foreign minister, Aziz Ahmed, traveled to Paris, London, and Washington soon after the Indian bomb explosion in search of guarantees and returned empty-handed. Thereafter, he concentrated on developing a Pakistani nuclear option as a necessary strategic and political weapon—one that would also serve to demonstrate Pakistan's leading position in the Third World. He thus made the decision to initiate the program which, by his own admission, he hoped would make Pakistan a nuclear power by the early 1980s.

THE ISLAMIC CONNECTION

It was indeed fortunate for Pakistan that, as Bhutto developed an Islamic link to press the Pakistani case in Washington, the quadrupling of the oil revenues enormously altered the economic and political clout wielded by some of these Muslim nations. Saudi Arabia and Iran thereafter became important not only in Islamabad, but also in Washington.

Bhutto was successful in his pursuit of a role in the Islamic movement for a variety of reasons. First, he had built a strong reputation for his pro-Islamic sentiments. This was more a consequence of his pre-1972 anti-Indian and anti-Hindu statements than his projection of pro-Arab and pan-Islamic views. To Muslims, Bhutto identified the Indo-Pakistani struggle as essentially a Hindu-Muslim quarrel. Therefore, it affected not only Pakistan, but every other Islamic nation. The 1971 war in particular became for him not merely a matter of Indian national interest asserting itself to seek hegemony in South Asia, but also a necessary consequence of hundreds of years of anti-Muslim hatred manifesting itself through the destruction of the Islamic state.

Second, Bhutto was one of the first leaders to speak of the Third World with its newfound unity—and the wealth of some of its ranks—as acting in unison to challenge the superpowers who had "bled" these nations as their erstwhile colonies. While the shah of Iran led the fight for raising oil prices that enriched OPEC, and King Faisal used the oil weapon to influence U.S. policy toward Israel, Bhutto spoke of widening the struggle to encompass all issues in North-South relations:

> With the terms of trade of the oil-producing countries, which will lead to a rapid increase in their financial resources, an unprecedented shift will occur in the global monetary and financial balance of power. The Third World can now participate in councils of the world on an equal footing with the developed countries and will be able to acquire a due measure of influence and control in international financial and economic institutions.[20]

In this way, Bhutto identified the oil-rich Muslim countries with the rest of the Third World and spoke of new opportunities that had arisen because these countries could infuse life into faltering economies and in the process also help themselves.

> The concept implicit in this approach is not that of aid as a form of charity from one developing country to another. The concept is that of mutually supportive economic activity in countries of the Third World

which would complement their individual resources and give them collective strength.[21]

Thus, Pakistan—a Third World nation—could be useful in adding to the overall strength in return for assistance to shore up its economic and diplomatic position. Bhutto was successful in selling this argument and he hammered away at the opportunities that had been opened up because the "Muslim countries are now so placed as to be able to play a most constructive and rewarding role for cooperation among themselves and with other countries of the Third World."[22]

Third, Bhutto had been able to bring his earlier experience with Pakistan's "bilateral tri-lateralism," namely, good relations bilaterally with each of the three superpowers, to bear on cultivation of friendly ties with three important Muslim countries, Saudi Arabia, Iran, and Libya. As he paid homage to Saudi Arabia for being the center of the Islamic world, and King Faisal as the keeper of the Faith, he cultivated the shah of Iran as an enlightened monarch and an old friend of Pakistan, and Libya's Colonel Qadaffi as a special person whose unannounced arrivals were always welcomed with a great deal of pomp and ceremony.[23]

Fourth, Bhutto took the lead in organizing an Islamic Conference and was, until his death in April 1979, its first president. An Islamic Summit, the second ever, was called for February 1974 in Lahore, Pakistan, and attended by 37 countries. The meeting was sponsored jointly by Pakistan and Saudi Arabia. Though its immediate goal was the liberation of Jerusalem and Arab lands held by Israel, the agenda was even more ambitious and encompassed the role of the Muslim states in global perspective. Bhutto was the chairman of the conference and delivered to it perhaps his most eloquent and moving address. This was a new Bhutto, bending his old talents to new purpose. Here he did not resort to the haranguing and crude language that was common to his public speeches. Rather, he donned the mantle of a Muslim scholar, and through the call he made in the larger interests of Islam, he tried to display in himself the virtues of which he spoke: "If he is a true Muslim, he is at once Eastern and Western, materialistic and spiritual, a man of enterprise as well as of grace."[24]

Bhutto benefited from his ability to champion the Islamic causes and identify himself as the personification of the most populous Muslim country in Western Asia, Pakistan. This helped him raise considerable amounts of money from the leaders of oil-rich Islamic states, who perceived him to be a dynamic force and with whom he enjoyed great personal popularity. (This popularity was later reflected in the fact that there were a great many appeals for clemency on his behalf and his execution led to a downward trend in Pakistan's relations with the Muslim world, a trend that was reversed only by the Soviet invasion of Afghanistan.) The necessity of close relations with Muslim countries has been voiced by every Pakistani leader and recognized by scholars of Pakistani foreign policy,[25] and Bhutto was the man of the moment who, when it became a real possibility, seized the initiative and brought the relationship to fruition.

Closely tied to Bhutto's policy of cultivating the Muslim bloc was his policy of identifying Pakistan with the Third World movement. This too was an old idea. Previous Pakistani leaders had all tried, in one form and another, to play a role in the Third World forums. Their efforts, however, had gone largely unrewarded for the following reasons: Pakistan suffered from its erstwhile image of unquestioning alignment, in the fifties and early sixties, with the United States. Pakistan's efforts to shed this image were hampered by the continuing antagonism between India and Pakistan. This was especially so since India had been very successful at cultivating itself as the champion of Third World causes. Whenever necessary, it invoked Pakistan's alignment with the United States to help deny Pakistan the corresponding access to the Third World forums.

Aware of this background, Bhutto worked out a successful strategy to gain Pakistan its long-denied entry into the inner sanctums of the Third World movement.[26] First, by clever public relations tactics, he set out to destroy the myth of Indian nonalignment. Bhutto cited the Indo-Soviet treaty of 1971 to identify what he considered near-total alignment of India with the Soviet Union. In this venture, Bhutto was greatly assisted by the PRC, who had itself worked hard to gain access to the Third World movement and whose goals in decrying the Indo-Soviet axis paralleled those of Pakistan.

As Bhutto worked to reduce India's prestige in the Third World movement, he embarked simultaneously on an active campaign to focus the movement's attention on its connections with the Islamic world. Islam's declared principles of concern for the less fortunate, absence of caste system, condemnation of racial bias, and its outward-looking philosophy to engage in a "struggle for a more equitable world order," were cited.[27] Thus, Bhutto projected Pakistan as a natural leader to champion Islamic and Third World causes, because he saw Pakistan's political and economic destiny linked to this bloc.[28] He personally sought a role in the multifarious forums where the Third World gathered to talk of the East-West issues or the North-South problems.

Bhutto achieved considerable success in these endeavors, whereby he used the Islamic links to help gain access to the Third World movement, and the latter to further cement Pakistan's ties to the Islamic world. These ties, along with the Third World connections, enabled Bhutto successfully to resist Washington's pressure on the important nuclear issue. It also made it enormously more difficult for the French to renege on their contractual agreement to supply a nuclear reprocessing plant. The French came under heavy U.S. pressure to cancel the deal, but given France's very considerable dependence on Middle East oil and its lucrative commercial interests in the Arab World, the existence of the Pakistani connection with these nations successfully checkmated the U.S. pressure. The success of Pakistan's policy on this issue is further evident from the fact that it was only after Bhutto's fall and the decline of the Pakistani clout in the various forums—at least until the Soviet invasion of Afghanistan—that the French broke their agreement. Washington's persistent efforts had finally been rewarded.

THE FALL OF BHUTTO AND CHARGES OF U.S. INVOLVEMENT

It was a confident Bhutto who declared on January 7, 1977, that national and provincial elections would be held on March 7 and March 10, respectively. There were a number of reasons for the decision to go to the polls a year earlier than was necessary, including a good spring wheat harvest, increased rice exports, and a decline in the rate of inflation. Ironically, Bhutto also desired to please the new Carter administration by demonstrating that Pakistan was the "only" democracy in South Asia, a pointed reference to Mrs. Gandhi's declaration of "emergency" and the concentration of power in her hands in the face of domestic discontent, and to the military government established in Bangladesh following the assassination of the leader of its independence movement, Sheikh Mujibur Rahman.

Bhutto and his advisers were confident of a total victory for the PPP. This confidence was based on its widespread identification, meticulously maintained and officially orchestrated through the mass media, as a "people's government," meaning a government that was determined to break the hold of the elite, even though reality militated against this identification. For example, Bhutto explained his induction of several key members of the landed aristocracy into the ranks of the PPP as an acceptance by the elite of their reduced status rather than a sellout (as was charged by Mubashir Hasan) by the PPP.[29]

Election results, which gave the PPP nearly four-fifths of the National Assembly seats against the Pakistan National Alliance (PNA),[30] a combined opposition constituting nine political parties, resulted in an almost unlimited confidence on the part of Bhutto.[31] Since he had overlooked the basic discontent of the many groups that he had carried in the 1971 election, he could not fully comprehend the cause or the source of agitation. The tendency on the part of Bhutto's advisers not to offer an honest evaluation of the situation and its seriousness was partly to blame. They, in turn, became yes-men, ever eager to please with optimistic assessments because of the notion that Bhutto subscribed to the Greek tradition that the bearer of bad tidings bears responsibility for them!

The PNA took to the streets charging massive electoral fraud, but at first Bhutto refused to take the situation seriously and believed that the agitation was a temporary phenomenon. Thus, he did not throw in the powerful FSF against the PNA nor did he declare martial law in the initial stages, preferring instead to rely on the civilian police to maintain public order. The opposition easily overwhelmed the police and the subsequent escalation of the use of force was interpreted by the PNA as a sign of Bhutto's weakness, which, in turn, rapidly escalated the charges against him.

A call for a general strike in Pakistan's major cities was made by the PNA leadership. The success of the strike resulted in continuous agitation after March 14, 1977. The PNA charged that Bhutto had rigged the elections. The PPP vehemently denied any such activity, although in private the leaders admitted "widespread, but small-scale rigging by overzealous local officials overstepping the law in their mistaken belief that it would please the authorities."[32] These riggings were described to be "harmless and ineffective" overall, except in approximately 20 or so cases (out of a total of 150 seats won by the PPP). Indeed, Bhutto made efforts to admit as much by encouraging the relevant defeated candidates to file complaints with the "election commissioner" with the discreet suggestion that the commissioner would look favorably on them.[33]

The PNA saw this as a sign of weakness on Bhutto's part and pressed their public protest further. They openly defied a government regulation banning public meetings, demanding fresh elections to follow Bhutto's resignation from office, charging that his presence in power made a mockery of free and impartial elections. Bhutto refused on the grounds that he was a twice-elected leader of "the people" whom the PNA had no authority to remove. He retaliated by ordering arrests of the top PNA leadership. This action, however, failed to stem public protest because a second line of leaders rapidly emerged to take charge. Bhutto finally responded by bringing out the FSF and the ensuing confrontation resulted in widespread bloodshed. After some 300 deaths and a much larger number of injuries were recorded, martial law was once more imposed in the major cities of Pakistan.

The politics of protest that characterized Pakistan after March continued unabated through June even though Bhutto agreed to hold talks with the PNA. His spokesman in these talks was Hafeez Pirzada, who represented Bhutto's viewpoint but was able to display more flexibility than could the beleaguered prime minister. It was accepted by most knowledgeable Pakistanis that the talks were a tacit admission of wrongdoing on the part of the PPP and that fresh elections would have to be held. An impasse was reached on the details of this process and as PPP and PNA supporters battled each other in Lahore on July 3, the military took charge amidst rumors of an impending civil war. On the night of July 4/5, after returning from a reception at the U.S. embassy, Bhutto was taken into "protective" custody by the military. Another coup d'état had been completed in Pakistan.

It was said in Pakistan that, in the final weeks of his administration, the only intelligence source that Bhutto trusted was the Soviet ambassador. Bhutto's trust in the Soviet embassy for information concerning Pakistan was an outgrowth of his firmly held belief that Washington was directly involved in the PNA agitations. Bhutto's advisers felt that the United States was going to stir up agitation even if there had been no rigging of the elections. Bhutto and his inner circle of advisers often cited Kissinger's remarks of August 1976, when he came to Islamabad to urge an end to the nuclear reprocessing plant agreement, saying that it would be better for Bhutto to reach an agreement with the Ford administration because: "If Carter comes in, he will make a horrible example of you." The anti-Bhutto movement of March-July 1977 was thus seen in the Bhutto camp as reflecting deliberate U.S. policy to "make a horrible example" of what they considered its independent-minded and nationalistic prime minister who would not compromise on an issue of such great interest to the nation.

The declaration of martial law was the direct outgrowth of the political stalemate that had developed after the March 1977 elections, for which the leaders of the principal political parties shared the responsibility, although as the party in power, the PPP was the main offender.[34] Had it scrupulously avoided irregularities, according to unbiased estimates it would have still emerged as the majority party, albeit with a considerably reduced margin. It paid for its greediness and lack of integrity with the deterioration of law and order and finally its dismissal from power by General Mohammad Zia-ul-Haq, whom Bhutto had promoted over more senior officials because of his presumed loyalty to Bhutto and his standing with certain Arab leaders; also, the fact that Zia did not represent the Sandhurst tradition in the senior Army ranks was important to Bhutto, who, according to one adviser, "wanted very much to break with that tradition."[35]

Bhutto's declaration of martial law in April in the major cities also hastened his fall. The military had assumed that Bhutto, who claimed to have subordinated the army to civilian control and who had also created in parallel his own military instrument (the Federal Security Force), would not need the army to do his dirty work. The army' had relinquished its domestic political power, but in return it did not want to be dragged in once again to bail out the political leaders. After March 1977, however, this tacit bargain appeared to break down; and as a result, intolerable conditions were created for the army. Its units were brought into direct confrontation with street demonstrators, and they either had to open fire on unarmed Pakistani citizens or face the taunts of the demonstrators concerning the army's shabby record of performance, both against the civilians and the Indian Army in East Pakistan. These confrontations infuriated the younger officers, who felt neither responsibility for the army's disgraceful behavior in East Pakistan nor any hand in the imposition of the martial law that they were now being asked to police. They felt humiliated. Their anger was in part directed against their own senior officers, who were not present at the scene and who supported a regime that called on the army to shoot down its own citizens.

Army resentment against the Federal Security Force also ran high. The FSF was created in line with Bhutto's concept of counterbalancing power and diminishing the importance of the army, especially for the maintenance of law and order. While the army tolerated the FSF, there was a good deal of resentment against the special status it enjoyed and the rapidity with which it had acquired this status. Its chartered duties were to provide protection for VIPs, supervise crowd control, and combat internal subversion. Its strength stood at almost 20,000 men, and it was equipped with the most modern arms and possessed the most sophisticated communications network in Pakistan. The army, in contrast, had had great difficulty in finding even the funds to maintain their dilapidated equipment. In the words of one army major: "My unit has only one working jeep. The FSF has hundreds of new ones, and they have the latest in everything."

One of the first actions of the army after taking over the government was to disband the FSF. The testimony given by its former chief, Masood Mahmood, to the Lahore high court revealed how Bhutto used the FSF against his political opponents. Indeed, its role has been likened to the Gestapo by General Zia himself.[36]

There were also more mundane issues, affecting the pocketbooks of military officers, which cast Bhutto in a bad light with them. In January 1977, the government, in response to rapidly escalating inflation, increased some pay scales and retirement stipends as well as other fringe benefits for civil and military services. But there was a wide discrepancy in the benefits received by civil and military personnel, and the officer corps concluded that this was one more case of shabby treatment meted out to the army by the Bhutto government. Similarly, the officers were affronted by a land redistribution measure announced just before the elections. The much-heralded land reform of 1972 had affected only about 5 percent of the agrarian population. In a move designed to appease a particular pressure group before the elections. Bhutto announced that holdings of nonirrigated land would be restricted to 100 acres. Senior military officers, who in the past had been compensated for their services with awards of land, interpreted this as yet another encroachment on their rights, since it meant that some of them would have to part with their land.

From another perspective, national economic collapse seemed imminent by July 1977, as months of rioting and absenteeism had already cost the country some $400 million in lost production. Inflation during the preceding nine months was running at the rate of 26 percent. Pakistan's indebtedness to foreign countries was dangerously high, with nearly 30 percent of its export earnings going to service debts. With declining income, lost production, and a general reluctance of foreign donors to extend any aid, something had to be done quickly. Martial law thus presented itself as a measure of last resort to arrest the decline.

There was also an external dimension to the imposition of martial law in 1977. This had to do with the confrontation between Bhutto and President Carter over the nuclear reprocessing plant agreement between Pakistan and France. Carter tried to dissuade Bhutto from proceeding with the project, as had President Ford (who had even promised to consider Pakistan's request for A-7 bombers, as a quid pro quo, if the latter gave up the deal with France). When quiet persuasion failed, Bhutto was warned that the Symington-Glenn Amendment called for cutting off all aid to countries that built reprocessing plants. Pressure was also put on France to cancel the agreement with Pakistan, but it did not fully succeed for reasons enumerated earlier (although the French did slow down the delivery of crucial blueprints and related technology to what an official of the Pakistan Atomic Energy Commission privately described "as barely a trickle").[37] While this earned Bhutto's displeasure, he was really enraged by what his advisers have described as "destabilization moves by the United States" aimed at toppling Bhutto.[38] Curiously, these charges have been denied with somewhat less than the customary zeal and conviction by the diplomats in Islamabad. Indeed, they acknowledged diplomatic "indiscretion" with regard to making "contacts with opposition leaders." According to these sources, their actions, though indiscreet, did not amount to overt interference in the internal affairs of Pakistan. Nevertheless, when Air Marshal Asghar Khan—a right-wing opposition leader, who headed the "Isteqlal-e-Pakistan" party—declared himself in favor of renouncing the Nuclear Option, and noted that the controversial fuel reprocessing plant on order from France was, in his judgment, unnecessary for the needs of Pakistan, Bhutto's advisers cried foul. They saw a U.S. hand behind this announcement and spread the word that the U.S. was actively seeking Bhutto's downfall because the PNA had secretly agreed to forsake the nuclear option.[39]

The Pakistani-American relationship further deteriorated with the announcement that Washington had suspended any further consideration of the possible sale of A-7s to Pakistan. The official reason given was the imposition of the "martial law decree," and the prevalence of "unstable conditions" in the country.

The normally buoyant diplomatic community in Pakistan, which had in early 1972 much welcomed Bhutto's arrival and Yahya's departure, was uncharacteristically glum during this period. In July 1977, after the military took Bhutto into what they called "protective custody," there were audible sighs of relief. Indeed, in private conversations, I heard mentioned the word "refreshing." Coming from a seasoned Western diplomat, this was a curious adjective being used to describe conditions brought about through a military takeover!

Blame for Bhutto's fall is placed by some on a desire of the Panjabi elements to perpetuate their power;[40] others cite the economic difficulties that plagued Pakistan under Bhutto[41] when the consumer price index rose 87 percent from the time he took over in December 1971 to March 1975.[42] Still others, though less publicly, have blamed Bhutto himself for his own downfall. "Bhutto's emphasis on politics above policies, and personal power above programs, made him a victim of his own megalomania."[43] Additionally, in more mundane terms, Bhutto's imperious manner, his belief in his own infallibility, and the terror that he struck in the hearts of those who worked around him, cut him off from the usual warning channels so necessary for the preservation of men in powerful positions. Through an instinctive human defense mechanism, his advisers were themselves forced to close their eyes and block their ears lest they should see or hear anything that spelled disaster for Bhutto and his policies. And even if they did, they remained tongue-tied. Deprived thus of warning signals, corrective actions were either not taken or they were too late in coming.

Bhutto's downfall, therefore, owed itself mostly to "internal" factors. Nevertheless, immediately after his overthrow, it was clearly observable that both the military and the opposition, the PNA, expected to receive a "favorable hearing" from the United States. It is for this reason that, during Carter's years of presidency, Pakistanis generally found U.S. condemnation of their "nonelected leaders" and "undemocratic processes" to be rather hypocritical. Because the United States was perceived as having been actively involved in Bhutto's overthrow even though he had been an elected leader, simply because his nuclear policies were anathema to Washington, Carter's sermons on human rights and international morality had a hollow ring in Pakistan.

GENERAL ZIA AND U.S. POLICY

The change in Islamabad affected the policies of the Carter administration. Washington expected Bhutto's deposal to result in a downplaying of the nuclear option, since both the military and the PNA were considered to be less committed to it. On the other hand, human rights, another Carter favorite, was expected to surface as an irritant because martial law, by definition, denied one of the basic human rights: the right to a democratically and freely elected form of government.

The martial law authorities foresaw the human rights issue cropping up early in their dealings with the U.S. administration. They were, however, aware that following the March 1977 elections, Bhutto had come down hard against his political opponents and had ordered several thousands of, what he called, "troublemakers and their collaborators" jailed. This, coupled with the bloodshed that followed the imposition of the martial law, had run Bhutto afoul of the human rights bureaucracy in the State Department. Bhutto, however, had decided to ignore the U.S. displeasure on this score, since he suspected U.S. collusion in the instigation of the street demonstrations. With this background in mind, Zia ordered many of those imprisoned by Bhutto without due process of the law released. Indeed, the Martial Law Administration (MLA) of General Zia was reported by U.S. officials to have improved the human rights situation by not only releasing such political prisoners, but also by allowing political parties (except for Bhutto's PPP) to function.[44] The MLA brought in a civilian component into the military administration. However, it declared that, under the 1977 martial law, the constitution would remain in force even though invoking the constitution to challenge martial law regulations would not be permitted.

Carter's lack of consistency in the exercise of international diplomacy has been much talked about. His dealings with Pakistan, however, provide a particularly telling example of how the flow of events was helped along certain directions, presumably to suit Carter's game plan for the region. Yet, once the movement had occurred, opportunities were missed and newfound friendships were allowed to sour.

Bhutto's Pakistan had run afoul of Carter's nuclear nonproliferation policies. His replacement by the military, if not actually aided, was, nonetheless, actively not discouraged. Under the circumstances, a certain sensitivity to the needs of those who followed could well have been used to advantage, not only for furthering the U.S. interests in the region, but also to help the regional powers solve some of their own problems. The latter could well have been achieved by helping bring about a rapprochement between India and Pakistan—a happening that did not seem impossible to achieve under Prime Minister Morarji Desai.

Instead, Carter hurled two diplomatic thunderbolts at Pakistan. The first was contained in a public statement made by Deputy Secretary of State Warren Christopher in New Delhi in July 1977 that said Washington expected India to play a "leading" role in South Asia. This electrified Islamabad, startling it out of its stupor to recognize that the U.S.-Pakistani alliance relationship had withered on the vine. What Christopher said in 1977 was no different from what the Soviets had been pressing on Pakistan since 1965. His statement was thus seen as conclusive proof that Washington had "abandoned" Pakistan to the wolves, leading to a sense of isolation that was punctuated by reliance on Chinese friendship[45] and recognition that the future of Pakistan lay with the conservative Arab states who alone could underwrite the costs of Pakistan's independence and security needs.

The second thunderbolt was clothed in the form of a deliberate diplomatic snub. Carter pointedly excluded Pakistan from his itinerary when in December 1978 he visited both Teheran and New Delhi. Pakistani officials recognized that this action downgraded earlier U.S. commitments to Pakistan and considered the exclusion a corollary of Brzezinski's "regional leaders" concept, under which India and Iran were regarded as regional leaders. Their preëminence was expected to lead to a general pacification of the region, thus making Washington's presence unnecessary. Top officials in Islamabad were appalled that Carter would seriously entertain thoughts of a "great power withdrawal" from the region, considering the communist takeover in Afghanistan in April 1978 and the Soviet Union's ever more heavy involvement in the region.

All of this was taken by Zia and his entourage to reflect a basic U.S. failure to face up to the new dimension of politics in Southwest Asia. They spoke of the ostrich syndrome whereby the U.S. had deluded itself into believing that the problem would simply disappear. Senior U.S. officials, whose responsibility it was to forestall crisis or any growing threat to Western interests, also seemed to reflect an inability to acknowledge a divergence of interests with Moscow in Southwest Asia.[46] Fixed to the idea that "it is not in the interest of the Soviet Union to destabilize the area," Carter refused to believe that Soviet preponderance might lead to a move to secure the southern flank.

Domestically, throughout 1978 the MLA remained more benevolent than it was to become later. General Zia's promise of elections and encouragement of non-PPP political activity put Pakistan in the category of countries where the status of human rights was not considered to be a cause for alarm. This all ended, however, in the weeks preceding Mr. Bhutto's conviction on charges of ordering the murder of a former PPP associate and a Cabinet minister, when Martial Law Authorities made many arrests among the PPP leadership and their supporters.[47] The hanging of Mr. Bhutto in April 1979 was the final straw. The human rights issue was once more in focus and Pakistan's military rulers, according to the Bureau in the State Department, were now among the worst violators.

During the early part of summer 1979, political action focused on the then pending elections, which Zia had set for November. The PPP, and those leaders who had been incarcerated earlier and had not been disqualified from participating in future elections, tried to keep a low profile, urging all political parties to do nothing that might lead to a postponement of the November elections. The sole exception was Bhutto's daughter, who continued to provoke the MLA with talks of "rivers of blood" flowing in Pakistan to avenge the death of her father.[48] Bhutto's hanging had indeed resuscitated the fortunes of the PPP, with images of a martyred Bhutto replacing earlier accusations of an intolerant and politically corrupt leader.

In July 1979, Zia came out with a set of additional restrictions on the scope of the eagerly awaited November 1979 elections. These consisted of proposals for constitutional change, incorporating a permanent role for the military in the political system.

The unveiling of Zia's proposals amounted to the dropping of a bombshell. The expectations that had been building for a return to civilian rule and political normalcy were shattered. The politicians, ever fearing the change of rules to something less propitious to their election, cried foul.

Thus broken, calm did not resettle spontaneously. Early in October, with a wave of arrests, the Martial Law Authorities clamped down hard again. It was a prelude to Zia's speech of October 16, 1979, which banned political activity and dissolved all political parties and indefinitely postponed the elections. He also ushered in the return of full-fledged censorship and expanded the powers of the military courts at the expense of the civilian adjudication procedures.[49] The Carter administration viewed this turn of events as boding ill for U.S.-Pakistani relations. In particular, the State Department, which had just embarked on bilateral discussions on regional security issues with Pakistani officials, feared that human rights problems would lead once again to a worsening of relations.

The timing of Zia's speech of October 16, 1979, was inopportune not only because it foreclosed the possibility of an improvement of relations, at which both the Pakistani Foreign Office and the State Department had so recently been at work, but also because it came at the heels of the announcement awarding the 1979 Nobel Prize for Physics to a distinguished Pakistani physicist, Abdus Salam (who shared it with two professors at Harvard). Thus, the event for the celebration of an achievement par excellence by a son of Pakistani soil was overshadowed by the bad publicity generated by the unfortunate turn of events in Pakistan.

Washington's unhappiness with Pakistan over the postponement of elections was real and, in part, justified. It nevertheless lacked a deep understanding of how the military was not the only culpable party. The political parties in Pakistan are not the repositories of implicit trust that they are supposed to be. Their actions are often self-serving, short-sighted and, indeed, undemocratic.

The more substantial reason for Washington's unhappiness with Zia, however, was his continuing stubborn refusal to take practical steps that would convince the United States of his disavowal of the nuclear option. The Pakistanis saw this as a red herring. Instead, they called Carter to task for ignoring the real menace across their frontier, namely, the rapidly escalating Soviet stake in Afghanistan.

Carter's implacable lack of concern at the widening Soviet stake in Afghanistan began to take its toll in Pakistan. Zia's advisers argued that, since the United States could no longer be aroused to take note of Soviet inroads in Southwest Asia, Pakistan's interests would be best served in making peace with the Soviets.

These thoughts were uppermost in the mind of General Zia, who decided to mend fences with Moscow since all of his efforts to engage Washington in a discussion of the Soviet threat in Afghanistan had been in vain. The transfer of the respected Pakistani ambassador to the United States, Sahabzada Yaqub Ali Khan (who was reported to be close to President Zia) to Moscow did not go unnoticed in Washington, but his replacement, Sultan Mohammad Khan, was a man who had close U.S. ties and not much was made of the change. Soon thereafter came the Soviet invasion of Afghanistan, which President Zia categorized as a deliberate and well-prepared move that was undertaken only because the United States had been ineffective and had signaled a lack of interest in Afghanistan particularly, and in the region generally.[50]

General Zia saw a fundamental flaw in Washington's lack of will and inability to stand by its allies, calling its record in Pakistan "patchy at best." Even after the Soviet invasion, attempts by either side to communicate ran into difficulties. Carter stressed the severity of the Soviet actions, launched the Carter Doctrine, and pledged that "any attack by any outside force to gain control of the Persian Gulf region will be regarded as an assault on the vital interests of the United States of America. And such an assault will be repelled by any means necessary, including military force."[51] Pakistani leaders did not really believe that Carter had the will to act decisively. In this context, the 1980 U.S. offer of $200 million in economic aid and $200 in military assistance was seen as being woefully inadequate. When Brzezinski visited Islamabad in February 1980, he was told that it was "not the quantity of aid but the quality of the U.S. commitment" that was important. A few planes or 100 tanks were not the issue. What was crucial, however, was whether the United States would give its word to defend Pakistan and keep it. The model cited was that of the Chinese: "They did not give that much aid, but their word is as good as gold with us." Short of such an undertaking, the United States was not able to attract Zia to accept the aid because of his firmly held view that the "Americans wanted to give a little aid, let Pakistan burn its bridges forever to the Soviet Union, and then leave it in the lurch." Unable to obtain a firm commitment from Washington, Zia shrugged off the offer with not only the famous comment that it was peanuts, but one that is more telling: "The United States has foreign relations but no foreign policy!"

OBSERVATIONS

When the 1971 war ended, Washington hoped to reap some benefits from its support during the crisis. In the early phase of the Bhutto period, the Nixon administration was content to let Bhutto rehabilitate Pakistan's image in the world, feeling that international acceptance of the "new" Pakistan would redound to the policy advantage of the United States by wiping out the negative international response to the 1971 "tilt." Nixon and Kissinger continued to view Pakistan as part of a larger picture of which the Sino-Pakistani relationship was an important component, and in this sense the U.S.-Pakistani relationship in the 1972–77 period was active, particularly between 1972 and 1975 when the arms embargo was lifted.

Bhutto's attempts to influence U.S. policy were focused on ensuring a U.S. commitment to Pakistan that in his view would enhance the argument for lifting the arms embargo. Bhutto sought an end to the arms embargo for a variety of internal as well as external reasons. He courted Nixon and Ford in order to get them to affirm that the territorial integrity of Pakistan was important to the United States. He saw this as a prelude to the lifting of the arms embargo. If Pakistan's continued survival with its present borders was important to the U.S. national interests, and if that survival was difficult without fresh infusions of arms, then how could the United States deny Pakistan the right to purchase the necessary weapons?

However, the lack of an institutionalized basis for the relationship continued to plague U.S.-Pakistani relations. The absence of any military program disallowed the military channels of access that had been useful until 1965. The Bangladesh war had all but ended whatever goodwill existed for Pakistan within the State Department. Thereafter, the State Department pushed for an early recognition of Indian preëminence in the subcontinent and for letting affairs there fall into a regional pattern that would preclude any need for U.S. involvement. Bhutto continued to rely on key personalities in the White House for favorable action on resuming arms sales. He stressed Pakistan's importance to the United States, but Nixon was caught up in Watergate matters and was reluctant to lift an embargo that he saw as being fundamentally opposed by the Senate liberals who had opposed his earlier pro-Pakistani "tilt" and who usually constituted the pro-India lobby. For this reason, it was not Nixon but Ford who finally lifted the embargo. Because the groundwork had already been laid, and because Kissinger was a key member of the Ford administration, Ford was able to move fairly quickly on the arms issue.

Once Pakistan signed the reprocessing plant agreement with France in March 1976 (after the arms embargo had been lifted), State Department officials began to put pressure on Ford and Kissinger to come down hard on Pakistan in order to influence its policy away from a pursuit of the nuclear option. Kissinger's August 1976 trip to Islamabad was an effort in this direction. The White House sweetened the pressure by offering Pakistan A-7's if it gave up the reprocessing plant. The State Department would have preferred to simply use threats of aid cut-off. But Bhutto saw the nuclear option as necessary and as constituting "a clear threshold of national interest" that could not be sacrificed in exchange for the A-7's.[52] Carter's personal commitment to the nonproliferation policy made it easier for State Department and Arms Control and Disarmament Agency (ACDA) officials to keep tight reins on the issue and one discerns a definite hardening of U.S. policy, as will be subsequently detailed.

There were several ways in which Bhutto tried to influence Washington's policy. First of all, he launched a major public relations campaign to improve Pakistan's image. Second, he used his relations with the shah and the Saudi monarchy to persuade U.S. presidents not to come down too hard on Pakistan. As one former Pakistani foreign minister reminisced, "Faisal had a soft corner for Pakistan and saw legitimate Pakistani security concerns that required arms purchases from the United States." Bhutto also made good use of the Third World movement as a forum for airing grievances against U.S. pressure on the nuclear issue. Third, noting that some of his more left-leaning advisers (e.g., Mubashir, Rahim, Meer) were unacceptable to both the Saudis and the U.S., Bhutto used it as a convenient pretext for his sacking them in 1974. His real motivation for this act had more to do with denying these men a role in future PPP policy for internal reasons of political control.

Communication flows, as reflected in the two Bhutto state visits to Washington, would depict greater intensity flux in favor of the United States, but these visits must also be weighed in context of their domestic payoff for Bhutto. In both instances he was able to win a good deal of public support for having succeeded in getting an U.S. commitment to Pakistan's territorial integrity and for having arrived at the formula that has been subsequently followed. It was also a useful diplomatic signal that Pakistan was not without a friend in the United States and that regional nations should take appropriate note.

Thus, it can be argued that, despite Pakistan's failure to develop any ongoing influence with the United States, it did succeed in acquiring instrumental influence as a means of achieving its goals in at least two key areas after 1972: one, the lifting of the arms embargo; two, a commitment by the United States to Pakistan's territorial integrity and a place for Pakistan in U.S. foreign policy. While the rapid confrontation that developed on the nuclear issue after 1976 downgraded the commitment, the Soviet invasion of Afghanistan revived it. Washington's heavy-handed tactics did not secure the scrapping of the Pakistani nuclear option: they merely raised its costs and helped postpone the day of its fruition.

NOTES

1. Richard S. Wheeler, *The Politics of Pakistan: A Constitutional Quest*, Ithaca, NY: Cornell University Press, 1970, p. 264.
2. Herbert Feldman, *From Crisis to Crisis: Pakistan 1962–1969*, London: Oxford University Press, 1972, p. 314.
3. Henry Kissinger, *The White House Years*, Boston: Little, Brown, & Co., 1979, p. 907.
4. Zulfikar Ali Bhutto, *The Myth of Independence*, Lahore: Oxford University Press, 1969, p. 43.
5. Accusing India of neocolonialism in its worst form. Herbert Feldman, *op. cit.*, p. 127.
6. For details of the Simla Accord, see Shirin Tahir-Kheli, "Bilateralism in South Asia," *World Affairs*, Vol. 136, No. 1 (Summer 1973), pp. 74–87.
7. Bhutto, *op. cit.*, p. 186.
8. Zulfikar Ali Bhutto, *Marching Towards Democracy: A Collection of Articles, Statements, and Speeches*, Karachi, Pakistan Publications, 1972, p. 13.
9. *Ibid.*, p. 39. Excerpt of a speech given at a public gathering in Lahore on March 8, 1980.
10. Interviews, 1978. The Pakistani Foreign Office does not discuss the offer of the base in Gwadar, but Bhutto's advisers were quite open about it.
11. Interviews, 1977 and 1978.
12. For a discussion of the evolution of post-1971 Pakistani politics, see Gerald A. Heeger, "Socialism in Pakistan," in Helen Desfosses and Jacques Levesque (eds.), *Socialism in the Third World*, New York: Praeger, 1975.
13. Shahid Javed Burki, *Pakistan Under Bhutto, 1971–1977*, New York: St. Martin's Press, 1980, p. 115.
14. *Pakistan Times*, August 17, 1973.
15. *Department of State Bulletin*, October 15, 1973, p. 482.
16. Interviews, 1976 and 1977.

17. When King Khalid, who replaced Faisal, visited Pakistan, Bhutto put on a grand sports display for which North Vietnamese teachers coached Pakistani athletes. King Khalid was apparently visibly upset at the "socialist display" by Pakistan in his honor and almost walked out.

18. The Indian action of May 18, 1974, struck a severe blow at the previously developing understanding between New Delhi and Islamabad by awakening anew in Pakistan the suspicion of Indian intentions generated by nearly three decades of overt and covert hostility underlined by three wars. L. F. Rushbrook William, *Pakistan Under Challenge*, London: Stacey International, 1975, p. 207. It also gave "every nation a pretext to set off nuclear explosions with little more justification than they were merely investigating new methods of opening beer cans." Lord Chalfont in Rushbrook William, p. 206.

19. *Christian Science Monitor*, May 30, 1974.

20. Zulfikar Ali Bhutto, *The Third World: New Directions*. London: Quartet Books, 1977, p. 85.

21. *Ibid.*, p. 86.

22. *Ibid.*

23. For example, Qadaffi expressed a liking for Pakistani dress for women and Mrs. Bhutto supplied this traditional dress for Qadaffi's wife.

24. *Ibid.*, p. 88.

25. For example, see Keith Callard, *Pakistan: A Political Study*, London: Allen and Unwin, 1957, pp. 18 and 314; S. M. Burke, *Pakistan's Foreign Policy: An Historical Analysis*, London: Oxford University Press, 1973, p. 65.

26. Interviews, 1975 and 1976.

27. Bhutto, *The Third World*, p. 100.

28. Even though only 13.7 percent of Pakistan's total exports are to the Islamic countries, 55 percent of Pakistan's overall exports are to the Third World nations. IMF/IBRD figures, cited in *Dawn*, May 17, 1980.

29. *Musawat*, Lahore, May 17, 1976.

30. See 1977 Elections, National Assembly.

PPP		*PNA*		*Independents*	
No. of Seats	% of Total	No. of Seats	% of Total	No. of Seats	% of Total
155	77.5	36	18	9	4.5

Total Seats: 200
Source: *Overseas Weekly Dawn*, Karachi, March 13, 1977.

31. Bhutto referred to the PNA as "a cat with nine tails."

32. Interviews, 1977.

33. *Ibid.*

34. Issues relating to the election are covered in Lawrence Ziring, "Pakistan: The Campaign Before the Storm," *Asian Survey*, Vol. 7 No. 7 (July 1977), pp. 581–98; Marvin Weinbaum, "The 1977 Elections in Pakistan: Where Everybody Lost," *Asian Survey*, Vol. 17, No. 7 (July 1977), pp. 599–618; and Anwar Syed, "Pakistan in 1977: The 'Prince' is Under the Law," *Asian Survey*, Vo. 18, No. 2 (February 1978), pp. 117–25.

35. See Shirin Tahir-Kheli, "The Military in Contemporary Pakistan," *Armed Forces and Society*, Vol. 6, No. 4 (Summer 1980), p. 646.

36. *The New York Times*, September 7, 1977.

37. Interviews, 1977.

38. Interviews, 1979 and 1980.

39. Interviews, 1977.

40. For example, see Saleem Ahmed Qureishi, "An Analysis of Comtemporary Pakistani

Politics: Bhutto Versus the Military," *Asian Survey*, Vol. XIX, No. 9 (September 1979), pp. 910–21.

41. W. Eric Gustafson, "Economic Problems of Pakistan Under Bhutto," *Asian Survey*, Vol. XVI, No. 4 (April 1976), pp. 364–80.
42. *Ibid.*, p. 375.
43. Interviews, 1977.
44. Department of State, *Human Rights Report to Congress*, 1978.
45. Even the shah of Iran had been pressing Pakistan in 1977 for concessions to India on transit trade-land routes through Pakistan.
46. Informal talk in Philadelphia, 1978.
47. In which the minister's father was mistakenly killed instead.
48. There were unsubstantiated reports in Pakistan that in an effort to get a stay on Bhutto's execution, his wife and daughter had secretly asked the United States to arrange for his release and reinstatement. In return, Bhutto would drop the nuclear reprocessing plant—which the family believed had brought him down to begin with.
49. For the text, see *Pakistan Affairs*, Vol. XXII, Washington, DC, November 1, 1979, Pakistan Embassy.
50. Interview with author, Islamabad, July 8, 1980. The Soviets, in a practice run, had been reported to have moved 10,000 soldiers in a fleet of Antonov-22s to South Yemen and Ethiopia several months prior to the invasion. Jiri Valenta, "The Soviet Invasion of Afghanistan: The Difficulty of Knowing Where to Stop," *Orbis*, Vol. 24, No. 2 (Summer 1980), p. 212.
51. Address to the Joint Session of Congress, January 23, 1980.
52. William H. Lewis, "Political Influence: The Dimensional Capacity," in Stephanie G. Neuman and Robert E. Harkavy, eds., *Arms Transfers in the Modern World*, New York: Praeger, 1980, p. 186.

4

ARMS AND INFLUENCE

That arms and influence are correlated is undeniable. The degree of "closeness" and "directness" of the correlation, however, is not trivially obvious. Indeed, it is a matter of some considerable scholarly interest and debate.

U.S.-Pakistani interaction provides a particularly fecund case study for the evaluation of this correlation. Accordingly, in the present chapter, we shall examine the relationship between the United States and Pakistan with a view to checking the validity of the arms-influence correlation and, if possible, establishing some measure of its strength. It is convenient first to give a narrative of the arms relationship between these two countries.

Pakistani perceptions of national security entailed a major commitment to military expenditures, the feeling traditionally being that "one cannot have enough security." The table below (Table 1) reflects the importance assigned to defense in the Indian subcontinent.

The arms embargo following the 1965 war with India was put into effect by the Johnson administration, both in order to limit the duration of the hostilities and to punish Pakistan for what the United States considered to be unacceptable behavior on the latter's part (that is, infilitration across the armistice lines into the Indian-held part of Kashmir). Despite the cessation of hostilities, and the signing of the Taskent accords, the virtual unwillingness of the Johnson administration to lift the embargo[1] and resume the previous arms relationship rankled the Pakistanis. In this context, the 1968 change of administration was greatly

Table 1. Military Expenditures as Percentage of Annual GNP

	1963–64	65	66	67	68	69	70	71	72	73	74	75	76	77	78
Pakistan	3.2	5.3	4.5	3.7	5.7	5.9	5.8	6.4	6.7	6.6	5.7	6.2	6.1	6.1	5.1
India	4.7	3.8	3.6	3.3	3.1	3.0	3.0	3.5	3.5	2.9	3.0	3.4	3.3	3.2	3.2

Source: Arms Control and Disarmament Agency (ACDA), World Military Expenditures and Arms Transfers, 1963–1978.

welcomed in Pakistan, particularly since Nixon was viewed to be an old and trusted friend.

THE ROAD BACK

The visit of President Nixon to Pakistan on August 1, 1969 was important for the restoration of better relations between the two countries. No arms sales were promised because the 1965 embargo was still in effect. However, once Nixon asked Yahya's assistance as a channel extraordinaire to Peking, the situation was bound to change.

On November 8, 1969, the House Foreign Affairs Committee, with the encouragement of the White House, urged the administration to reconsider its ban on lethal *matériel* to both India and Pakistan. The rationale for requesting the change was that the ban on military sales had caused India and Pakistan "to turn to the Communist world to obtain what they consider[ed to be] their legitimate defense needs."[2] There was particular concern over the modest $30 million agreement that Pakistan had concluded with the USSR. The agreement was viewed as being significant because it signaled a breakthrough in Soviet-Pakistani relations. Moreover, it seemed ominous because it was cemented by Pakistan's closing of the U.S. base in Peshawar.

While the administration declared that it did not intend to renew arms deliveries to Pakistan, it nevertheless felt that some modification in its policy was warranted. As such, the United States offered to make a "one-time" limited exception that would help Pakistan, yet would not constitute "an opening of the gates."[3] Moreover, as President Nixon noted in his State of the World Message, "[this] modest exception should not upset the military balance in the area and accelerate an arms race."[4] The President lamented the fact the U.S.-Pakistani relations had moved away from their previous level of "close association" to a point where Pakistan had formed equally good relations with both the Soviet Union and China. The "once only" exception proposed the supply of 300 armored personnel carriers (APCs) to Pakistan at a total cost of $50 million. Considering the increasing hostility in the Senate toward Pakistan because of the mounting repression in East Pakistan, the decision was indicative of Nixon's generally sympathetic feelings toward the country that had hailed him as "an old friend."

The APC offer was rationalized by the White House on the basis of several factors. First, it noted India's continuing receipt of arms from the Soviet Union and Eastern Europe while Pakistan's equipment was below par by comparison. Moreover, the point was made that an old ally deserved some consideration.[5] Second, the argument was put forth that only a resumption of arms—no matter how limited—would enable Washington to maintain "a constructive political relationship with Pakistan."[6] (Nixon and his immediate staff fully subscribed to the view that Washington had necessarily to approach Islamabad in a sympathetic manner, if the former was at all to influence the latter's behavior.) Third, hope was expressed that the reopening of the pipeline would prevent Pakistani dependence on other sources of arms supply and would also give Washingon much needed leverage. (In other words, the 1965–69 period had convinced the White House that while the delivery of arms may not amount to much influence, its absence certainly ensured the denial of even an opportunity to influence.)[7] Of course, what was left unsaid was perhaps the most crucial point: namely, the usefulness of Pakistan as a secret channel to Peking.

Initially, the White House planned something for each of Pakistan's three services: APCs for the army, 50 F-5 fighters for the Pakistan Air Force (PAF), and three or four maritime patrol craft for the Pakistan Navy (PN). The package was designed, in the words of one U.S. State Department official, "to tell the Pakistanis that we still loved them." However, plagued by problems of bad press and congressional pressure to penalize Pakistan for its brutality in East Pakistan, only the APC deal went through, and that on a strictly "cash-and-carry" basis.

Nixon's largesse toward Pakistan could not bear further fruit in 1971 because of opposition both within the executive branch and on Capitol Hill. His difficulties were understood in Pakistan even by Yahya himself. According to Pakistani officials who were around him, Yahya—in his more lucid moments—would wax poetic about Nixon's friendship and daydream that the future held great reward for Pakistan (a reference presumably to Yahya's role in forging Sino-American rapprochement). Yahya subscribed to the theory that Nixon, as well as his National Security Adviser, Henry Kissinger, were both "profoundly grateful" to him, as indeed the latter has himself admitted.[8] And even though no quid pro quo was established,

Yahya felt that the success of the China opening would, at the very least, improve the climate and make the United States more receptive to Pakistan's needs.[9] On a grander scale, it would, according to Yahya's game plan, fundamentally alter the strategic balance in South Asia, as the hostility between the United States and the PRC gave way to normalization and active collaboration. Yahya's (and presumably Pakistan's) place would be secure in this emerging relationship. Moreover, Yahya dreamed that the United States would at last begin to make a distinction between friend and foe and forsake its misguided neutrality in Indo-Pakistan affairs and hug closer to Islamabad. Others within the Pakistani elite, military members in particular (e.g., General Pirzada and General Omar), did not share Yahya's sanguine feelings and feared that the U.S. would soon forget any favors done for them by Pakistan and revert to their habitual "India worship."

Meanwhile, the disastrous course set by Yahya in East Pakistan began to take its toll. Nixon was subjected to increased pressure in Washington to respond firmly against the military repression in East Pakistan. Consequently, fissures opened up in U.S. policy. On the other hand, a dichotomy developed between the executive and the legislative branches on the issue of arms for Pakistan. U.S. law clearly required a cut-off in arms supply to any country using U.S.-made weapons for anything other than for defensive purposes. While Nixon was willing to overlook this clause on the basis of the fact that East Pakistan was, in strict legal terms, only an internal matter that was being internationalized by Indian actions, Congress was not so inclined. On the other hand, opinion within the executive branch itself was divided. Unaware of the behind-the-scenes China initiative, the bureaucracy could not comprehend the president's understanding of the Pakistani viewpoint. Within the Nixon White House, the prevalent feeling was: "The United States and Pakistan had a common philosophy and understanding of the area."[10] However, the regional bureau in the State Department charged with responsibility for South Asian matters, as well as the Office of the Secretary of Defense, both agreed with members of Congress that no arms should be supplied to Pakistan.

At last, with great reluctance, Nixon gave in, and an arms embargo was clamped down on Pakistan in April 1971, with the following results: first, the United States put a hold on deliveries of Foreign Military Sales (FMS) items from Defense Department stocks; second, the State Department suspended issuance of new licenses and forbade renewal of expired licenses for items on the munitions list and for other FMS sales; third, the United States held in abeyance any action on the "one-time exception" arms-supply order that had been issued earlier.

According to Pakistani perceptions, the availability of the U.S. arms was the *raison d'etre* of the alliance. As such, the imposition of the embargo once again shook the very foundations of the relationship. Nixon fully appreciated the seriousness with which the Pakistanis viewed this action. Without attracting attention, he worked hard to assuage the Pakistani sensitivities. In particular, an effort was made to release the APCs, to which Pakistan had already obtained legal title when restrictions to their purchase were temporarily lifted under the one-time exception arrangement. Notwithstanding Nixon's quiet efforts, the physical delivery of the APCs was stretched from 1973 all the way to 1975.

Despite the brevity of the 1971 war, the U.S. arms embargo remained rigidly in place until April, 1972, when the window was opened a tiny bit to let through some spare parts and a small quanitity of non-lethal (end) items. Although Islamabad had hoped for far more, the new president, Zulfikar Ali Bhutto, expressed his gratitude and welcomed even the limited U.S. sales to Pakistan because they had a place in Bhutto's scheme of things. While hoping to lessen Indian hostility through the rapprochement at Simla,[11] there remained a military dimension to Bhutto's policy that was a result of his continued desire to demonstrate Pakistan's status as a medium-range military power.

STATE VISITS, REGIONAL PRESSURES, AND ARMS

Bhutto was unsure of Indian intentions despite the Simla agreement, which he had co-authored and which was tantamount to a recognition of Indian preëminence. In the same self-contradictory vein, Bhutto's delight at the humiliation of the military at Indian hands was circumscribed by his concern that a completely emasculated army did not fit into his grandiose plans for playing an important role among the Islamic and Third World nations. Accordingly, it was in search of ways to strengthen the military dimension of his policy that Bhutto paid his official visit to Washington in September, 1973.

Riding on the crest of the Shanghai Communiqué, which acknowledged Pakistan's importance, Bhutto was in the fortunate position of being part and parcel of Nixon's China policy, which evoked much pride in Washington as well as in Islamabad. Nixon's gratitude and appreciation for Pakistan was epitomized by the official U.S. statement that: "The independence and integrity of Pakistan is a cornerstone of American foreign policy."[12] While similar sentiments had been expressed on previous occasions, their expression in an official format was especially important in 1973 because in Pakistani perceptions it gauged the extent of the U.S. commitment.[13] The commitment was useful to Bhutto even though at the same time he continued to display independence from the United States, following the Chinese formula by withdrawing from SEATO and recognizing the ousted Sihanouk regime in Cambodia.[14]

Bhutto was lavishly entertained by Nixon, and the atmosphere of the 1973 visit was extremely cordial. Privately, the Pakistani delegation was not expecting the arms embargo to be lifted at that time. They were fully aware of the residual ill–will in Congress toward Pakistan and the general disenchantment with arms transfers to an area that had twice seen major fighting within a six-year period. In addition, Nixon was becoming increasingly preoccupied with the unfolding drama of Watergate and was in no mood to take on Congress by proposing any arms sale for Pakistan.

While Abdul Hafeez Pirzada was a senior member of the prime minister's delegation, he did not have any impact on foreign policy issues. There, Bhutto considered himself to be the foremost expert. The executor of his decisions was Aziz Ahmed, minister of state for foreign affairs, who was a former career civil servant, having served as foreign secretary when Bhutto was foreign minister under Ayub Khan (1963–66). A certain amount of coaching of Bhutto's daughter, Benazir, was also going on during the visit, as she sat in with Bhutto on his meetings with various dignitaries. By and large, this was a public relations visit, designed to improve Pakistan's image and to provide Bhutto exposure as a world statesman. Bhutto's acute sensitivity to public relations gimmickry (a valuable asset for those who wish to do business with United States democratic institutions) is evident in his establishing a chair for Pakistani political studies at Columbia University (where academic opposition to Pakistan in 1971 had been particularly strong) during the course of his visit. The chair was to be funded by the government of Pakistan.

The 1973 visit laid the groundwork for the eventual lifting of the embargo. It was an integral part of the plan to influence Washington to do something it was loath to do, i.e., rearm Pakistan. For personal and technical reasons alluded to earlier, Nixon was unable to lift the embargo, but the stage was set for his successor to rule favorably on the matter after Nixon's resignation in August, 1974.

The ending of the arms embargo in February, 1975 was a hard-won prize for Pakistan. Its lifting also provides a classic case study of what we shall call "inverse gradient" influence flow. Such a flow occurs against the "power gradient." Accordingly, it implies the influencing by a weak state of the actions of a strong world power. However, before addressing the issues, and describing the events that led up to the reopening of the arms pipeline, it is useful to recall briefly the rationale for instituting the embargo and continuing it from 1971 to 1975.

Several reasons were advanced in U.S. congressional circles for action against arms sales to the subcontinent. First, there was unhappiness with the use of U.S. arms by Pakistan against India—arms that were ostensibly given for use against communist countries. Second, the embargo suggested itself as an even-handed policy toward both India (formally neutral, but a signatory to the "friendship" treaty with the Soviet Union) and Pakistan (a U.S. ally). (That it was not entirely even-handed was obvious because it pleased the pro-India lobby in Congress and greatly angered the Pakistanis.) Third, the embargo was an outgrowth of growing exacerbation with the entire U.S. arms export policy. Congress was becoming gravely concerned with the U.S. role as the "arms merchant of the world," which it saw as contributing to the instability of friendly purchasing countries. Moreover, the process, in turn, carried an inherent danger of drawing the United States into regional conflicts where U.S. supplied arms might end up being used. The record of Indo-Pakistani relations with periods of open warfare was held up as a specific example of the dangers of arms transfers.

None of these conditions had changed in early 1975 as Bhutto worked for renewed arms supply. With Gerald Ford in office as president, and Kissinger providing continuity in foreign policy, the White House was aware of Pakistani bitterness and also of the heating-up of the situation on the Pakistan-Afghanistan border. However, Congressional sentiments against resumption was a factor in executive-legislative relations against which Bhutto had to work. Bhutto took a measure of the complexity of the U.S. political situation and tackled the issue by a combination of what amounted to cosmetic public relations activity and clever manipulation of the United States' diplomatic psyche. He began to talk in lofty tones about the "shared goals" of the two democracies and the "commonality of the threat" faced by them. In this spirit, he found it useful to revise the defunct CENTO—which in the past he had been thoroughly averse to—as a "critically important alliance."

In addition, both Iran and Saudi Arabia, which had emerged as important actors in the region, were approached to plead the Pakistani case in Washington. While the shah's moves to project Iranian power into the Persian Gulf area made some of his smaller neighbors nervous, they did not disturb Pakistan. Rather, because of the realization that there was no question of competing with the massive arms buildup embarked on by Iran at a cost in excess of some ten billion dollars (which the Iranians could afford because of the quadrupling of their oil revenues after 1973, but which the Pakistanis could not even dream of emulating), Bhutto took the eminently sensible tack of riding cheaply in Iran's slipstream. Bhutto, who was not personally impressed with the shah, nevertheless whetted his ego by acknowledging Iran's preëminent role in Southwest Asian defense and, thus, in effect, extracted what was tantamount to an offer of a security umbrella. As a concrete realization of this umbrella, the shah helped with the stabilization of Baluchistan (the Baluchi insurrection, although rag-tag and disorganized, continued to plague Bhutto throughout his years of leadership). Indeed, as the situation deteriorated in 1977, Iranian AH-IJ Huey-Cobra helicopters manned by Iranian pilots flew missions against Baluchi guerilla camps. (The insurgency, which lasted from 1973 to 1977, was ended only after Bhutto's departure, when President Zia reached an "uneasy truce" with Baluchi leadership in November 1977.)[15]

Within the context of joint security, the shah gave Pakistan almost $850 million in economic and military assistance, and also offered a tempting $2.5 billion deal to Daud for Afghan development. Given the linkage in the security of Iran/Pakistan and Afghanistan, the Iranian monarch's pressure on Kissinger and Ford to support Pakistan through arms sales was seen to be in Iran's self-interests. Thus, it was entirely natural that between 1973 and 1975 the shah should be a firm supporter of Bhutto's requests to Ford and Kissinger for arms sales to Pakistan.

The shah's contacts were with the president and the secretary of state (he would not stoop to deal with anyone lower), as were Bhutto's (he had fewer choices). Both these U.S. leaders understood the geopolitical concerns of the shah and his preoccupation with Soviet power and Soviet support for Iraq and Afghanistan. The carte blanche given Teheran by Washington made Iran the largest buyer of military equipment in the developing world (spending almost 27 per cent of its budget for defense.)[16] By comparison, Pakistani requests were negligible. However, Bhutto firmly believed that U.S. concern with Iran impinged on U.S.-Pakistani relations because the twain were inseparable. As he stated to Kissinger: "If there are small bangs, it does not matter. If there is a big bang, then [the U.S.] cannot consider Iran's security separate from Pakistan's."[17]

Saudi Arabia was the other pillar of support for Pakistan within the Islamic bloc. Saudi financial aid was crucial for economic projects as well as some military purchases. However while the Saudis provided some cash, they stayed away from involvement in any specifics of the arms deals with, perhaps, the sole exception of a short-term consideration of a planned Pakistani purchase of self-propelled howitzers. When it became clear that the howitzer deal would cost $68 million, the Saudis felt that the figure was too high and lost interest. However, they remained impressed with the argument that Pakistan's legitimate defense needs required arms purchases from the United States and their position on this issue was extremely important in Washington.

Bhutto's efforts, combined with the pressures the shah and the Saudis brought to bear on Washington, finally bore fruit. Kissinger's appreciation of Pakistan's strategic location, fitting snugly into his geo-political equation for Southwest Asia, was clearly an important factor. Moreover, the Ford-Kissinger predilection not to abandon an old ally helped bring about the favorable outcome. Despite the State Department's adamant opposition to the reopening of the arms supplies for Pakistan, under Kissinger's management it curiously befell the State Department "to do something new for Pakistan."[18] Beyond the usual affirmations of U.S. interest and concern, the lifting of the arms embargo was the concrete step that made Bhutto's February 1975 visit to Washington a crowning success.

In addition to getting the U.S. embargo lifted, Bhutto also managed to convince some Muslim countries to finance Pakistani arms purchases. For example, Libya supported Pakistan by giving it $150 million in economic assistance and nearly $200 million for military purchases between 1975 and 1976. In return, Pakistan supplied military personnel under contract, particularly to the Libyan Air Force, where they were involved in the operation of MIG 21s, 23s, and perhaps some Mirage fighters. In addition, Abu Dhabi sponsored the largest of the arms deals financed with Arab money. It funded the direct purchase of 32 Mirage Vs for the PAF at a cost of $330 million and contracted for Pakistani crews to operate an additional 24 that were bought for the Abu Dhabi Air Force with the caveat that, in the case of an emergency, these too would be made available to PAF. The total cost of the deal was nearly $650 million.[19]

Assistance from all of the above sources enabled Pakistan to purchase arms from France and China in order to maintain what Bhutto, as well as the military, considered minimal levels of preparedness. Arab assistance also provided the Pakistanis with the only possibility of coping with the situation, since French arms were extremely expensive. Moreover, the French demanded cash payment in advance of delivery—and cash was what Pakistan did not have a great deal of at all.

Bhutto returned home triumphantly. He impressed upon the military not only his success in Washington, but also his ability to raise funds for their shopping list of military hardware. To the public at large, he offered improved relations with the West, in general, and Washington, in particular. At this juncture, Bhutto also attempted to reassure India, which feared that the willingness of the United States to consider arms sales "would result in an unrestricted flow of arms to Pakistan."[20] This, he said, would not be the case because of severe limitations imposed by Pakistan's "financial constraints and obstructing conditions" laid down by Washington.[21]

1975–76 ARMS SALES: A LIMITED PROMISE

The much heralded lifting of the arms embargo indeed did not result in the opening of the flood gates for U.S. arms. It could not because of the monetary constraints continually faced by Pakistan as well as the defensive nature of the weapons systems that U.S. policymakers were prepared to consider for sale. But the greatest difficulty arose when Pakistan signed an agreement with France for the sale of a nuclear reprocessing plant. The March 1976 nuclear agreement impinged immediately on the issue of U.S. arms sales to Pakistan.

Kissinger paid his last visit to Pakistan in August 1976, amid growing concern in Washington that the French government had opened the way for a Pakistani access to the nuclear threshold that the United States considered to be fundamentally dangerous in view of India's demonstrated nuclear weapons capability. Kissinger explained to Bhutto that while he understood the security framework within which Pakistan was operating and appreciated its legitimate defense needs, pursuit of the nuclear option would detract from Pakistani security rather than enhance it.

To sweeten U.S. pressure and to impress on the Pakistanis the fact that the Republican administration had no quarrel with Pakistan's search for security within an acceptable framework, Kissinger made an offer to sell Pakistan 100 A-7 jet fighters in exchange for the abandonment of the reprocessing deal with France. The very fact that the offer was made was indicative of the declining ability of the United States to influence Pakistani policy. During the vernal days of the relationship, United States disapproval would have virtually guaranteed cancellation of any such deal.

The Kissinger offer was received very favorably by officers of the PAF. In particular, its commander, Air Marshal Shamim, was enthusiastic. The A-7 was considered to be "the foremost power symbol of medium and small powers,"[22] and the air force was well aware of its superior performance capabilities. The military considered the fighter plane offer as a far more concrete step toward strengthening defense against India than a rather nebulous nuclear program. Moreover, subscribing to the theory that "a bird in the hand is better than two in the bush," the military much preferred to have the fighter then (for, according to Kissinger's offer, it would presumably have been made available expeditiously), than to wait for a problematical nuclear program that was not expected to bear fruit for at least a decade, at the earliest.

Despite eagerness on the part of the military to accept Kissinger's offer, Bhutto was reluctant. His vision of a nuclear Pakistan seemed much grander than one with a few new planes. Besides, as a politician he knew that, because of India's entry into the nuclear club, Pakistan's research program had a popular appeal. Its abandonment, on the other hand, he felt might redound to his political disadvantage. Nevertheless, he agreed to put forward discreet feelers to test U.S. willingness to make good on Kissinger's offer. From his experience he knew that the United States spoke with many different voices. Not only was there a divergence of views between the legislative and the executive branches, but within the executive also there were major disagreements.

Bhutto's fears were soon confirmed when the bureaucracy raised a hue and cry, describing the offer of sale of the A-7 as a "bribe." Opposition came from both the Bureau of Politico-Military Affairs (Pol-Mil) and the Bureau of Near Eastern and South Asian Affairs (NEA) at the Department of State, claiming that the sale of A-7s would set an ugly precedent and leave the United States open to future blackmail by countries using threats of nuclear technolgy acquisition.[23]

The only major military sale made to Pakistan after the lifting of the embargo was negotiated in 1976. Pakistan purchased self-propelled howitzers and two surplus destroyers. Bought at their junk value of $225,000, the destroyers were nonoperational at the time of purchase. An additional $16 million was spent in order to refurbish the two destroyers at U.S. shipyards. Pakistani crews came to the United States for fifteen months of training in 1977. The total cost of the deal was $37 million, which included some $19 million in munitions, torpedoes, and anti-submarine rockets. Originally, Pakistan had asked for six destroyers of the same make, which would have enabled the Pakistan Navy to retire the WW-II vintage ships it operated. But Islamabad was unable to secure the additional four because of the Congressional ban on naval transfers.

THE ARMS EXPORT CONTROL ACT: NEW RESTRAINTS

While arms sales as a means of maintaining "general political influence"[24] had become an accepted part of U.S. diplomacy, provided they did not harm other goals, the advent of the Carter administration added impetus to the imposition of new constraints resulting from a growing feeling that the amount of influence acquired by the United States was not really commensurate with the level of arms transfers. Furthermore, Mr. Carter had pledged throughout his campaign that the United States could not simultaneously claim to be the world's leading peacemaker and remain the world's largest arms merchant.

Once in office, Carter moved to implement his promise to reduce U.S. arms transfers, which he expected would rapidly result in decreasing the threat to peace around the world. Despite the existence of other sources of arms transfers, the United States would, in the Carter view, set an exmple by unilaterally moving toward a reduction in its arms trade. President Carter also objected to the fact that arms sales had increasingly become a major U.S. foreign policy instrument. In a statement on arms transfer policy, Carter vowed that henceforth arms sales would constitute an "exceptional foreign policy implement, to be used only in instances where it can be clearly demonstrated that the transfer contributes to our national security interests."[25] Apart from applying controlling channels and setting a ceiling figure for arms transfers (fourteen NATO allies, Japan, New Zealand, and Australia were exempted from the controls) and moving the locus of decisions on arms transfers from the Pentagon to the State Department, the new policy also changed the climate of arms transfers by stating that henceforth the "burden of persuasion will be on those who favor a particular arms sale, rather than those who oppose it."[26]

The above policy was predicated on the assumption that U.S. security assistance programs operated in an international environment in which there were a large number of nations whose security needs were peripheral to the East-West confrontation. However, the United States was to reserve the right to undertake arms transfers in the form of a major response to threats facing friends and allies.[27]

Details of the new policy indicated the variety of channels and the number of controls that were to be brought to bear: the Arms Export Control Board (AECB), the Policy Review Committee (PRC) of the National Security Council (NSC), as well as the NSC itself, to name a few.[28] Despite these announced checks, however, as time passed all indications pointed to the fact that rather than being an exceptional foreign policy implement, U.S. arms transfers continued to be made routinely with the application of very little restraint. For example, between May and September, 1977 (the first four months after the policy was announced), the administration notified Congress of forty-five planned arms sales to eighteen countries at a cost of over $4.1 billion. FMS, in fact, increased from $11.3 billion in 1977 to $13.5 billion in 1978.[29] There were only *two* cases where requests for arms were turned down during this period. One of these was, of course, Pakistan's request to purchase 110 A-7 fighter aircraft. The other was an unusual request for 250 fighters of the still undeveloped genre, F-18, by Iran. This request was denied on the basis that no weapons could be developed solely for export, and no purchase of the F-18s were planned by DOD at that time. Thus, the sum total of Carter's much touted arms transfers curtailment policy was the unique denial of the Pakistani request for A-7s! The curiousness of this happenstance did not go unnoticed in Islamabad, especially since the Pakistanis were, according to their perceptions, only taking the United States up on its own (i.e., Kissinger's) recent offer.

To placate Pakistani indignation, the Carter administration attempted to offer an explanation and made an alternative offer. The explanation centered on the advanced performance characteristics of the A-7, with its forward-looking infrared (FLIR) system that provided it a night and all-weather attack capability against armor and other targets. Thus the denial was explained to have been based on the concept of "non-introduction of a sophisticated weapons system in South Asia."[30] The alternative offer consisted of the relatively obsolete, and clearly harmless, A-4s or the limited range F-5s. Aware of India's possession of the MIG-23s and their projected acquisition of the deep penetration Jaguars, Pakistanis were impressed neither with the explanation nor with the alternative offer. The A-4s and F-5s were rejected disdainfully as a "waste of money."

The offer of the A-7 by the Ford administration and then its denial by the Carter administration did little to enhance the image of U.S. reliability and was later to have an impact on U.S.-Pakistani relations. That the A-7 offer was formally reneged by Washington in June, 1977, when Bhutto was becoming mired down in the post election storm that began to envelop him, did not help the United States in Islamabad. Instead, the U.S. action fed the anti-American paranoia rapidly building up in the Pakistani government, particularly within the ranks of Bhutto's supporters and close associates. Taken together with continuing U.S. pressure on the nuclear issue and the mounting belief within the Bhutto camp that the United States was deliberately undermining the Bhutto regime, Washington's denial of the A-7s was interpreted as a signal to the Pakistani military that Bhutto could no longer provide the weapons they wanted. The fact that the military finally moved to oust Bhutto within a month of the U.S. decision to deny the A-7s confirmed to Bhutto's inner circle the "fact" that the United States was behind the army's move against them.

Despite previously expressed views on Capitol Hill that it was necessary to curtail arms transfers, Congressional reaction to Carter's arms transfer policy was somewhat skeptical so far as the unilateral imposition of ceilings for FY 78 and the expectation of other nations following the U.S. example were concerned.[31] This skepticism was reasonable in view of the fact that, although Soviet arms sales to Third World countries were nominally lower (declared value, $2.5 billion in 1976, but actual value close to $4.5 billion) than those from the United States ($8 billion in 1976), the trend for the United States was down while that for the USSR was up.[32] It was thus assumed that even if U.S. sales declined, those from other nations, including the Soviet Union, would not. However, the increased built-in controls that were implicit in the new Carter administration security assistance posture were in general welcomed by Congress.

Legislation on FMS subsequently adopted by Congress impinged heavily on Pakistan's ability to purchase what it wanted from the United

States. The Arms Export Control Act (PL 94-329) was passed on June 30, 1976 and went into effect on September 1, 1977. It required that certain sales (over $1 million) be notified to Congress and that others be subjected to Congressional veto. In the latter category were all arms sales of $7 million that consisted of "major defense equipment" (MDE) or a total package (spare parts, defense services or items) costing $25 million or more. MDE consisted of "any item of significant combat equipment on the United States' munitions list having a nonrecurring research and development cost of more than $50 million or a total production cost over $200 million."[33]

An additional constraint was also applied to Pakistan, which felt itself singled out both by general antiweapons sentiments in Congress and by what it perceived to be an animus against it by the State Department and the Arms Control and Disarmament Agency (ACDA). The third restriction was the Symington-Glenn amendment to the Security Assistance Act of 1977, which forbade military and economic assistance to any country receiving "nuclear-enriched equipment" not subject to multilateral management under the International Atomic Energy Agency (IAEA) safeguards. While Pakistan was not actually in this category, its agreement with France for a reprocessing plant was deemed to subject it to the Symington-Glenn amendment. Accordingly, it was under this provision that all assistance to Pakistan was terminated in April 1979.

U.S. military representation in Pakistan through MAAG had already been reduced after the arms embargo of 1965. Yet, this aspect of the interaction was further curtailed to what only seven lone members of the MAAG team could provide in the way of advice, training, or information. After the 1976–77 legislation, Congress ordered MAAG personnel "not to discuss new weapons systems with host country officials without prior approval" and required close supervision by the State Department through the U.S. ambassador.[34] In addition, even Pakistani officers who trained in the United States were forced to terminate their program in 1979 because the United States refused to bear the $500,000 annual costs. It was a short-sighted move at economizing because these contracts were beneficial to both the United States and Pakistan.

We might pause here to recall that Pakistan put in an enormous effort to have the 1971 arms embargo lifted. Moreover, great jubilation was occasioned in Islamabad at its lifting in 1975. However, the changes that subsequently occurred in Washington militated against the fulfillment of Pakistani expectations. Indeed, by the middle of 1977, as the Bhutto regime was abruptly brought to a close, it was clear that the embargo had ended only in name and not in substance. Despite the change of personalities in Pakistan, this feeling has persisted.

Because of the difficulty of obtaining U.S. arms, Pakistan continued to

TABLE 2: Indian Arms Purchases in Billions of Dollars°

Supplier	1960–69	1970–79
Eastern Bloc[†]	2.960	5.675
Western Nations[‡]	1.765	5.926
TOTAL	4.725	11.601

Source: Interviews, 1978–79.
°The unit used is the 1979 U.S. dollar.
[†] Eastern Bloc—primarily the USSR, but also Eastern Europe and Yugoslavia.
[‡] Western Nations—France, the UK, USA, West Germany, etc.
NOTE: Figures given are those announced by India and the USSR. These figures have been traditionally underestimated in terms of their real world market value. Accordingly, the Eastern Bloc purchases for 1970–79 are worth approximately $12 billion.

search for other markets for its purchases. In Islamabad the acquisition of military hardware was rationalized on the basis of the continued Indian threat, coupled after April 1978 with a renewed threat from Afghanistan. Combined with the dual perception of the threat was the seemingly assured and continuing Indian access to external sources of arms, as indicated in the above chart.

By the mid-70s, India's technological base had expanded and matured. The building of the nuclear bomb was a case in point. In more conventional terms, India was now able indigenously to manufacture sophisticated weapons systems for both its army and air force. In contrast, Pakistan had little indigenous capability for weapons manufacture or, indeed, for their upkeep. Moreover, in comparison with India, Pakistani resources were limited, as were its sources of weapons supply. The PRC was one source whose terms were favorable, but the weapons fell far short of the sophistication of Western or Soviet systems. To fill the gap, Pakistan turned to France. French hardware was expensive and it was primarily financed from the assistance given Pakistan from the Muslim bloc. Additionally, Islamabad moved to acquire some measure of domestic production, e.g., the Chinese built a facility to service the T-55/59 tank fleet. However, it was hampered in making a substantial gain toward self-sufficiency because of the unavailability of high quality steel and the lack of an adequate technological base. Pakistani difficulties were compounded by the chronic shortages of foreign exchange and the perennial desire for a "quick fix." Maneuverability was thus limited to an attempt to reduce the leverage of any one supplier by making a virtue of a necessity and opting for multiple sources of weapons supply. This, in turn, complicated the picture because of the requirement for varied spare parts, training bases, etc. Because Islamabad could not forswear the need for U.S. arms it had to keep its options open even in periods where leaders vowed "to expunge all foreign and especially U.S. influence."[35]

Despite the vicissitudes in U.S.-Pakistani relations, one side or the other raised the arms question either directly or through third parties. The last such contact (prior to the Soviet invasion of Afghanistan) made by the Carter administration came from Undersecretary of State for Security Assistance, Science, and Technology Lucy Benson who, in the course of her visit to Pakistan in November 1978, carried a U.S. proposal for selling 70 F-5s (to replace the obsolete F-86 Sabers), Hawk ground-to-air missiles, armed helicopters, and antitank weapons at a total cost of $500 million, to be delivered over a period of three years. This offer was taken in Islamabad as the carrot in U.S. attempts to influence Pakistan's nuclear policy. Yet, Islamabad chose not to forget the fact that Carter and the State Department had turned down the sale of A-7s in 1977 as an offensive attack aircraft and had counteroffered with the F-5, which was presumed to be a defensive interception weapon. What surprised the Pakistanis was the insensitivity and the shortness of memory displayed by the U.S., which had chosen to forget that the centerpiece of this offer, the F-5, was regarded as a waste of money.

Rather wistfully, Pakistanis mentioned instead the F-15. Interest in the F-15, however, was never entertained in Washington, which led the Pakistanis to believe that India always would have the final veto over U.S. arms sales to their country, at least under Carter.

From the perspective of the United States, the Benson offer was indicative of the "reservoir of goodwill for Pakistan" and a recognition that its defense needed some shoring up.[36] From Islamabad's point of view, the offer was long overdue. However, its quality was below par. Moreover, it was unacceptable because it was tied to the nuclear program[37] and was considered to have been discriminatory since India had not been forced to make similar commitments. In addition, Islamabad was not interested in the F-5, which was not considered to be sophisticated enough to compete with India's MIG 23s and 25s or the Jaguar for which the Indians were negotiating with the British. Since the proposed F-5s were to be sold for cash rather than to be provided under some assistance program, the Pakistan military, in particular, felt that 15 Mirage Vs were a better bet in terms of capability, parts, and cost. The F-5 was an old aircraft developed by Northrop in the late 1950s (1,500 of which had been sold to some twenty-seven countries). From the U.S. arsenal, if not the F-15s, then the A-7 with its all-weather attack capability, was considered by PAF to be the minimally acceptable offer. According to PAF, France was also a safer source for spare parts so long as Pakistan was able to pay the rather exorbitant prices they charged for them. U.S. supplies were subject to the whims of political control and were perceived as unreliable. Only their high quality and reasonable price were the commending factors. Thus it was important not to accept another aging weapons system from the United States. (The PAF Sabers, being totally obsolete, were a constant reminder of what could happen.) Regarding Carter's new directives limiting arms transfers, the Pakistani military considered that even the new policy called for a continuation of sales of sophisticated weapons "in support of allies' self-defense needs."[38] Hence, the fact that the United States would not consider selling viable arms systems to Pakistan was taken as a reflection of a total lack of any genuine concern for Pakistani vulnerability and of continued U.S. preoccupation with unwarranted Indian sensitivities.

CRISIS IN AFGHANISTAN: A U.S. SHIFT?

After news of the proposed fuel enrichment plant from France became public, any offers of weapons sales from the United States became coupled to it. The attempts of either side to influence the policies of the other became locked in a test of wills where a shift could only be occasioned either by Pakistan's abandonment of its nuclear option or by the United States overlooking it. For Pakistan, it was one national interest weighing against another (nuclear versus conventional). In Washington's perceptions, the Pakistanis had no viable option except to come around because a single (or even a few) nuclear devices were hardly an acceptable substitute for conventional power and security.

Islamabad would not accept arguments against the nuclear option just as it had never believed the Carter administration's seriousness in maintaining its announced ceilings on arms (which were violated, in any case, as FMS figures for FY 1978 had risen to $13.5 billion).[39] Pakistan received no consideration in U.S. security assistance after April 1979. Indeed, the only aid it received was $40 million in the form of PL-480. Then came the Soviet invasion of Afghanistan on December 25, 1979, and the U.S. framework for assistance was changed overnight. President Carter stated to a joint session of Congress on January 23, 1980, that "any attack by an outside force to gain control of the Persian Gulf region will be regarded as an assault on the vital interests of the United States of America. And such an assault will be repelled by any means necessary, including military force."

Carter felt that the Soviets had threatened U.S. vital interests by sending 80,000 Soviet troops into Afghanistan. And even if years of Soviet buildup had not been a clear indication of aggressive intentions, deployment of Soviet troops in Afghanistan was clearly unacceptable. Carter viewed Afghanistan as a watershed. In his administration's view, it "lent powerful emphasis and powerful force to the rationale we believe supports our policy . . . to respond to the clear inimical, long-term trend in power relationship."[40] The area was considered to be vital because 33 per cent of the oil imported by the United States came from there. Corresponding figures for Western Europe and Japan were 66 per cent and 75 per cent, respectively. The argument of economic survival was buttressed by a strategic view of the Soviets as a power on the offensive, mopping up regimes from Angola to Ethiopia and Yemen to Afghanistan.

Claiming that he had discovered the true and aggressive nature of the Soviet Union only as a consequence of the Afghan invasion, Carter sought to give an appearance of firmness by his condemnation of the Russians, and urged strong measures. But his actual options in military terms were limited. Grain embargo, Olympic boycott, and travel restrictions were insubstantial responses except, perhaps, as symbolism to the American psyche, which needed awakening after the post-Vietnam paralysis. Equally, they presented themselves as real actions to a vacillating president who, for want of deeper understanding, had trusted the Soviets as a highly responsible, if not humane, super-power.

The fall of the shah and the presence of fifty-two U.S. hostages in Iran made any dealings with Iran impossible. The Saudis were nervous, and Carter was well aware of the fact that the stability of the Saudi ruling family was dependent on a precarious balance between an U.S. commitment and Saudi domestic sensitivities to an actual presence. The precursor of the Rapid Deployment Force (RDF), the 110,000-strong "unilateral corps,"[41] had yet to become functional even though a general outline was approved by Mr. Carter in August 1977.[42] While the idea of RDF gained institutional acceptance after the discovery of the Soviet brigade in Cuba in 1979, it was not until the Afghan invasion that a firm commitment was undertaken to make the United States the preponderant naval power in the Indian Ocean and to accelerate plans for the RDF.

According to reports of how the U.S. strategy toward the Persian Gulf region evolved, White House aides are said "to have been shocked by how few military options the United States had at its disposal."[43] The Afghan situation, according to a Carter official, had elevated the status of the Gulf region to that of Western Europe, Japan, and South Korea, "areas where Washington is prepared to risk a conflict to contain Soviet influence."[44] This being the case, one of the few immediate military moves open to Washington was to revive its military relationship with Pakistan.

The Carter administration had boxed itself in by its earlier pronouncements and policies regarding the negative correlation between aid to Pakistan and the latter's nuclear policy. Yet, the exigencies of the situation demanded some backing away. After a great deal of consultation within the State Department between the Secretary's Office, the NEA, and ACDA, and between State and the White House, the immediate military response to "the gravest crisis confronting the West since World War II" was unveiled.[45] It comprised two annual doses of aid, each consisting of $100 million in economic aid plus $100 million in military hardware, to be provided to Pakistan over a two-year period.

NEA, the Bureau of Near Eastern and South Asian Affairs, and ACDA, which had worked with Congress on the April 1979 ban based on the Symington-Glenn amendment, began contacting Capitol Hill on proposed aid to Pakistan. NEA obtained promises that Congress would be sympathetic to the Pakistani aid package. The expectation was that the "nuclear proliferation issue will be shoved aside by the more urgent issue of regional stability."[46] The assistant secretary and various lower-rank officers within NEA made regular visits to Capitol Hill to convince Congress that a change on U.S. aid policy toward Pakistan was in order.

Having secured appropriate assurances from Congress, the Carter administration also moved to ease other issues that had plagued U.S.-Pakistani relations by removing U.S. objections to Pakistani pleas for debt rescheduling, and reviewing earlier refusals to supply fighter aircraft. When Agha Shahi, the foreign policy adviser to General Zia, came to the United States in order to attend the UN General Assembly Session (which on January 17 overwhelmingly condemned, by a vote of 104 to 18 with 18 abstentions, the Soviet invasion of Afghanistan), he preceded the UN session with consultations in Washington on the Afghan situation and attempts to formulate a coordinated response.

Pakistan was an important factor in fashioning U.S. policy on Afghanistan. As its neighbor and as a country with whom the United States had a bilateral agreement that had stipulated a U.S. response (even though the wording of the agreement was cleverly adroit in lacking specifics), it could use its nonaligned status to plead the case at the United Nations and also invoke its Islamic and Third World credentials to canvass for a condemnation of the Soviet Union in world forums. Such expressions of condemnation, and the resulting isolation of the Soviets, were important to Carter, for he wished to wipe out charges of weak and naive leadership in the Iranian crisis by appearing to move forcefully in responding to the Afghan situation. Thus it was important for him to bring Pakistan back into the fold and convince it to actively cooperate with the United States. This is the reason why so much energy was expended on Pakistan and why Pakistan's inability to forget the previous record of the Carter administration was so gravely resented by the White House. The commitment to Pakistan was also meant to signal U.S. resolve to Saudi Arabia, which was also expected to help meet the costs of weapons supply to Pakistan.

To assuage Pakistan's doubts about the seriousness of U.S. intensions, munitions lists began to be formulated. The Pentagon and Brzezinski were once again willing to talk of selling used U.S. Navy, Air Force, and National Guard A-7s to Pakistan, but ACDA and officials from within Pol-Mil in the State Department who had turned down the earlier request in 1977 were still reluctant. There were also bad feelings amongst some in Pol-Mil as well as in NEA about the burning of the U.S. embassy in Islamabad by unruly mobs (who erroneously suspected U.S. involvement in the desecration and the taking over of the Prophet's mosque in Mecca by Saudi dissidents). They complained of delay in the arrival of Pakistani troops to rescue the stranded U.S. diplomats and the off-handedness of Zia who "was (rumored to be) off cycling in the bazaars of Rawalpindi" as the embassy burned to cinders around the beleagured diplomats.

Pentagon teams drew up lists of weapons that could be made available to Pakistan. The A-7 became a sensitive item because of the previous refusal (both governments were reported by senior officials to be "hypersensitive" to rebuffs). But Pol-Mil, ACDA, and the Indian Desk officers in the State Department contended that India would resent any A-7 sale unless both its range and payloads were reduced (which, in turn, would anger Pakistan because of its perceptions that the Indians had a veto on U.S. arms sales). Appropriately downgraded A-7s could have been readied within a month (from Eglin AFB at Florida) at a total cost of $500 million for 80 such aircraft, spares, support, and training.

The list of weapons drawn up (at White House's request) by the Pentagon (which involved the Office of the Secretary of Defense (OSD), the Services, and Pol-Mil in the State Department) included the Redeye man-portable infrared guided missile, the improved Hawk antiaircraft missile, and the TOW wire-guided antitank missile.[47] The list was to be presented to the Pakistani government in Islamabad in early February, in order to demonstrate U.S. resolve in meeting the Soviet challenge. At the same time, Washington wished also to indicate that the United States was cognizant of Indian sensitivities: "We seek good relations with both. Our assistance to either is not directed at the other."[48]

Much to Washington's surprise, Islamabad gave a cool reception to U.S. overtures. It was reticent at first and thereafter reluctant to get involved with the aid offer of $400 million, of which only $200 million was for military aid. When Zia characterized the offer as "peanuts," the U.S. response was one of shocked incomprehension. As usual, Pakistan began to receive bad press on the issue. This time around, however, there was very little understanding of the background of insecurities that lay behind Zia's attitude. Years of difficulty over arms sales, a deep sense of betrayal at the imposition of arms embargoes, "heightened by what was perceived to be hypocrisy in U.S. nonproliferation policy" (in view of U.S. benevolence toward the Indian nuclear program) had caused a questioning of U.S. reliability in all matters.[50]

Carter tried to allay Zia's fears by reaffirming the 1959 Agreement of Cooperation with Pakistan in his speech before Congress. It was symbolism but, it was nonetheless important because Pakistan had raised questions of a congressional (as opposed to an executive) understanding. The reasoning behind such a move was the realization that Pakistan had suffered from the personalized nature of its relationship with Washington and that congressional commitment would provide much-needed continuity. Zia wanted a formal treaty, ratified by Congress. The State Department, however, from the Office of the Secretary all the way down to the Pakistan Office (PAB) within the NEA, all felt it to be a totally inappropriate request on Zia's part. An impasse was rapidly reached whereby Zia, noting that the invasion of Afghanistan had "brought the Soviet Union to our doorstep,"[51] stated that in the absence of "active participation" by the United States, Pakistan may have to adapt itself to the new reality: "If you live in the sea, you have to learn to swim with the whales" became a part of his lexicon. Citing the fact that: "history has taught us not to harbor any illusions"[52] regarding U.S. participation, Zia looked toward China and the Islamic nations for support.[53] By the time the meeting of 35 Muslim countries took place in Islamabad on January 27 and 28, 1980, Pakistan had still not accepted the U.S. offer of aid. The conference condemned the Soviet invasion of Afghanistan, suspended Afghanistan from the Islamic Conference, withheld recognition from the Babrak Karmal regime, severed diplomatic relations with Afghanistan pending a total Soviet withdrawal, and urged all Muslim states to support Islamic countries neighboring Afghanistan.[54] Although some of the radical Arab states worked at the conference to avoid antagonizing the USSR, the prevailing sentiment was overwhelmingly anti-Soviet.[55]

Coinciding with the rapidly moving events was Secretary of Defense Harold Brown's visit to China. Planned in the summer of 1979 for January 1980, it was meant to be a dramatic, visible proof of the improving relationship between the two countries. Coming as it did in the midst of the Afghan crisis, it took on increased importance for Pakistan, especially as Brown stated: "Afghanistan gives the visit added significance. My Chinese hosts and I will be discussing the Soviet invasion . . . and the necessary actions that each will be taking."[56] Brown's talk of "parallel responses" sounded sweet to Pakistani ears because their experiences with China had generally been so positive. However, while the Chinese assured Pakistani leaders that Sino-Pakistani cooperation occurred outside the Sino-American framework, they advised coöperation with the United States. They could not do otherwise, considering that Peking had been actively seeking assistance from the best sources (and particularly from the United States after normalization of relations) for its four modernizations. It was undoubtedly in the PRC's interest to get a U.S. commitment to the security of Southwest Asia and U.S. offers to Pakistan had the potential of moving toward the same.

In order to underline the importance attached to Pakistan in the Carter administration's response to the Soviet invasion of Afghanistan, Zbigniew Brzezinski, the national security adviser and Deputy Secretary of State Warren Christopher traveled to Islamabad. They held two days of discussions there on February 2 and 3, 1980, with President Zia and Foreign Affairs Adviser Agha Shahi. The joint representation from the White House and State Department was taken positively by Islamabad. It was seen as being indicative of a coördinated policy. In any case, Brzezinski's notions of the Soviet threat were more akin to those held in Pakistan, and the fact that he led the delegation was symbolically important in view of past problems with Warren Christopher (in particular, his call for recognizing Indian preëminence on the subcontinent).

The discussion centered on general strategic issues, their impact on the region and matters relating to bilateral relations between the two countries. That a serious situation had been created was not disputed by either side. Problems arose on the nature of the U.S. commitment as the U.S. team sought to assure their Pakistani counterparts of Washington's seriousness. Pakistan was adamant on this point and the feeling has persisted in Islamabad (indeed, Zia reiterated this in his interview with this author) that the "quality of the commitment outweighed specific quantities of aid." The fact that Zia personally participated in these discussions was taken by the U.S. team as an indication of the gravity of his concern.

Once again, Pakistan promptly raised the treaty issue. By asking for a treaty commitment, duly ratified by Congress, Pakistani leaders were trying to redress problems that their alliance relationship with the United States had faced since 1954. Experience had taught them that anything short of such a commitment created in the long run more problems than it resolved. These leaders shared a strong feeling that the 1959 bilateral agreement, which was duly reaffirmed by the United States, provided too many loopholes in the definition of the "threat" and the assistance Pakistan could receive subsequent to it. Islamabad continued to be uneasy with India because of the fact that major issues in Indo-Pakistani relations still remained unresolved. Somehow, Zia and his advisers believed that a treaty relationship would force the United States to resolve the dilemma of wanting to help Pakistan but holding back due to Indian sensitivities. In this connection, 1971 was mentioned in Pakistan as an illustration of "Soviet controlled aggression," which had not activated the bilateral agreement because the State Department had maintained that it was only an "executive agreement." It was, therefore, queried by the Pakistanis that: were a similar contingency to arise as a result of Afghanistan, could

Pakistan be sure of U.S. intentions? Agha Shahi explained: "While a treaty by virtue of its ratification by the U.S. Senate is binding on successive governments, an executive agreement which lacks such ratification is binding primarily on the administration which enters into it."[57]

The U.S. team visiting Islamabad was not alone in its opposition to formalizing the agreement into a treaty. For example, sentiments by key witnesses before the Senate Foreign Relations Committee acknowledged that the United States "purposely kept the amount and type of arms (to Pakistan) in relative simplicity so as not to cause difficulty in the area, particularly with reference to India."[58] George Kennan's remarks to the committee were even stronger: "I have never seen the wisdom of our military involvement with that country (Pakistan). . . . All of this seems to be of questionable wisdom not only from the standpoint of our relations with the Soviet Union, but also from the standpoint of our relations with India"[59]

Secretary of State Cyrus Vance went before the House Foreign Affairs Committee on February 5, 1980, to talk about the foreign assistance programs. He clarified what the Carter administration had in mind for Pakistan. It would "address the immediate danger" and request "an exception to existing legislative restrictions so that we can join with others in responding swiftly to Pakistan's security needs."[60] While indicating that this request did not mean a lessening of commitment to nonproliferation (so indicated to the Pakistanis), Vance left the impression that it signaled U.S. desire to counter Soviet expansion by helping Pakistan.

All this activity in Washington as well as Islamabad was interpreted quite differently in Moscow; that is, as laying "a long-term foundation for the policy of U.S. interference in the affairs both of Pakistan itself and of other Near East and Middle East countries."[61] The Soviets accused the United States of trying to involve the Saudis in building up the Pakistani military position and using the Afghan situation as a pretext. They also said that Brzezinski's visit to the Khyber Pass had led to an increase in the "banditry in Afghanistan."[62] According to TASS, the entire aid package for Pakistan was "a ploy to provide the Afghan insurgents with arms, thus turning Afghanistan into a base against the USSR."[63]

A U.S. military team whose task it was to establish Pakistani weapons requirements traveled to Pakistan as the visit of the Brzezinski team was drawing to a close. There were a number of lists drawn up consisting of what the United States was prepared to give and what the Pakistanis felt they minimally needed. The discrepancy between the two sets was enormous. When the Pakistanis finally produced their own list, it was what one U.S. official called a "wishful shopping list" costing in the region of $11 billion. Included in it were radar, aircraft, antitank missiles, armed helicopters, tanks and APCs, light field artillery and self-propelled guns.[64]

An impasse was reached in the months that followed.[65] While Carter continued to say: "The measures we've taken against the Soviet Union since the invasion will remain in effect until there is total withdrawal of Soviet troops from Afghanistan,"[66] Zia noted sarcastically that: "On such occasions, practical steps are more significant than mere statements."[67] And while Vance indicated the U.S. position: "The nature of our economic and security assessment will depend both on Pakistan's needs and our own resources,"[68] Kissinger summed it up best for the Pakistanis: "Somewhere, somehow, U.S. foreign policy will have to find a way of rewarding friends and penalizing opponents."[69] Thus, Pakistan rejected the aid offer. Stunned and peeved, Carter would not revise it. Thus, it was left to his successor to come up with a more acceptable offer.

THE REAGAN ADMINISTRATION'S AID PACKAGE

The change of administration in Washington has augured well for the renewal of a U.S.-Pakistani dialogue. The difficulties of the relationship under Carter would not disappear overnight, but a philosophical change has been evident on both sides. Typically, a Republican administration is more favorable toward understanding the security underpinning of the relationship with Pakistan. Reagan's administration sees the Soviet move into Afghanistan as militating in favor of a rejuvenation of a stronger and more active U.S.-Pakistani relationship. The centerpiece of the new relationship is an economic and military aid package of approximately $3 billion extending over a six-year period. The rationale for the 1981 aid package is remarkably similar to that articulated in 1954. As stated by James L. Buckley, under-secretary for security assistance, science and technology, the thrust of the Reagan administration's policy is: "to recognize that arms transfers, properly considered and employed, represent an indispensable instrument of American policy that both complements and supplements the role of our own forces."[70]

The six-year aid agreement calls for the rapid restoration of U.S. military aid to Pakistan.[71] The mere fact that it includes the offer of selling forty F-16 fighters along with the aid package (only six of which are to be delivered within one year of signing the agreement) is symptomatic of the sensitivity of this administration to years of Pakistani frustrations at being offered nothing but "trash" (a snide reference made by a senior PAF officer to an earlier U.S. offer of F-5s instead of the A-7s). Even more telling is a comment made by the Pakistani foreign minister, Agha Shahi, that: "We do believe in the determination of the new U.S. administration to strongly support the independence of Pakistan."[72] In other words, Islamabad has perceived that the "quality of the commitment" has undergone a change under President Ronald Reagan. The fact that the quantity offered is considerably in excess of the Carter package of $400 million has also helped in the dialogue, particularly since the Pakistanis made it plain early in the discussions that the Carter offer lacked credibility in terms of meeting the magnitude of the threat.

The dialogue between the Pakistanis and Reagan officials has been, in the words of Secretary of State Alexander M. Haig, "unusually cordial and productive."[73] But attention has focused on the F-16 as providing the test of Washington's seriousness. Islamabad wants at least three squadrons of the aircraft and wants them to be delivered expeditiously. In order to discuss the issue as well as to formulate the rest of the package, a Pakistani military delegation came to Washington in July 1981. It was not pleased to learn that the first deliveries of the F-16 could not be promised until after the end of President Reagan's present term.[74]

From the Pakistani perspective, the entire aid package seems to revolve around the F-16 issue. Having given up their earlier insistence on a security treaty duly ratified by Congress, the Pakistanis feel they cannot accept the package piecemeal because of local sensitivity to past shifts in U.S. behavior. U.S. arguments that the time lag in F-16 delivery does not reflect a downplaying of the Pakistani relationship have not dispelled fears in Islamabad that once again the United States is asking for a commitment from Pakistan *now* for deliveries of critical arms to be made on a "never-never" basis. Accordingly, Pakistan has been reluctant to burn its bridges to the Nonaligned Movement and, indeed, to the Soviet Union.

The Reagan package acknowledges that the nonproliferation issue, while still a concern, is no longer a major stumbling block. As stated by the State Department spokesman David Passage: "This administration believes that by addressing those security concerns which have motivated Pakistan's nuclear program and reëstablishing a relationship of confidence with it offer the best opportunity in the long run for effectively dealing with its nuclear program."[75] The administration won support for its policy when the Senate Foreign Relations Committee modified aid restrictions against Pakistan and the Senate panel approved legislation permitting President Reagan to waive the aid restrictions. However, because the aid package requires approval each year for the appropriate component to be shipped that year, any progress by Pakistan on its nuclear option could still jeopardize this package. It is also for this reason that Pakistanis have expressed such misgivings about delaying the transfer of F-16s. They fear that if by then the Pakistani nuclear program should not appear to be bearing fruit, the prize (namely, the F-16s) may well be withdrawn. On the other hand, should the nuclear program appear to be heading for a success, the provisions of this aid package would force the Pakistanis once again to make a choice between the aircraft they feel they need and the nuclear option they would have worked so hard to exercise. Notwithstanding the existence of these misgivings, the shift in U.S. arms policy toward Pakistan has come in spite of, and not in lieu of, the nuclear program.

OBSERVATIONS

The relationship between arms and influence is a close one in the case of the U.S.-Pakistani interaction. The correlation was established at the very outset as it was clearly indicated by Pakistan that the United States would have to offer substantial arms assistance in return for Pakistani membership in pacts and the pursuit of joint interests along the "Northern Tier." It was a marriage of convenience. Dulles wished to line up as many adherents as was possible, and the Pakistanis recognized that Washington was a logical source of assistance.

The decision to turn to the United States for arms, was not however, based solely on the belief that it was the only available source, but was a spillover of a shared philosophy. In other words, the partnership did not evolve simply by default. Rather, it was a considered and deliberate commitment. However, there were obvious and key differences, the differing view of India being the most salient one, and identical perspectives were never the hallmark of the alliance. Both Pakistan and the United States decided early in the relationship to overlook the fundamental incongruity in their differing perspectives on what constituted the "threat." In so doing, Pakistan was not averse to subscribing to an anticommunist alliance, especially because of the Western socialization of its elite and their discomfiture with the USSR as a totalitarian nation-state with its antielitist, and equally importantly, antitheistic Marxist ideology.[76] Thus, joint interests led to a symbiotic but turbulent relationship, with its many ups and downs.

As stated earlier, the military aid in substantial quantities was the glue that nurtured the symbiosis. Its absence increased the centifugal tendencies and loosened the bonds holding the relationship together. However, it was a narrower concept of influence over specific issues and not a broad gauge response by Pakistan to U.S. needs, which led U.S. policymakers (during the latter half of the thirty-odd years of their interaction) to complain of the high cost of their Pakistani involvement. Pakistan, on its part, was willing to make important sacrifices, especially during the *prima veral* period spanning the earlier years of the relationship. (For instance, Pakistanis decided to forego the natural development of strong friendly ties with the Muslim-bloc nations during the 1950s in favor of the U.S. connection. Similar cold shouldering of the Soivet Union, however, came more naturally to the Pakistanis.) In contrast, when issues of national security and "survival" became involved (as they did, according to Pakistani perceptions, in the case of their quarrels with India), the United States was, in general, not able to exercise any crucial, restraining influence.

U.S. ability to influence Pakistani policy declined markedly after the special arms relationship was broken in 1962 by the supply of U.S. arms to India, which Pakistan regarded as its most dreaded antagonist. This action, perhaps more than any other, mirrors the fundamental importance of arms to the U.S.-Pakistani relationship and the negative effect it engendered when the arms were, instead, supplied to one who was perceived as the enemy.

Having reviewed the evolution and dynamics of the arms relationship between the United States and Pakistan, there remains the task of examining its correlation, or the lack thereof, with influence. To this purpose, it is convenient to work with the following hypotheses:

1. That arms bring the supplier influence; conversely, that a decrease in the supply of arms leads to a diminution in influence; additionally, that imposition of arms embargo by a traditional arms supplier is destructive of whatever influence it has acquired, and that the longer the embargo lasts, the greater the destruction of this influence;
2. That the easier the terms of trade for the supply of arms, the greater the influence of the supplier; additionally, that once the recipient country learns to expect a certain set of terms of trade, any worsening in them is destructive of the supplier's influence;
3. That the greater the supply of arms, the greater the supplier's level of influence;
4. That the higher the sophistication of arms, the more durable the influence of the supplier;
5. That while responsiveness (by the supplier to requests for arms sales) in itself does not necessarily lead to an enhancement of its influence, a failure to respond is destructive of whatever influence the supplier country already has in the recipient country; and finally,
6. That arms sales enable the supplier to affect the behavior and outlook of the military elite in the recipient country.

That a limited correlation existed between U.S. supply of arms to, and its influence with, Pakistan is amply confirmed by the account given above. The limitation is built in because of the quantities involved (hypothesis number three) and the Pakistani threshold of national interest that precluded overall influence. In other words, while the United States was able to get a base at Peshawar, managed to wean Pakistan away from both the nonaligned (a fairly sought-after club in the 1950s) and the

Muslim blocs and got general compliance in its diplomatic statements, postures, and policies against the Soviet Union, it was unable to shape Pakistani responses to its own advantage in all cases. For example, Pakistan chose not to address the threat from China (a very strong theme in U.S. foreign policy in the 1950s and 1960s) and would not shift its primary concern from India, nor would it free Pakistani military personnel for duty elsewhere along the Northern Tier.

That a decrease in arms supply leads to a commensurate decline in influence certainly held true in this relationship. Indeed, it is possible to pinpoint the turning point in the U.S.-Pakistani relationship, after which the ability of the United States to influence Pakistani policy decreased significantly. Relations took a turn for the worse after the 1961 review by the Kennedy administration that entailed a decline in the arms commitment. Even though the Pakistanis had always been unhappy with the pace as well as the size of deliveries, it was mostly a matter of relative unease on the part of the Pakistanis and also an attempt by them to infuence U.S. policy to increase the size of the arms package. Only after the 1962 arming of India (without the promised consultation with Pakistan) did the decline in U.S. influence in Pakistan begin. The arms embargo of 1965 was a major shock because the Pakistanis found it hard to believe that an ally of the United States that was totally dependent on U.S. arms (which Washington acknowledged) would be allowed to "twist slowly in the wind" while India went ahead and rearmed itself.

Finally, addressing the last part of the first hypothesis, we recall that the 1965 embargo impinged on U.S. ability to influence Pakistan in many ways. For example, it ended the access that Washington enjoyed, both through MAAG and at senior levels of policymaking. The relationship with the Pakistani military was shaken by the embargo in 1965 and destroyed by the one following the 1971 war. By wiping out its *raison d'etre*, the embargoes downgraded the alliance relationship. The 1971 embargo was deeply resented by the political/civilian elite as well, because they felt that the United States was callous in not acknowledging the reality of the Soviet involvement with India after the 1971 Indo-Soviet treaty. All of this surfaced during the 1980 Pakistani request that the United States upgrade the 1959 Executive Agreement because Islamabad belatedly recognized that its total reliance on the White House had left it exposed to Congressional and State Department criticism.

The second hypothesis, i.e., that the greater the supply of arms, the greater the supplier's level of influence, is also confirmed in the case of the U.S.-Pakistani arms relationship. As indicated above only when the level of arms supply was at its peak period, i.e., 1954–61, could the United States be said to have had substantial influence in Pakistan (within the limitation already spelled out). In Pakistan's case, the military relationship spanned a wide spectrum. Beginning, as it did, with small-scale direct assistance (MAP as well as grants), it increased eventually to the tune of over $900 million" (between 1955 and 1965). Then came the abrupt freeze. Additionally, U.S. arms policy underwent a directional change: from outright grants to loans and then to sales on "cash and carry" basis. Once the sales policy was instituted (and the lifting of the 1971 arms embargo in 1975 came under its aegis) the U.S. ability to influence was even further diminished (refer to hypothesis 2, above). This was due to the fact that Pakistan learned to expect the arms on favorable terms. Now it had to dig deep to find the necessary cash, which cut into its ability to purchase arms and was resented. In any case, soon after the embargo was lifted in February 1975, Pakistan ran into difficulty with arms purchases from the United States because of the nuclear reprocessing plant agreement it signed with France in March 1976. Islamabad's unwillingness to sacrifice its nuclear option (because it too was considered to be beyond the threshold of national security interests) made any meaningful arms relationship with the United States a moot point.

The fourth hypothesis, namely, the higher the sophistication of arms, the greater the influence of the supplier country, is only partly confirmed because it can be applied only in the post-1975 period. While it may have been true that from time to time the Pakistani military complained that they were receiving fairly obsolete equipment from the United States, they never really made it an issue in their relations with Washington so long as arms were part of an aid package. However, once Pakistan had to pay cash for its arms, like many other countries, the acquisition of the best possible weapons system or the most advanced aircraft that money could buy (and that Pakistan could pay for) became the goal. From Islamabad's point of view, the pursuit of such a policy made sense. It could, after all, already get less sophisticated arms from the PRC at very favorable terms. Accordingly, it needed the United States only for the supply of more advanced weaponry. The case of the A-7 aircraft amply illustrates this point. Had the United States sold the A-7 at the time that it was first offered in August 1976, they might have been able to come out ahead in terms of influencing the post-Afghan invasion relationship. By reneging on that promise, by offering instead the F-5 that Islamabad all along considered to be an unacceptably low performer, Washington destroyed the credibility of its policies. The turning down of the aid offer of January 1980 as "peanuts" has to be viewed in this context. Zia would not be swayed by Brzezinski's argument in 1980 that the $200 million in military aid, to be given over a two-year period, was "only the beginning." The Carter administration's vacillation on the A-7 made promises of better things to come, if a commitment were first made by Pakistan, sound hollow indeed. That the argument for the denial of the A-7 was based on a possible threat to India (and not finally on the nuclear issue, which had been side-stepped) made it sound ludicrous in Islamabad because of India's possession of MIG 23s and 25s and its deal with Britain for the supply of the Jaguar. In the final analysis, Zia was not willing to surrender the veto (over U.S. arms sales to Pakistan) to New Delhi.

The fifth hypothesis, i.e., while responsiveness in arms sales does not necessarily lead to an enhancement in influence, a failure to respond is destructive of any prevailing influence, is amply confirmed in the U.S.-Pakistani context. The deep psychological letdown felt by the Pakistani elite, particularly by its military, at what they perceived as the U.S. failure to consider Pakistani needs in instituting the 1965 arms embargo and its failure to lift the embargo in the face of continued Indian supplies, is only matched by the shock of arms aid to India in 1962. Moreover, in the face of a steady flow of Soviet arms to India in the months preceding the momentous signing of the 1971 "friendship" treaty that turned into a veritable flood in the weeks after the treaty was signed (and as the Indian Army prepared to move into East Pakistan), the United States 1971 arms embargo was bitterly resented in Pakistan. Somewhat in the same vein was the arms sales cut-off instituted by Carter in April 1979, on the premise that Pakistanis had not foresworn their interest in the nuclear option. By itself this cut-off might not have galled the Pakistanis as much as did the fact that simultaneously Carter also pressed for continuing the shipment of enriched uranium supplies to India, where tangible evidence for the development of the nuclear option already existed. This duplicity was destructive of whatever residue of U.S. influence in Pakistan still remained. Even the shock of Soviet troops on the Pakistani doorstep did not wipe out the bitterness felt by the military. By 1980, the United States had acquired negative influence in Pakistan as years of perceived letdowns make it impossible to resuscitate the relationship.

Hypothesis six, that is, arms sales enable the supplier to affect the behaviour and outlook of the military elite of the recipient nation, is confirmed in this study. Arms sales provided the United States with an opening to Pakistan through its military establishment and it was arms sales that sustained the relationship and provided the United States with whatever influence it had. Contact with MAAG and the training of Pakistani officers in the United States under the International Military Education and Training Program (IMET) also gave, at relatively modest cost, easy U.S. access to future influential members of the Pakistani elite. As stipulated in the *Military Assistance and Sales Manual*, IMET was expected to promote rapport between the U.S. military and its foreign counterpart. Another goal was the promotion of better "understanding" of the United States, its institutions, and its people.[78] IMET's goals were reached because it generated a great deal of goodwill for the United States in circles that counted. Therefore, its termination denied the United States an important channel to the Pakistani military, and vice-versa for access to the U.S. military establishment. Once the power to effect arms sales was shifted from the Defense Department to the State Department, Pakistan fared badly in terms of aid and, reciprocally, the U.S. lost influence in Pakistan.

To conclude, the arms relationship over the years can aptly be summed up from the Pakistani perspective in the words of former Secretary of State Henry Kissinger: "To be an enemy of the United States can be dangerous but to be a friend is downright hazardous!"

NOTES

1. In April 1966 U.S. supplies were recontinued but were limited to spare parts and "nonlethal (end) items," that is, anything that was not a weapon itself or a major component of a weapon, e.g., cargo and utililty vehicles, radar, communication equipment, etc. Medical and transport equipment was supplied in early 1967.
2. *The New York Times*, November 9, 1969.
3. Interview, senior U.S. official, 1979.
4. *The New York Times*, February 26, 1971.
5. Interview, senior member of the Nixon White House Staff, 1971.
6. *Ibid.*
7. The United States sold Pakistan $453 million worth of military equipment during the 1955–65 period and gave it an additional $650 million worth of arms under the Military Assistance Program (MAP) during the same period.
8. Henry Kissinger, *The White House Years*, Boston: Little, Brown & Co., 1979, p. 849.
9. Sultan Mohammad Khan, Pakistani ambassador to Washington from January 1979 to January 1981, and foreign secretary in July 1969 when he saw Kissinger off for Peking at Islamabad, writes: "It was a measure of Chinese confidence in Pakistan and its foreign policy that they accepted this channel, in "Pakistani Geopolitics: The Diplomatic Perspective," *International Security*, Vol. 5, No. 1 (Summer 1980), p. 28.
10. Interview with a senior staff member of the Nixon White House, 1980.
11. Detailed in Chapter Three.
12. *Department of State Bulletin*, October 15, 1973, p. 482.
13. For example, by Kissinger at Lahore on August 8, 1976, *Department of State Bulletin*, September 6, 1976, p. 318.
14. William J. Barnds, "Pakistan's Foreign Policy: Shifting Opportunities and Constraints," in Ziring, Braibanti and Wriggins, eds., *Pakistan: The Long View*, Durham, N.C.: Duke University Press, 1977, p. 394.
15. Selig F. Harrison, "Nightmare in Baluchistan," *Foreign Policy*, No. 32, (Fall 1978), p. 139.
16. Barry Rubin, *Paved with Good Intentions: The American Experience and Iran*, New York: Oxford University Press, 1980, p. 158. Also, Leslie M. Pryor, "Arms and the Shah," *Foreign Policy*, No. 31 (Summer 1978), pp. 62–63.
17. *Pakistan Times*, August 9, 1976.
18. Interview, former Senior State Department official, 1979.
19. The International Institute for Strategic Studies, *The Military Balance: 1979–80*, London: IISS, 1980, p. 106.
20. *New Directions*, London: Quartet Books, 1977, p. 98.

21. *Ibid.*
22. Ingemar Dorfer, "Arms Deals: When, Why, and How?" in Stephanie G. Neuman and Rogert E. Harkavy, eds., *Arms Transfers in the Modern World*, New York: Praeger, 1980, p. 202.
23. Leslie Gelb, "Arms Sales," *Foreign Policy*, No. 25 (Winter, 1976–77), pp. 12–13.
24. *Ibid.*, p. 19.
25. Congressional Research Service (CRS), *Implications of President Carter's Conventional Arms Transfer Policy*, Washington, D.C.: U.S. Library of Congress, September 22, 1977, p. 11.
26. *Ibid.*
27. Paul Y. Hammond, David J. Louscher and Michael D. Salomon, "Controlling U.S. Arms Transfers: The Emerging System," *Orbis*, Vol. 23, No. 2 (Summer 1979), p. 319.
28. *Ibid.*, also, Jo L. Husbands, "How the United States Makes Foreign Military Sales," in Neuman and Harkavy, eds., *op. cit.*, p. 157.
29. *Ibid.*
30. Statement by Department of State, June 3, 1977, *Washington Post*, June 4, 1977.
31. CRS, Implications of President Carter's Conventional Arms Transfer, *op. cit.*, p. ii.
32. U.S. Congress, Committee on Foreign Relations. *Report to Congress on Arms Transfer Policy Pursuant to Sections 202 (6) and 218 of the International Security Assistance and Arms Export Contract Act of 1976*, 95th Congress, 1st Session, U.S. Government Printing Office, Washington, D.C., p. 4.
33. PL 95–105, Arms Export Control Act, Foreign Relations Authorization Act, approved August 17, 1977, Fiscal Year 1978.
34. Hammond, *op. cit.*, p. 343.
35. Geoffrey Kemp, "Arms Transfers and the 'Back-End' Problems in Developing Countries," in Neuman and Harkavy, *op. cit.*, p. 272.
36. Interview, U.S. official, 1979.
37. Once the French cancelled their nuclear reprocessing plant agreement in August 1978, Pakistan hoped that Washington would lessen the pressure. While the Benson visit could be viewed as an outcome of the cancellation, the feeling in Islamabad remained that further promises were sought on nuclear policy.
38. CRS, *op. cit.*, p. 91.
39. Harold Brown, Secretary of Defense, *DOD Annual Report*, FY 1980, p. 225.
40. Statement by Mathew Nimetz, undersecretary of state for security assistance, science and technology, Department of State, Current Policy No. 221, September 16, 1980, p. 2.
41. *Washington Post*, June 22, 1979.
42. *The New York Times*, January 25, 1980.
43. *Ibid.*
44. *Ibid.*
45. Statement by President Carter, *The New York Times*, January 24, 1980.
46. *Business Week*, January 14, 1980, p. 131.
47. *Aviation Week and Space Technology*, January 14, 1980, p. 12.
48. Statement by former Secretary of State Cyrus Vance, *Department of State*, Current Policy No. 153, March 27, 1980, p. 3.
49. *The New York Times*, January 18, 1980.
50. Francis Fukuyama, "The Security of Pakistan: A Trip Report," *RAND*, N-1584-RC, September 1980, p. 24.
51. Interview with Arnaud de Borchgrave, *Newsweek*, January 14, 1980, p. 32.
52. *Ibid.*
53. Interview with author, July 8, 1980.
54. *Department of State*, "Soviet Invasion of Afghanistan," Special Report No. 70, April 1980, p. 3.

55. Alvin Z. Rubinstein, "Soviet Imperialism in Afghanistan," *Current History*, 19 October 1980, p. 83.
56. *Ibid.*
57. Speech on March 5, 1980, *Pakistan Affairs*, Vol. XXIII, Washington, D.C., March 16, 1980, p. 5.
58. Statement by Clark Clifford, former Secretary of Defense and special presidential emmissary to India in January/February 1980. *U.S. Security Interests and Policies in Southwest Asia*, Hearings, Senate Foreign Relations Committee, 96th Congress, Washington, D.C., US GPO, 1980, p. 15.
59. *Ibid.*, p. 49.
60. *Department of State Bulletin*, Vol. 80, No. 20, March 1980, p. 36.
61. *FBIS*, Sov-80-024, Vol. III, No. 024, February 4, 1980.
62. *FBIS*, Sov-80-026, Vol. III, No. 026, February 6, 1980.
63. *Time*, February 11, 1980.
64. Fukuyama, *op. cit.*, p. 28.
65. Lord St. Brides, "New Perspectives on the Hindu Kush," *International Security*, Vol. 5, No. 3, Winter 1980/81, p. 170.
66. Address to the American Society of Newspaper Editors, Washington, April 10, 1980, *Department of State*, Current Policy No. 159, April 10, 1980, p. 3.
67. *The New York Times*, April 18, 1980.
68. Statement before Senate Foreign Relations Committee, March 27, 1980, *Department of State*, Current Policy No. 153, March 27, 1980, p. 3.
69. Address to American Society of Newspaper Editors, Washington, April 10, 1980, *The New York Times*, April 11, 1980.
70. Testimony before the Senate Foreign Relations Committee, July 28, 1981, *Department of State*, Current Policy No. 301, July 28, 1981.
71. *The New York Times*, September 16, 1981.
72. *The New York Times*, April 22, 1981.
73. *Ibid.*
74. *International Herald Tribune*, July 18–19, 1981. The Air Force has been adamant that it not be called on to pay a heavy price for Pakistan.
75. *The New York Times*, June 15, 1981.
76. See Ph.D. dissertation, Shirin Tahir-Kheli, "Pakistani Elites and Foreign Policy Toward the Soviet Union, Iran and Afghanistan," University of Pennsylvania, 1972.
77. *U.S. Security Interests and Policies in Southwest Asia*, Hearings, Senate Foreign Relations Committee, 96th Congress, Washington, D.C., US GPO, 1980, p. 145.
78. *DOD, Military Assistance and Sales Manual*, DOD 5105. 38D.

5

NUCLEAR POWER AND POLITICAL FALLOUT

The complexities of the U.S.-Pakistani relationship have been reflected in their clash over nuclear policy. Despite U.S. encouragement in launching Pakistan's Atomic Energy Program in the mid-1950s, Washington reacted negatively to overt and covert attempts by Islamabad some two decades later to enter the select group of nuclear "haves." This nuclear path has been strewn with a plethora of problems. Pakistan's claim that it simply wanted to master the full nuclear energy cycle was challenged as the U.S. perceived Pakistan to be the "test" case for its "nonproliferation" policy. Washington desperately wanted to influence Islamabad's nuclear effort. In this pursuit, it used both the carrot and the stick to nudge a recalcitrant Pakistan away from attempting to cross the august nuclear threshold. Pakistan, however, was unswayed by either of these approaches. Indeed, even "the sanction of overwhelming physical force, by the United States directly or through third parties," which has remained a factor in Pakistani calculations, has done little to keep the Pakistanis from continuing on the course they set several years ago.[1]

THE PAKISTAN ATOMIC ENERGY COMMISSION

When it was established in 1956, the primary goal of the Pakistan Atomic Energy Commission (PAEC) was the generation of nuclear energy and the utilization of nuclear isotope technology for industry, agriculture, and medicine. Scientific research, although a fundamental component of the program, was not geared to the development of a nuclear weapons capability. The case for nuclear power seemed sound, because it offered another alternative to the energy shortage that has plagued Third World countries in general, and Pakistan in particular. With eradication of chronic hunger and poverty as the goal, the energy-deficient developing countries expected nuclear power to provide a crucial underpinning for their efforts at economic development. Pakistan's rationale was similar, and the fact that availability of energy on a per capita basis remained one-tenth of the world average and one-sixtieth that of the U.S. has dramatized the lag that had to be made up.[2]

The United States was not averse to Pakistan's commitment to nuclear energy. Indeed, under the "Atoms for Peace" program inaugurated by the U.S. Washington supported Pakistan's entry into the UN International Atomic Energy Agency (IAEA) when it was established in Vienna in 1957, and helped elect it to the Board of Governors. From its inception, the Pakistani nuclear program was intimately dependent on the United States. Pakistani students were trained in various Western countries. In particular, several U.S. nuclear research institutions (including Oak Ridge, Brookhaven, and Argonne) entered into bilateral arrangements with Pakistan to help train its personnel for a role in the programs of the PAEC. This relationship expanded further as membership in CENTO and SEATO increased Pakistani access to U.S. assistance programs.

THE RATIONALE

However, in pursuit of nuclear technology, Pakistan was only one of many such countries that felt development to be a prerogative as well as a necessity and that the West, led by the U.S., had to be mimicked.[3] As the relationship with Washington unfolded in the mid-1950s, Pakistan increasingly looked to the U.S. for support and found no reason to believe that there would be any basic incongruity between its pursuit of nuclear know-how and U.S. policy. There was little or no indication during this period that Washington recognized the possibility that today's nuclear-powered nations may be tomorrow's nuclear powers in terms of their ability to acquire a nuclear weapons capability. The nuclear issue was fairly typical of the big-brother attitude adopted by the U.S. and welcomed by Pakistan in the 1950s.

Pakistan launched it nuclear power generation program by placing an order for the 137 Mega Watt of electric generation capacity (MWE) Karachi Nuclear Power Plant (KANUPP) from Canada in 1965. By the time the plant went critical in 1971, Pakistan had already completed the necessary training and preparatory phases of the program (unlike neighboring Iran where the shah simultaneously launched the building and the training phases). The KANUPP was a heavy-water moderated, heavy-water cooled reactor using only slightly enriched natural uranium as fuel. The foreign exchange cost of KANUPP was $50.6 million, which was financed through a Canadian soft loan of $23 million and credits of $24 million.[4] Japan supplied the turbo-generators, providing credits of $3.6 million. Pakistan's nuclear program called for a second power plant with capacity of 400 MWE to be in operation by 1981 and another single or dual purpose plant to be built near Karachi in 1983–84.[5]

The planned expansion of nuclear power in Pakistan was predicated on the availability of only a limited number of viable alternatives. Only 14 percent of Pakistan's annual consumption of oil is met from domestic sources. Proven reserves of coal amount to 72. 5 million tons but the coal is of low quality and is high in sulphur content. While Pakistan is relatively richer in natural gas reserves (608.87 billion cubic meters), nearly 50 percent of the gas in spent on power generation,[6] and most of this gas is found in the Baluchistan province with its myriad political problems and its great distance from the more densely populated industrial areas of the country. Equally important, while hydro-electric power generation offers promise, only 876 MWE, out of a total potential for 18,000 to 25,000 MWE, have yet been developed. Furthermore, considerable technical and escalating cost problems, associated with the plant siting as well as power transmission, have been encountered.[7]

Yet, it cannot be demonstrated conclusively that the pursuit of nuclear technology through the acquisition of nuclear power is simply motivated by the economics of the enterprise. Indeed, the inherent costs of the nuclear undertaking cannot be fully assessed until the issues of nuclear waste disposal and the health and environmental risk factors are properly evaluated. Clearly, therefore, sound economic reasoning is not the sole motive force behind the clamor of Third World nations to seek nuclear generation facilities concomitantly with the development of other energy resources. The attraction of nuclear power lies primarily in the perception of the elite in these countries that it is "glamorous." In addition, it is thought to lead in the long run to energy independence. The high initial costs of training, development, and the physical plant are considered entirely worthwhile. Moreover, it is argued that the burden becomes easier to bear as the scientific-technological base in the country reaches maturity and makes the entire venture an indigenous one.

Thus, to seek only economic explanations for why various developing countries opt for nuclear energy is to miss the point. The situation is no different in the case of Pakistan.

The economic arguments offered by the Pakistanis are, nonetheless compelling. Various members of Pakistani governments, under Ayub,

Bhutto and Zia, have stressed the following theme: (a) The oil import bill for Pakistan is escalating (for 1980, imported oil is estimated to have cost Pakistan $1 billion). The national economy is staggering under this burden and can be expected to fail if the costs continue to rise, (b) Because of the high costs of imported energy, the country remains energy poor. The industry and agriculture are accordingly constrained and the productivity falls still further. This in turn makes the economy weaker—and the vicious cycle becomes ever more vicious as the ability to pay for imported energy is, in the process, further decreased.

THE AYUB YEARS

The need for a viable nuclear power generation program was stressed throughout the Ayub years. However, there was little, if any, thought given to the development of a nuclear weapons option. This is corroborated by the meandering course the Pakistani nuclear program has followed.

Ayub, as President, was the author of the nuclear power generation program and the first such reactor was specifically sanctioned by him. Despite its high cost, Ayub saw the program as a necessary prerequisite to the various modernization schemes he had set under way. Decisions regarding the nuclear program were made at the highest levels of the Pakistani government, although perceptions sometimes differed with regard to specific needs. For example, Dr. Nazir Ahmad, the first chairman of PAEC (1956–61) and Dr. Raziuddin Siddiqi, member of PAEC, proposed in 1958 that Pakistan should acquire the CP5 type of reactor for research, while the prevailing view was that the swimming-pool type was less expensive and simpler to handle. The latter type of research reactor, with only a tiny 5MW peak operating capacity, was subsequently built in 1962–63 at the Pakistan Institute of Nuclear Science and Technology (PINSTECH) in Nilore near Islamabad. Had the Pakistanis planned a nuclear weapons capability earlier in the program, they could have pushed for the acquisition of appropriate nuclear technology in the late 1950s and early 1960s when, in the words of one Pakistani scientific leader: "not only technical help but also financing was easily available."[8]

In addition to the basic experimental work in nuclear science, which was organized at PINSTECH, the PAEC set up a number of other facilities. For example, so-called "radiation centers" were established at Lahore, Tandojam (Sind), Faisalabad, Karachi, Islamabad, and Peshawar, where radio-isotopes and x-rays were utilized for agricultural, medical, and industrial purposes. In all phases of the Pakistani nuclear program, the U.S. was generally helpful until a series of events occurred in the 1970s that led to divergence between U.S. inclinations and Pakistani policies.

THE SECURITY FRAMEWORK OF A
CHANGED NUCLEAR POLICY

The loss of East Pakistan at Indian hands in 1971 was taken by Islamabad as a graphic reminder of the precariousness of Pakistani security. Given the ability of Indian Armed Forces to "free" any of the remaining constituent territories of Pakistan at will, and the continuing difficulty of the Indo-Pakistani leadership to evolve a peaceful, coexistent *modus vivendi*, it was hard for the Pakistani elite, as well as the public, to feel confident about the future integrity and security of their country.

Despite the shock of dismantlement, the post-Bangledesh era began on a relatively positive note when a welcome reprieve was offered by the Simla Accord, signed by Bhutto and Mrs. Gandhi. However, despite the toning down of the rhetoric on both sides, a nagging sense of insecurity (born out of defeat and the emasculation of its armed forces) persisted in Pakistan.

A different, but not altogether untraumatic shock was registered when two years later (in 1973) the OPEC price hike caused the cost of imported oil to skyrocket. However, this trauma was shared by the United States, which had the additional problem of an oil embargo to contend with. Now, the U.S. began to subscribe to an apocalyptic vision of a world held hostage by a number of newly important but unstable countries who might even become armed with nuclear weapons, if not developed indigenously, then acquired through surrogates. The resulting polarization of the "haves" and the "have-nots" demonstrated the vulnerability of the U.S. and other industrial nations to a group of Third World countries who had previously been taken for granted. This vulnerability manifested itself in the determination to limit the scope of the power of oil-rich developing countries, which could otherwise be used in ways detrimental to Western (and thus world) interests. The group of newly rich oil producing countries, a majority of whom happen to be Muslim, could not be denied their newly found economic power so long as the demand for oil continued unabated. But they could, and certainly ought to, the U.S. felt, be kept from acquiring nuclear wherewithal, with its potential for causing trouble later. Since the majority of nations in the above category lacked the necessary infra-structure to build a credible nuclear program, Pakistan was seen by Washington as the missing link in the chain for the acquisition of nuclear weapons by these countries. That the region encompassing the oil wealth was marked by East-West as well as Arab-Jew rivalries was a further destabilizing factor.

Then came the birth of the Indian nuclear bomb in May, 1974. Pakistani fears for its own security, which were lulled briefly by the Simla Accord, were re-awakened with a thunderous jolt, as though the man-made quake in the Rajasthan desert had registered ten, rather than a mere four, on the Richter scale.

While the West's unhappiness with the Indian test was genuine, it was, nevertheless, short-lived. Washington soon started worrying: "If Indians build the bomb, can Pakistanis be far behind?" Therefore, partisans coined a catchy phrase, the "Islamic Bomb," which was bandied about with remarkable abandon by the media and officials alike.

The Pakistanis, however, reacted in a different vein. Bhutto, who had been minister for fuel, energy and natural resources when Ayub committed Pakistan to its nuclear energy and research program, was prime minister in May 1974. Bhutto characterized the Indian explosion as a "fateful development" for Pakistan's security, saying: "The explosion has introduced a qualitative change in the situation prevalent in the sub-continent."[9] This statement lies at the heart of Pakistan's search for a nuclear umbrella following the Indian test. Bhutto sent his foreign minister, Aziz Ahmed, to various Western capitals. Aziz Ahmed's charge was to explain that consistency in Western concerns for nonproliferation demanded a positive response to Pakistan's request for protection against possible nuclear "blackmail" from India.

Aziz Ahmed's pleas fell on deaf ears. No guarantees whatsoever, even in the form of nonbinding verbal soothsayings, were forthcoming.° Aziz Ahmed returned home empty-handed because the United States, as well as other Western nuclear nations, wished not to get physically involved (any guarantees were perceived to imply a physical involvement) in matters that, according to their judgment, did not directly impinge on their national interests. That this was a short-sighted approach was implicit in Aziz Ahmed's diplomatic brief. The nuclear genie was now out of the bottle in South Asia. And its immobilization demanded some visionary responses from those in Western capitals who considered it their business to work against nuclear nonproliferation the world over.

Having exhausted his supplications for diplomatic-nuclear support against, what Bhutto considered a very real possibility, Indian nuclear

---

°It should be remarkable indeed if a consummate diplomat like Bhutto really put any stock in Western guarantees against nuclear blackmail. He would be aware that it was laudable for him to have sought them, but it would be obvious to him that their pursuit was not worth the effort undertaken. For even in Europe, which is supposed to rely on the U.S. nuclear arsenal for deterring and repelling any possible Soviet attack, these guarantees are viewed with considerable skepticism. And compared with Europe, a nuclear attack on Pakistan can be expected to cause much less of a soul-searching in Washington. Clearly, therefore, what Bhutto really hoped to achieve was to bring Indian nuclear activities under closer focus in the United States with the hope that super-power attention would exert a restraining influence on any nuclear moves by India (against Pakistan).

blackmail, Bhutto found himself with no alternative but to seek the elusive spirit himself. The development of a Pakistani nuclear option thus became a case of reassurance à la Britain, France, China, or India. It was also a case of Bhutto worrying that India might extract political concessions by "threatening to use nuclear weapons in the event that concessions are not granted."[10] Bhutto now gave the green light for Pakistan's development of a nuclear option. The decision fell on Munir Ahmad Khan, who had replaced I. H. Usmani as chairman of the PAEC in March 1972 after the latter was dismissed, apparently over a problem compromising Pakistan's friendship with China. Despite Usmani's enormous talent for engendering self-serving scientific publicity in the Pakistani media, he was, nevertheless, a product of the Indian Civil Service (ICS). The golden rule under which the British Raj, and the ICS, operated (namely, "divide and rule") was still a successful formula for attaining firm control over subordinates in Pakistan. However, the inspired leadership that the budding scientific community needed was nowhere in evidence, except that provided by Abdus Salam of Imperial College, London. Accordingly, any attempts to compare Usmani's role in the PAEC with that of Homi Bhabha[11] in India are entirely specious. Nevertheless, Usmani grasped the magnitude of the opportunity that the concept of Pakistan going nuclear offered. He used the media tirelessly and with considerable effectiveness touted the theme of nuclear development for Third World countries such as Pakistan. He, nonetheless, carefully circumscribed any concrete achievements of these goals and kept his fences mended with the U.S., whose wishes and desires for the PAEC had begun to diverge from those of Bhutto's Pakistan.

Munir Khan came to the PAEC from his post as director of the Reactor Section in the Secretariat of the IAEA. While there were other actors in different aspects of the overall nuclear research program under Bhutto, the move to speed up the capability and to attempt to develop a nuclear option (despite any demonstrated lack of feasibility) was Bhutto's own decision. In Pakistan, as indeed in India,[12] the head of the government is the final supervisor of the nuclear program, with a general "lack of public pressure on government policymaking" on these matters.[13] Accordingly, Bhutto was under no obligation to make public the deliberations on this subject.

Bhutto, nevertheless, continued his international compaign to secure viable guarantees against possible nuclear blackmail by India. To this end, he ordered the Pakistani Foreign Office to lobby extensively within the UN for the establishment of a "nuclear (weapons) free zone" in South Asia. This proposal was opposed by India with the argument that if such a decision were to be made, it should come only from the relevant nations of the area rather than be imposed by international will. And the relevant nations of the area had irreconcilably different perspectives on the issue considering that amongst them India alone possessed the capability to manufacture nuclear weapons!

Thus the India factor, which precluded Pakistan from becoming a signatory to the Nonproliferation Treaty (NPT), was immensely enhanced after 1974.[14] In addition, it is also important to remember that at that same time, Pakistan's relations with Afghanistan were also very tense. "Sandwiched between Afghanistan and India, with the Soviet Union waving a stick from a not-too-far distance," Pakistan felt that its security problem had become acute and it sought to multiply its options.[15] The security incentive ranked foremost in Pakistan's decision to develop a nuclear option, which in turn made it a nonnegotiable item in its policy. In this framework, the nuclear option was seen in Pakistan as providing an "ability to deter a militarily superior rival."[16] Also, to a lesser extent, the nuclear capability was viewed as a possible opportunity to end the vicious cycle of dependence on external sources of arms supply and the capriciousness of the suppliers.[17] The argument put forward for India that: "In a world in which naked power unfortunately dominates the resolution of vital issues involving the security of nations, the case for India producing such [nuclear] weapons is extremely strong" seems also to have been uppermost in Bhutto's mind.[18] Even though the strategic balance after 1971 weighed heavily in India's favor, it did not do so "to the point where India maintains an overwhelming predominance and war is unlikely."[19]

The prestige and status factors inherent in the decision to develop a nuclear option have been consistently overrated in the case of Pakistan. The chain effect of nuclear proliferation was more the issue (i.e., the security threat from a nuclear-weapons-equipped India) rather than a matching "Islamic Bomb" to compete with a "Hindu Bomb."[20] Indeed, Pakistanis were well aware that the possession of a demonstrated nuclear capability, in and of itself, is no guarantee of a seat in the councils of the world, India being a case in point. Other factors, such as the gross national product (GNP), carry more weight in substantiating any nation's claim to a position of power and prestige (for instance, compare India and Japan). Pakistan's indigenous effort to develop its own nuclear option was thus an act of desperation and a "recourse to a last resort."

If the elusive nuclear option was at one end of the security spectrum, pursuit of the more concrete, conventional arms supplies was at the other. The U.S. figured prominently in both calculations and for this reason Bhutto stated in early February 1975, just prior to the lifting of the U.S. arms embargo, that Pakistan's nuclear weapons policy was under "constant review" and depended on whether Washington provided Pakistan with sufficient conventional weapons.[21] But there were few expectations in Islamabad that this would actually occur. When the embargo was lifted in late February, and it became clear that support for Pakistan would be considerably offset by sales of U.S. military equipment to India, the decision was made in Pakistan that military sales (because of various limitations) were more an appendage to, rather than a substitute for, the nuclear policy.[22]

THE REPROCESSING PLANT AND U.S. PRESSURE UNDER FORD

Against this backdrop Pakistan signed (on March 18, 1976) an agreement with France for the sale of a fuel reprocessing plant to be erected in Pakistan. This agreement instantly ran into difficulty with Canada, which was particularly sensitive to nuclear issues in South Asia following its great embarrassment at Indian hands. (Indians are believed to have diverted the plutonium produced by their Canadian-supplied reactor, despite the existence of some safeguards, to build their first nuclear device.) Canadians, who had supplied the KANUPP power plant to Pakistan, immediately cut off all shipment of fuel supplies for this reactor. Having been stung once, they were not prepared even to accept stringent international as well as bilateral safeguards on the KANUPP.

The U.S. reaction was equally strong. They took the signing of the Pakistan-French deal on the reprocessing plant as a signal that Pakistan wanted to acquire a weapons capability. Accordingly, they put pressure on the French, along with the Pakistanis, asking for the deal to be cancelled.

Having secured the lifting of the arms embargo by the U.S., Bhutto may have misjudged the seriousness of Washington's commitment to nuclear non-proliferation. A juggler in pursuit of several different options simultaneously, he may have reckoned on a combination of French nationalism and Saudi/Iranian influence in Washington to bail him out of the impasse.

For the U.S. nonproliferation policy to succeed, it was necessary to ensure a certain degree of uniformity in the export of sensitive nuclear technology. This consistency in turn required U.S. coordination with allied exporting countries. Almost immediately after Washington started to tighten controls it ran into difficulty. Historically, U.S. companies, General Electric and Westinghouse in particular, had been at the forefront of the export market. By the mid 1970s, however, France's Framatome and Germany's Kraftwerke Union were beginning to land lucrative contracts.[23] Given the growing mass sentiment against nuclear power in Europe itself, especially in Germany, the European governments needed the export markets for the nuclear power plant's manufacturing industries. For example, the German government "could not neglect the 13,000 workers at KWU, many of these highly skilled, nor the welfare of KWU's 300 subcontractors."[24] Thus the export of nuclear technology offered both the German and the French nuclear industry much-needed business. It also offered the governments of these countries a chance to recover their R&D costs; for instance, Germany had invested several billion dollars on the development of light-water reactors in R&D alone.

The Europeans (France and Germany) resisted Canadian and U.S. efforts to push for comprehensive measures, the lack of which, Washington complained, was circumventing the effectiveness of the Nuclear Suppliers Group.[25] The French were suspicious of U.S. motives and the Germans stated that "severe restrictions on exports could be counterproductive."[26]

Washington's reaction to the proposed French sale of a reprocessing plant was to undermine it along two fronts. The first was to apply pressure on Islamabad to reconsider its entire policy. The second approach was to pressure France into a unilateral cancellation of the agreement. These were the two complementary routes along which U.S. policy attempted to influence events. There were, however, many nuances that developed along the path as events unfolded.

The dilemma for Ford and Kissinger became particularly acute in 1976. An election year found Ford on the defensive on many issues, challenged first by the various opposition spokesmen and later by Jimmy Carter, the Democratic Party nominee for president. One of the primary issues of concern to Carter was the dangerous spread of nuclear weapons and the priority his administration would give to curtailing it. Ford was also sensitive to public impressions that he lacked demonstrated leadership, having become president under unusual circumstances without having had to expose his ideas and policies to the gruelling scrutiny of an election campaign. Moreover, Carter found it useful to be highly critical of Nixon, during the election campaign, for demonstrating a lack of any coherent policy or response to the Indian nuclear bomb test, saying that the Republicans had: "rewarded India with additional supplies of nuclear materials even though India, not an NPT party, used our past aid to explode a nuclear device."[27] Ford thus felt obliged to respond, particularly since he had only a year earlier lifted the arms embargo that was supposed to deal with Pakistan's legitimate defense needs. Ford also found it necessary to somehow placate the fears within the India lobby inside Congress and the State Department of another pro-Pakistan tilt in the making.

Following the French-Pakistani deal, attention immediately focused on the Canadian heavy-water reactor (HWR), KANUPP. Statistics were cited by Washington that many kilograms of plutonium per year could be produced if it operated at full capacity.[28] Present-day power reactors use slow neutrons for fissioning the active fuel ingredient, usually uranium

235. This process itself produces neutrons, which in turn are slowed down by the "moderator," thus sustaining the so-called chain reaction. The overwhelming majority of the fuel matrix, however, contains the relatively inert uranium 238. Very occasionally, this nucleus too gets inseminated by a slow neutron. This occurrence, followed by successive ejection of two electrons, results in the production of a new, highly toxic and fissionable nucleus, plutonium 239. Some of these nuclei do themselves get burned in the reactor. A few, however, remain lodged in the fuel matrix when spent fuel rods are removed. If these plutonium nuclei could be separated from the spent fuel rods, one would have a supply of plutonium. This chemical separation is more hazardous but less tedious than the corresponding physical separation of the fissionable uranium 235 from its natural background, uranium 238. The end product of both these efforts, however, is really equivalent—namely, the possession of a quantity of uranium 235 or plutonium 239, either of which can then be used as the necessary central critical core for a nuclear explosion.

Argument has generally been made that from its KANUPP operations in five years Pakistanis would have as much as a total of 500 kilograms of plutonium (within the matrix of the spent fuel rods) and hence the capability of making approximately a hundred nuclear bombs.[29] This argument is manifestly and transparently flawed. Indeed, it is quite as ridiculous as the corresponding one that asserts that since Pakistani reserves of naturally occurring uranium contain enough fissionable uranium 235 to construct a hundred thousand nuclear devices, within a decade Pakistanis will have the capability of blasting to extinction all life from the face of this earth.[30] The crucial difficulty in both these arguments is the assumption that the separation of the active ingredient from its inactive background can be done by Pakistan. Whether this separation is undertaken via the chemical procedures embodied in the reprocessing plants or through the tedious physical separation that is carried out by cascades of high-speed centrifuges is essentially irrelevant.

It is in this context that the possible acquisition of the reprocessing plant was seen by Washington as being tantamount to delivering the "weapon on a silver platter" to Pakistan. Pointing to the Pakistani announcement of 1973[31] that "abundant quantities" of uranium had been discovered, and aware of the growing congressional pressure, particularly from Senators Ribicoff, Glenn, Church and Percy, the Ford administration felt compelled to move to try and influence Pakistan's course of action.[32] Accordingly, the United States heartily approved the Canadian action to cut off the supply of fuel for KANUPP.

As the U.S. elections approached, the Ford administration became desperate in its efforts to show some positive movement on the Pakistani nuclear option. Kissinger personally journeyed to Pakistan in August 1976.

Islamabad was hard put to explain its rationale for acquiring a reprocessing plant as a measure of achieving nuclear fuel autonomy. Even though a fairly ambitious nuclear power program had been planned, the fact remained that only KANUPP was operational. (Moreover, in terms of fuel economics, the reprocessing plant could begin to pay for itself only when it supported some fifty-odd reactors of the size of KANUPP). Thus, the Pakistanis cited their intentions to implement a fairly grandiose plan for nuclear power generation and gave some convincing figures for the high cost of imported oil. Kissinger, however, refused even to talk about the economic rationale for the reprocessing plant, labelling this line of argument as "insulting to the intelligence of the United States."[33] Bhutto's pleadings that Pakistan desired to shed its dependence on politically sensitive foreign sources (including the U.S., whose unilateral moves had left Pakistan in various difficult situations over the years), were countered by Kissinger with the suggestion that the U.S. would endorse the building of a joint regional nuclear reprocessing plant (presumably in Iran) that would provide a guaranteed and stable source of fuel supply for Pakistani needs.

Despite the coaxing and cajoling, on the one hand, and the application of severe pressure, on the other, years of Pakistani frustration over arms embargoes and the collective perception, on the part of the political as well as military elite, that the United States had long ago abdicated its responsibility toward Pakistan's security heavily militated against the U.S. ability to dissuade Pakistan from its chosen course. Thus, while Kissinger cited the dangers inherent in Pakistan's nuclear policy, Bhutto maintained that it was a matter of national security involving intense nationalism, and that he (Bhutto) would not be forgiven by the masses if he were seen to be compromising it. Kissinger worked on Bhutto's vanity by praising his statesmanship.[34] But when Bhutto remained adamant that the nuclear reprocessing agreement was an "internal matter" that Pakistan would not reconsider, Kissinger is reported to have reminded Bhutto that it would be wiser to deal with an understanding Republican administration on an issue that was rapidly becoming pivotal in U.S. elections. The secretary of state warned that were the Republicans to lose because of their inability to influence Pakistani nuclear policy, then Carter as president would certainly "make a horrible example of you."[35]

When both threats and pleadings did not work, Kissinger tried to break the deadlock with an offer of 100 A-7s. This offer, he said, was to signal Washington's understanding of Bhutto's argument of Pakistan's security considerations, of which the reprocessing plant was only a symptom. The offer constituted a clever move because it immediately won over the military, which was susceptible to offers of arms sales as a ready means of augmenting their capability. In contrast, the nuclear program was considered to be a more hypothetical and distant option whose chief utility lay in the political rather than the military realm.[36] While Bhutto was quite aware of the Pakistani need for the A-7s and the military's desire to avail themselves of the opportunity offered by Kissinger, he was unwilling to accept an immediate quid pro quo: namely, A-7s for the cancellation of the reprocessing plant. However, as time passed, it became clear that Bhutto would have welcomed the ability to buy the A-7s, and the resultant reaffirmation of his trust in the United States would self-consistently have translated into a slowing down of the quest for the nuclear option. As it happened, this scenario was never played. The U.S. did not come forth on the A-7 deal, and Bhutto, in turn, offered the U.S. no satisfaction on Pakistan's nuclear program.

Washington's attitude hardened after the Kissinger visit. Carter's election was a harbinger of greater U.S. seriousness toward nonproliferation issues, in which Pakistan rapidly became a test case. The domino theory in nuclear proliferation became representative of U.S. policy. At the same time, "in order to obfuscate the real issue that nations are likely to go nuclear when they feel that they are likely to face threats from nuclear weapon powers," the U.S. focus remained riveted on the idea that prestige was a major factor in proliferation.[37] While there may have been a tendency in Pakistan to relate "international influence and nuclear power,"[38] the basic underpinning of the nuclear policy remained security, and, to a lesser degree, the desire to achieve near-autonomy in an important area: nuclear energy.

CARTER AND NUCLEAR POLICY: A MAJOR QUARREL

At the very least, the pressure applied by the Carter administration on Pakistan hardened the latter's attitude and pushed the issue within the rhetoric of intense nationalism. The Carter policy also forced Bhutto, and later Zia, to take a public stance that made compromise difficult without charges of bowing to external pressure. Throughout his tenure, President Carter focused on the nuclear issue as an outgrowth of his own beliefs and background. Furthermore, Carter's commitment confirmed in the minds of some Congressional leaders the need for institutionalizing controls against the spread of nuclear technology.

When attempts to influence Pakistani policy away from acquiring the reprocessing plant failed, U.S. attention was directed at France. At first, the French government was less than enthusiastic in welcoming U.S. interference. Earlier Gaullist governments had rejected U.S. measures as being ineffective and impinging on matters of French national sovereignty. In addition, Paris viewed Bonn's actions as contributing more directly to nuclear proliferation. Thus, Paris accepted nonproliferation, but only in principle, and only so long as it did not affect the French program.[39] However, after Chirac's departure as premier, changes began to take place in these perceptions. For one thing, the locus of proliferation concern was no longer Germany, but, as Washington never failed to point out, had shifted to the Third World, where Paris hoped to play a special role in the North-South dialogue. For another, France, which had become a major exporter of nuclear technology, increased its participation in the London Suppliers Group despite the economic stake in continued exports.[40]

The tenure of Jacques Chirac as premier was crucial to Pakistan because of his refusal to bow to U.S. pressure. His comment that the reprocessing deal was "an agreement between France and Pakistan and not subject to third-party interference" was hailed in Islamabad. Calling the deal a matter between two sovereign states, Chirac responded to Kissinger's calls for cancellation (made in Paris after the unsuccessful trip to Islamabad in August 1976) with the remark that there was no question of accepting U.S. pressure in an affair that concerned only France and Pakistan.[41] His public disagreements with Kissinger became well documented, contributing finally to his resignation as premier in August 1976.[42]

Once Chirac resigned, French nuclear policy moved under the supervision of Elysée Palace. Giscard immediately imposed direct control over all nuclear exports through the Council of Foreign Nuclear Policy (CPNE) established in September 1976. A new nuclear export procedure was announced on October 11, 1976, after Giscard's visit to the U.S., which was reported to have led to a "detente" on nuclear policy.[43] On December 16, 1976, the French government issued an order "discontinuing until further notice the export of reprocessing facilities."[44]

The shift in French policy, not universally welcomed in France,[45] was received with a sense of foreboding in Islamabad. While Bhutto recognized that Giscard was obviously less determined than Chirac had been to maintain national sovereignty at all costs, Giscard had moved to allow *no further* sales of reprocessing plants, which meant that the existing contract with Pakistan would still be honored. While the Pakistani government focused on this aspect of the policy, there were new indications that the French were slowing down the supply of necessary blueprints and holding back on the transfer of critical technology. Seemingly, then, while Washington's attempt to influence Islamabad had been singularly unfruitful, attempts to influence Paris were proving far more successful.

When Carter took office in January 1977, Giscard had basically come around to the U.S. point of view on the export of sensitive nuclear technology. This new policy became all the more apparent in Pakistan after 1977, when Paris intensified its pressure through offers of alternate technology, i.e., co-processing (which was as yet not fully developed and therefore, according to Pakistani perceptions, not a viable alternative), and an almost continuous raising of the costs of the plant and announcements of long delays in shipments of the sensitive components. The French went even a step further by resorting to economic blackmail when they insisted, in the summer of 1977, that Pakistan fulfill its various economic needs solely from France, if the reprocessing plant sale was to be consummated.

Islamabad's reaction to the newly emerging French policy was to stand firm and not to provide the French any satisfaction by voluntarily withdrawing from the deal. Instead, in a major media blitz, the Bhutto Government pointed out two things. First, it was stated that the Pakistanis had only "peaceful" intentions and the rising cost of dependence on oil made the development of a viable nuclear energy program an urgent imperative. In achieving this goal, Pakistan hoped to master the entire fuel cycle, i.e., use its indigenous uranium to fabricate fuel, build nuclear power plants using internal efforts, and utilize the reprocessing plant to recycle fuel. Second, it was made clear that Pakistan had fully accepted IAEA safeguards on the reprocessing plant, not only to cover that particular plant but also any others using French-supplied technology. Hence, the U.S. effort to block the reprocessing plant was depicted as a peevish, punitive move representative of Carter's general pique with Pakistan.

In Pakistan, the adverse developments on the reprocessing deal were seen as a successful attempt by the United States to frustrate Pakistan's "legitimate" search for security. Bhutto and his acolytes did not take kindly to this and, facing an election at home, Bhutto became increasingly anti-American and spoke of plots and conspiracies "hatched by the U.S." in seeking his overthrow because he, as a true nationalist, would not yield to Washington in a matter that he considered to be of vital importance to Pakistan's security. Toward the end of his tenure as prime minister, Bhutto repeatedly mentioned the episode of the reprocessing plant and the duplicity and the hypocrisy of Carter's sermons. Bhutto's argument was the following: Carter has just lifted the U.S. ban on the shipment of highly enriched uranium to India (announced in June 1977). This was done with full knowledge of the evident fact that the building and the stockpiling of nuclear weapons has continued in India. Yet, at the same time, Carter has chosen to come down so hard against Pakistan's nuclear effort despite Bhutto's acquiescence to all the IAEA safeguards built into the French agreement.

Bhutto viewed his ouster by the military in July 1977 as an extension of Carter's animus against him. Not only was the U.S. ambassador to Pakistan reported to have warned Bhutto against any further pursuit of the reprocessing plant, according to Foreign Minister Aziz Ahmed, even Secretary of State Cyrus Vance told him directly that Bhutto would not survive in power if he persisted in following his present course. While U.S. officials close to the issue have disclaimed that any such threat was ever made, the rumor has persisted in Pakistan. One official confided: "If the French premier (Chirac) can be removed in order to placate Washington, certainly the Prime Minister of Pakistan could be similarly treated."[46]

The conspiracy theory is given considerable credence within the PPP, especially since the beneficiary of Bhutto's overthrow was the military, which was considered to be less wedded to the reprocessing plant. But the military rapidly found itself unable to jettison the nuclear baggage, identified as it now was with "national honor as well as security." The military began to see it as one solution to the security threat facing Pakistan, not only from Afghanistan and India, but also the "ideological" war at home. As a result, within the military command most came "to accept the idea of a nuclear weapon with varying degrees of enthusiasm."[47] Indeed, General Zia reiterated Pakistani determination to go ahead with the deal, and he hoped France would similarly maintain its principled stand on the issue."[48]

Paris tried early in August 1978 to renegotiate the arrangement with Pakistan by offering an alternate nonproliferating but as yet undeveloped technology. A senior French official traveled to Islamabad to deliver a letter from Giscard. Zia's reply to the offer was to be crucial in determining the nature of the final agreement. When Zia stated that Pakistan intended to procure the nuclear reprocessing plant that it had signed an agreement for, the French efforts to achieve a diplomatic face-saving formula for the cancellation of the deal were left with no prospect for success.[49] Grudgingly, announcement was made of what had become all but a reality already: the reprocessing deal was officially dead. At long last the reprocessing plant thus became a certified casualty of U.S. commitment to nonproliferation and a measure of its influence, not in Islamabad but rather in Paris. Curiously, the announcement of the cancellation (on August 24, 1978) came not from Paris but from Islamabad. Giscard apparently felt himself susceptible to charges of a sell-out by the Gaullist right at home. It was also perceived to be damaging to France's image in the Third World because Bhutto had identified this matter as a North-South issue.[50]

It has undeniably been a consistent Pakistani public stance that the nuclear option is totally and implacably nonnegotiable, even in exchange for conventional security arrangements. However, as stated earlier in regard to Bhutto, if a clear and reliable arrangement existed whereby the Pakistani leadership could put its trust in the United States' commitment to the security of Pakistan, or be guaranteed a continuing access to alternative conventional arms supply, they would have seriously reconsidered their single-minded pursuit of the nuclear option. This was in all likelihood true of Bhutto—who was denied any chance of adopting this course of action due to the short sightedness of the Carter administration. It was even more true of Zia's government—which, in turn, was given a pitifully inadequate offer by Carter (a veritable case of "peanuts," according to Zia) and the matter was once again never put to an actual test. A case in point, which hints at upholding the above thesis, was the Pakistani reaction to the long-anticipated French decision to cancel the sale of a reprocessing plant. Despite the formalization of this decision in August 1978, Pakistan and France continued to hold talks not only on the plant but also on a possible sale of Mirage fighter jets. In a visit to Paris, Zia's foreign affairs adviser, Agha Shahi, stated that he would "try and find ways" to pursue French-Pakistani relations. Purchasing Mirages was certainly one option.[51] In other words, the French, with an offer of sale of Mirage Vs, had succeeded where the U.S., because of the retraction of the offer of A-7s, had failed in maintaining good relations despite the mortal setback to the Pakistani nuclear program. Continued good relations with France were predicated on Islamabad's perceptions that Paris was unencumbered by a pro-India lobby and was therefore in a position to deliver arms while Washington was not.

Bhutto, writing from his death cell, chalked off the entire saga of the military coup against him as a pyrrhic victory. Had he not been overthrown, he claimed, the French government would never have reneged on its promises for the sale of nuclear technology. The overthrow of his civilian government by the military was, according to Bhutto, bound to create massive disquiet but "the awesome implications of these developments were not weighed when there was a rush to join in the conspiracy to overthrow my government."[52]

CONGRESSIONAL LEGISLATION AND RESTRICTIONS

Legislative veto over transfer of nuclear technology evolved because of growing concern with proliferation in unstable areas of the world. The Carter administration deliberately cultivated Congressional involvement in nonproliferation as a corollary of its own efforts aimed at limiting the nuclear club to the present "haves." A unified policy was expected to yield greater results, and besides, it was one of the few areas of agreement between the White House and Capitol Hill.

Coordination with Congress went into effect at the same time that pressure was being applied by the executive branch on both France and Pakistan to cancel the agreement for the reprocessing plant. In Islamabad this pressure was not perceived as being a part of a comprehensive approach to control the spread of nuclear technology. Rather, it was seen as a convenient ploy to shift the blame on Congress, i.e., whenever an inept Carter administration wished to deflect criticism of its handling of the growing crisis in U.S.-Pakistan relations.[53] The seriousness of Carter's commitment to nonproliferation was, according to the Pakistani view, suspect because of serious and illogical discrepancies between the treatment meted out to India and Pakistan. Continued supply of U.S. fuel to India in the absence of fullscope inspection safeguards, in the hope of an Indian agreement "in the future," had cast doubts in Islamabad on the Carter administration's sincerity and its "common sense."

The International Security Assistance Act of 1977, which amended the Foreign Assistance Act of 1961 and authorized international security assistance programs for 1978, required changes that came to be known as the Symington-Glenn amendment (Section 670). This amendment dealt with nuclear reprocessing transfers and nuclear detonations and mandated that no U.S. funds were to be used for "providing military assistance," or "granting military eduction and training" or

> extending military credits or making guarantees, to any country which on or after the date of enactment of the International Security Act of 1977:[54]
>
> (1) delivers nuclear reprocessing equipment materials, or technology to any other country (except for the transfer of reprocessing technology associated with the investigation, under international evaluation programs in which the United States participates, of technologies which are alternatives to pure plutonium reprocessing); or
>
> (2) is not a nuclear-weapon state as defined in article 1 of the Treaty on the NonProliferation of Nuclear Weapons and which denotes a nuclear explosive device.[55]

This legislation was expected to put some teeth into the NPT that was notable for the non-participation of the countries most likely to proliferate. The passage of the amendment ensured an automatic cut-off of military as well as economic assistance, credits, training grants whenever Pakistan was seen to be in violation of the provisions of the United States nonproliferation policy.

The legislation was accompanied by a proviso that the president may furnish assistance otherwise prohibited under the act if he certified in writing to the House and the Senate that "termination of such assistance would be seriously prejudicial to the achievement of United States nonproliferation objectives or otherwise jeopardize its common defense and security."[56]

Thus, U.S. policy had come a long way since December 1953, when President Eisenhower had launched his "Atoms for Peace" program. The motivating idea then was to assist countries in the development of a civilian nuclear energy program. The U.S. had offered the fruits of a new technology without a great deal of attention to its pace, its economic and environmental costs and, in particular, its military ramifications. By 1978, Washington moved to correct these policies by building in restraints.

THE URANIUM ENRICHMENT PLANT: U.S. RESPONSE

The U.S. learned in the spring of 1979 that Pakistan was beginning to attempt to put together a clandestine plant for enrichment of uranium using the gas centrifuge method. In order to avoid arousing suspicion, the acquisition of this high technology was undertaken under false pretenses in several Western European countries, including Britain, the Netherlands, Belgium, Switzerland, and Germany.[57] An unidentified U.S. company also reportedly sold multi-phase high frequency inverters to Pakistan. U.S. officials launched an inquiry in October 1978 when they discovered in the midst of a labor dispute in Britain that a British subsidiary of a U.S. company (Emerson Electric) had been in the process of manufacturing inverters for a "Pakistani Special Project."[58] Indian sources, ever on guard against Pakistani motives, got wind of some of this and informed their officials in Vienna who, in turn, reported Pakistani purchases to the IAEA authorities. The U.S., having thus far been unable to influence Pakistani policy on the nuclear issue, came to the realization that Pakistan, after failing to secure a reprocessing plant, had put into operation its second (a more costly, tedious and, indeed, desperate) option to go nuclear: namely, that of physical, rather than chemical, separation of fissionable material.[59] This realization came as somewhat of a shock to the U.S. However, already armed with relevant Congressional legislation, the United States now moved quickly to impose sanctions.

Washington's surprise stemmed partly from its belief that the Pakistani military was less wedded to the nuclear option, and the expectation that for all intents and purposes the cancellation of the reprocessing plant by France in August 1978 had pretty much ended the saga of the nuclear option because Pakistani scientific know-how, although not totally non-existent, was nevertheless far too elementary at this stage to be able to construct a reprocessing plant domestically. On the other hand, the process of physical separation, though in principle available, was known to be even harder and the relevant technology completely inaccessible to Pakistan. With this as the background, the news of Pakistani attempts at construction of a physical enrichment plant brought characteristic consternation in Washington. Officials within the ACDA suddenly emerged confident that Pakistan indeed possessed the ability and the scientific know-how to see this process through to completion. Moreover, senior State Department officials convinced themselves that it was really only a matter of time—tens of months rather than tens of years—before Pakistan crossed the nuclear explosives threshold. Estimates from the CIA, State Department, and ACDA all converged to the same desperate conclusion that unless action was taken immediately, Pakistan would go nuclear within a year. Washington's policy, accordingly, swung into gear to thwart Pakistan's "menacing race" toward nuclear acquisition.

The U.S. exerted pressure on all supplying nations to cut off shipments for the enrichment plant and scrutinize all exports to Pakistan.[60] In addition, the cut-off in military assistance (which was already insignificant) and economic assistance (which was by now only $40 million) came automatically in April 1979 as a result of the Symington-Glenn amendment. Pakistan thus became the test case in Washington's commitment to nonproliferation and the use of sanctions to influence a country's nuclear policies. U.S. perceptions differed markedly from those of Pakistan on the nuclear issue and despite the hardship that U.S. sanctions wrought, particularly as the U.S. pressured other countries to also come down hard on Pakistan, there was very little to indicate that Islamabad was reacting positively to Washington's pressures.

Statements by the Department of State that it wished "to act in the spirit of the law, especially in view of the president's concern over nuclear proliferation" were largely a technicality in 1979. The U.S. had not signed any new aid agreements with Pakistan after July 1977.[61] Islamabad reacted by going over the usual ground of the "peaceful" nature of their nuclear program but acknowledged that research was indeed being carried out on uranium enrichment.

Hoping to maintain a dialogue with U.S. officials, Agha Shahi stated that he would go to Washington in October 1979. Convening a conference of Pakistani ambassadors to major countries, he told them to "counter propaganda against the peaceful nuclear plan," particularly since it posed no threat to any country.[62] He regretted the dichotomy inherent in what the U.S. saw as its "global policy interests" and what Pakistan considered to be "a vital national interest." These words were essentially identical to those used by senior members of the State Department throughout 1979.

Despite a feeling of frustration with the penalties occasioned by U.S. nonproliferation policies, senior Pakistani officials, including the president, the foreign affairs adviser, and the Pakistani ambassador to Washington, all continued to hope that the resolution of the nuclear issues would result in a "restoration of the traditional relationship." Even though Islamabad was aware of the hardening of the United States' attitude under Carter (Pakistan was, after all, expendable in an area where Iran and India were to be the predominant actors), hopes of reviving old friendships were still expressed. For example, the Pakistani ambassador to Washington, Sultan Mohammad Khan (who as foreign secretary had seen Kissinger off for Peking in 1969), said to a Congressional delegation heading for Pakistan in August 1979 that: "We are still eye-to-eye on many international issues and cooperate in the promotion of common objectives." Whenever differences and disagreements had appeared in the relationship, "the two countries in the past had been able to find ways to overcome them."[63] Congressman Lester Wolff, chairman of the House Subcommittee on Asian and Pacific Affairs, was the leader of the Congressional delegation. He stated subsequently that, although he was impressed by Zia, he remained concerned with "any further development of nuclear activity in Pakistan."[64] He also felt that the Indian prime minister, Morarji Desai, was "Gandhi reincarnated," and believed that India would suspend further development of nuclear weapons. Lamenting U.S. impotence in influencing events, Wolff characterized the U.S. as "the misunderstood lover," particularly in India.

Even prior to the arrival of the U.S. Congressional delegation, Zia once again addressed the issue of nuclear technology, declaring that "Pakistan would never compromise on its sovereignty." Repeating the refrain of the economic incentive to go nuclear, Zia stated: "Our economic aid has been affected but we have absorbed its impact and the entire nation supports the government's stand because it is united on this issue." Ruling out any possibility of compromising the national interest, Zia concluded: "We shall bear our vicissitudes ourselves. We shall lift our own burden. We shall eat crumbs but will not allow our national interest to be compromised in any manner whatsoever."[65] This was the strongest of Zia's statements on the subject and his version of Bhutto's "we will eat leaves and grass, even go hungry," but not accept pressure remark.[66]

Senator John Glenn, one of the members of the Senate Foreign Relations Committee most committed to nonproliferation issues, talked of his perspective on the Pakistan matter. Acknowledging the security concerns that motivated the Pakistani nuclear program, he stated nonetheless: "I would not like to see the development of nuclear weapons in Pakistan." While he confirmed U.S. commitment to Pakistani territorial integrity, he added that "proliferation" was not the answer to the problem of insecurity among "have-not" states. Responding to Pakistani charges of discriminatory treatment under the Symington-Glenn amendment, the senator responded that Pakistan's case "happened" to be the first one on which a decision needed to be taken. The next one was to be India.[67]

Reports were circulating in Pakistan in August 1979 that plans to acquire nuclear technology had military implications and thus the program had been separated from the country's nuclear power development program. Hence, the coordination of the effort for the enrichment plant was organized as a "special cell" of the Pakistan Ordinance Department and was headed by a major general in the Pakistan Army reporting directly to Zia and not the chairman of PAEC.[68] There was a great deal of anxiety in Islamabad in August 1979 that, having failed to influence Pakistani nuclear policy, Washington would shortly undertake covert military action against the nuclear facilities at Kahuta and Nilore near the capital. This move was expected either through direct U.S. action or as a commando raid by either the Israelis or the Indians. These rumors were taken seriously enough for PAF Mirages to overfly the facility and air defenses to be set up on an alert basis.

SECURITY PERCEPTIONS AND THE UTILITY OF NUCLEAR WEAPONS

The "copy cat" nature of Pakistani nuclear effort, emulating as it does (if not in substance, at least in terms of slogans) the nuclear program of India, manifested itself almost from its very beginning. This correlation was also present when, following India's lead, Pakistan too declined to be a signatory to the nuclear nonproliferation treaty (NPT). (The NPT went into effect on March 5, 1970, and to date has been ratified by 84 states.)[69] Washington has also not been unaware of this interrelationship. It has long suspected India to be the *raison d'etre* of the Pakistani nuclear program and has refused to put any credence in talk of Pakistani need for energy self-sufficiency to be the motivating force for the program. However, only in late 1979 did Pakistani officals drop the practice of referring to the Pakistani nuclear program as being exclusively related to energy needs in their dealings with senior U.S. officials.

The NPT defines a "nuclear-weapon state" as one that "has manufactured and exploded" a nuclear weapon prior to January 1, 1967. "Whether explosion is a test of possession or a test of willingness to explode,"[70] it remains an acknowledged part of the definition. The NPT system has been characterized as "an evolving system, dynamic and not fixed." [71] Pakistan should be seen as being representative of a group of countries who have felt that the NPT is discriminatory because it limits the "fruits of nuclear technology" to those who already possess it and it assumes that while present nuclear powers are inherently "responsible," any newcomers are not. Since all of the major nuclear powers are Western and many of the aspiring ones are not, this policy is indicative, according to the holders of the view, of the bias and superior attitudes displayed against the non-Western states. Accordingly, the NPT is viewed as being unstable over time because it affords "stronger states disproportionately inequitable privileges," which makes it difficult "to impose moral pressures on states refusing to comply."[72]

Bhutto, and later Zia, perceived the strategic nuclear weapon as a political rather than a military instrument, i.e., relevant in peacetime rather than in war by providing a deterrent against Indian attack.[73] Pakistani leaders do not believe that the development of the nuclear weapons option will by itself result in a destabilization of the area. They have said that the acquisition of a weapons capability could well follow the European pattern where, in the words of one analyst, it "was more significant for regional entente than for regional rivalry."[74] This belief is coupled to the image of a nuclear weapon as being a means of expanding available options and raising the costs of an attack on Pakistan.[75] However, since the leaders do not expect to have to use the weapon, very little thought has been given by the leaders in Pakistan to the failure of this deterrence or the resultant devastation ensuing from miscalculation.[76]

The nuclear issue goes to the very heart of Pakistan's perceptions of its security image. Pakistanis in recent years have viewed their vulnerability vis-à-vis India, the Soviet Union, and Afghanistan to be increasing. Indian superiority in conventional arms is unquestioned, and Pakistanis believe that in 1981 it stood at approximately fifteen-to-one in India's favor. (A more accurate ratio, that can be gleaned from third-party estimates of Indo-Pakistani armaments, is approximately half that, i.e., eight-to-one in India's favor.) In this regard, Pakistani military leadership cites the lessons of 1971 as being fresh in their minds. While they (the military in Pakistan) do not foresee another war over Kashmir, the traditional bone of contention in Indo-Pakistani relations, they do visualize future moves by India, coming in tandem with the Soviet Union (with help from their surrogates in Afghanistan). These moves, the Pakistani military suspects, will come after prior preparation of an appropriate political climate in Pakistan, aided and abetted by these outside parties, and will be directed at one or more of Pakistan's four provinces. Within such a framework, the possession of a *political* weapon is considered quite valuable. Moreover, considering the absence of any viable option to remedy the imbalance in conventional armaments, not only the weapon itself but firm control over the complete fuel cycle[77] is seen to be needed for redressing the balance that goes in favor of "naked power."[78] In this context, the January 1980 U.S. aid offer was turned down by Pakistan because of the belief that unless substantially increased and upgraded, the offer would detract from, rather than enhance, Pakistan's security. Equally unacceptable was the overt U.S. suggestion that the granting of the conventional arms package "could affect the pursuit of our nuclear research and development program."[79] As a general comment, it is clear that the security underpinning of the pursuit of the nuclear option points out the dilemma that the nuclear sponsors of the NPT face: "formal security guarantees for the nonnuclear signatories of the NPT may be impracticable, but, in the absence of security guarantees by the nuclear powers, there is likely to be a steady erosion of the nonproliferation front."[80]

The nuclear incentives for Pakistan have been compared and found similar to those on which U.S. and NATO policy was premised, i.e., that nuclear retaliatory power was needed to counterbalance superior conventional Soviet forces. Thus the Pakistanis claim that it can plausibly be argued that Pakistan has as much legitimate need for a nuclear deterrent as the U.S. had in the late 1940s and Western Europe and China have today.[81] Moreover, the Nixon Doctrine forced area states to seriously consider self-reliance, which meant that incentives also tended to increase as capabilities increased.[82] Pakistanis have viewed the U.S. as applying a "triple standard" with regard to Pakistan; i.e., not only does the U.S. differentiate between the nuclear "haves" and "have-nots," but it also chooses within the latter group, namely, between India and Pakistan.[83]

In the final analysis, the nuclear issue has been one of sovereignty and a test of Pakistan's ability to make decisions affecting its national policy. Islamabad wished to prevent the U.S. from having any, or as little as possible, influence over this issue. Accordingly, it braced itself against threats, bribes, and persuasion. Perhaps, therefore, the only "quid pro quo" that stands a chance of succeeding in coaxing the Pakistanis to put their nuclear effort on the "back burner" would be "adequate and viable" support that reduces their vulnerability to the preponderant Indian superiority in conventional armament. And even here, the Pakistanis are unlikely to permanently forswear the nuclear option. Rather, they would quietly defer it. But as bankers in an era of escalating interest rates would say: a loan deferred is a loan unpaid. So, in the words of a leading Pakistani, "a nuclear option deferred is indeed a nuclear option unexercised."[84]

THE IMPACT OF AFGHANISTAN ON
U.S. NONPROLIFERATION POLICY

The perceptions of the Carter administration shifted rather dramatically following the Soviet invasion of Afghanistan. The president declared that: "Soviet occupied Afghanistan threatens both Iran and Pakistan. This would threaten the security of all nations, including the United States."[85] As part of the U.S. response, Carter promised "military equipment, food, and other assistance to help Pakistan defend its independence and its national security against the seriously increased threat it now faces from the north."[86] Because the Soviet invasion shattered the basic premise of the status quo in East-West relations, and since the fall of the shah had not only sensitized Washington to the vacuum in U.S. policy in the area, but also vitiated the "regional leaders" concept, both the White House and the State Department recognized the need to mend fences with Islamabad.

A two-pronged approach was adopted. First, an aid package for Pakistan would be put together along with a reaffirmation of the sometimes nebulous U.S. commitment to Pakistan's territorial integrity. (Any aid for Pakistan would mean making an exception in Pakistan's case of the Symington-Glenn amendment, which the law allowed.) Second, knowing that India would react negatively to this move, the State Department would go ahead and approve two pending Indian requests for shipment of enriched uranium for Tarapur. Approval of the Indian request meant that the Carter administration would ignore the fact that a ban on nuclear fuels for India (because of its refusal to accept fullscope safeguards) was to become effective in March 1980. An intensive lobbying effort was launched by the administration on both these aspects of U.S. policy.

With regard to Pakistan, Deputy Secretary of State Warren Christoper answered questions dealing with the impact of proposed aid for Pakistan on the Carter nonproliferation policy this way: "We will not put aside the nuclear issue with Pakistan because it is a basic principle of this administration—but it is only one of several foreign policy issues." Hence, he argued, aid to Pakistan was necessary, disagreements over nonproliferation notwithstanding.[87]

Senator Charles Percy, who would have had a major part to play within the Senate in passing any aid package for Pakistan, offered his opinion that aid to Pakistan was indeed necessary (along with aid for Afghan rebels), in the absence of which the Soviets would "go through Baluchistan to oil fields in the Middle East." Given these conditions, Senator Percy (who had previously backed controls on nuclear proliferation) felt that Washington should make an exemption to its nuclear policy and accept Pakistani assurances (assuming they would be forthcoming) that it would not manufacture a nuclear weapon nor would it transfer sensitive nuclear technology elsewhere. The senator stated that he had told the State Department that he would be willing to sponsor or co-sponsor a bill on aid to Pakistan and had also told the same to the Pakistani ambassador in Washington. He expected that the aid bill would pass the Senate.[88]

These sentiments were echoed by Senator John Glenn, who had previously taken a very hard line against Pakistan on nonproliferation. He acknowledged that the Soviet invasion of Afghanistan had precipitated the need for the U.S. to review "various strands" of its foreign policy:

On the one hand, the United States has longstanding and highly important nonproliferation interests and objectives which it is seeking to pursue in its nuclear relations with India and Pakistan . . . . On the other hand, long-term U.S. interests in maintaining stable political and security interests in Southwest Asia have been accentuated by the Soviet aggression and the need for a clear U.S. response to it. The United States has been seeking to revive and strengthen that country's ability to defend its borders against Soviet incursions from Afghanistan.[89]

As a reading of the above statement illustrates, a basic change in U.S. perceptions occurred as a result of the Soviet invasion of Afghanistan. Even though senior State Department officials, e.g., Thomas Pickering, assistant secretary, Bureau of Oceans, International Environment, and Scientific Affairs, and Peter Constable (who had served in Pakistan), senior deputy assistant secretary, Bureau of Near Eastern and South Asian Affairs (NEA), wished to emphasize the need to help Pakistan, they added two caveats: "At the same time we have informed the government of Pakistan that we remain deeply committed to our nonproliferation policy,"[90] and "We have expressed to Indian leaders our desire for good relations with India."[91]

Constable stated that in discussions with Washington, Islamabad had offered two "significant assurances" on its nuclear program. These dealt with the fact that Pakistan would not develop a nuclear weapon and that it would not transfer sensitive nuclear technology to other countries. However, beyond these two specific issues, the U.S. was unable to do much more. Pickering acknowledged the limitation on U.S. ability "to influence the nuclear programs of India and Pakistan."[92]

Statements by the Department of Defense also reflected the basic dichotomy of the U.S. position that, as a senior State Department official said, expressed the fact that "nuclear proliferation is now in the background."[93] The secretary of defense, Harold Brown, summed up U.S. concern for stability in South Asia and the security of Pakistan in light of the Soviet pressure in Afghanistan: "We also are concerned, however, with the problem of nuclear weapons proliferation, even as we work to safeguard the legitimate security interests of the regional states."[94]

Congressional sources repeated the same argument: "The U.S. is concerned about Pakistani nuclear activities and has sought to discourage Pakistani acquisition of nuclear weapons. Future Pakistani requests for purchase of significant military equipment will be evaluated in light of those concerns as well as in terms of the external threat engendered by the Soviet invasion of Afghanistan."[95] Words of caution were also offered by some outsiders.[96]

The Carter administration's response on the issue of supplying enriched uranium fuel for India's Tarapur reactor was a matter of some urgency in light of events in Afghanistan. While senior State Department officials and the president himself felt it important to continue the fuel shipments to keep New Delhi placated, others were less sanguine. Senator Glenn was particularly anxious that India subscribe to IAEA safeguards prior to any further shipment of fuel. Because, he said: "India's hesitancy about going on with IAEA safeguards after the past performance of previous administrations is not very encouraging,"[97] a position completely in keeping with his earlier statements to a Pakistani correspondent and not dissimilar to Carter's statements when he was a candidate.

Islamabad followed these developments very closely, seeing in them once again the application of Carter's triple standards. It was aware that during 1978–80, the two-year grace period allowed India, two large shipments of enriched uranium fuel (running into tens of tons) had already been made. Then, in September 1978 and August 1979, India had applied for another two shipments. For Zia, the processing of these Indian requests was another test of the seriousness of Carter's commitment to nonproliferation. Previously, when he had complained to Washington about the one-sided sanctions against Pakistan, the answer had always been that until March 1980, India was not subject to controls and that only Pakistan was a test case.

In May 1980, the Nuclear Regulatory Commission (NRC) turned down the new Indian fuel applications, saying that they did not meet statutory criteria since full-scope safeguard requirements applied to any export beginning after March 10, 1980, irrespective of when the shipment had been planned to occur.[98] The applications were then referred to the president, who could authorize the exports, subject to review by the Congress. The criteria for overruling the NRC were based on the president finding that withholding the fuel would seriously prejudice U.S. nonproliferation objectives or would otherwise jeapordize its common defense and security. In June 1980, Carter invoked just such a predicament to overrule the NRC and to authorize the new shipments to India. Curiously, the most substantive arguments offered by Carter for this glaring breach of his self-avowed stance on nuclear nonproliferation were as follows: first, the United States had already shipped more than 200 tons of enriched uranium fuel to India's Tarapur reactor, which was, in principle, subject to some limited safeguards. To deny the additional fuel shipments (which were, in any case, not immediately needed for running the reactor since Indians still had substantial quantities stockpiled) would, Carter argued, be foolhardy because then the Indians would reject and violate even the limited safeguards and thereafter openly reprocess the spent fuel to recover explosive plutonium from it—which in turn would further undermine the U.S. nonproliferation objectives. Second, both the president and the State Department contended that supplying India with fuel for Tarapur in the absence of full-scope safeguards would actually support U.S. nonproliferation policy.[99] According to this argument, supplying fuel would buy time for the U.S. to convince India to accept international safeguards in the future. Otherwise, warned Secretary of State Muskie: "If one party to an agreement abandons it, the other party surely is free not to feel bound by it."[100] Third, the Soviet invasion of Afghanistan and events in Iran had affected U.S. security interests in South and Southwest Asia deeply. The shipment of fuel to India was therefore "the best way to influence India to adopt policies beneficial to U.S. interests" and was going to be taken by the Indians as a "crucial indicator of the seriousness with which we view our relationship with them."[101]

Inhabited, as it is, by large numbers of lawyers, Washington felt no qualms about offering the foregoing arguments to support the administration's predilections. In Islamabad, however, this line of reasoning sounded surrealistic! At the very least, it appeared to be double talk.

Congressional response to Carter's overruling of the NRC was music to Islamabad's ears. Despite intense lobbying by the White House, the House of Representatives voted 298 to 98 in mid-September 1980 to uphold the NRC decision and to disapprove the shipments. However, after President Carter personally telephoned several senators from *Air Force One*, the Senate voted 48 to 46 to approve the sale of 38 tons of additional enriched uranium fuel to India on September 24, 1980. During the more than seven hours of debate, proponents of the sale used the president's arguments to support their case. Opponents of the sale, Senator Glenn foremost amongst them, said: "If we back down at the first test, especially in the case of India, the country with the worst history of any of our trading partners, what does that do to the credibility of our nonproliferation policy?"[102] Several other senators opposed the sale on the ground that the administration had criticized the Swiss nuclear exports to Pakistan, calling their attitude strictly "legalistic."[103] Senator Boschwitz of Minnesota said: "it was a contradiction, on the same day in which we are criticizing Switzerland, to support the sale to India."[104]

Despite the shipment of fuel, India complained of delays (even though Indian stockpiles of fuel for Tarapur already covered a full ten-year period) and notified the U.S. that they would proceed to reprocess spent nuclear fuel from Tarapur. This Indian decision had to be made by Mrs. Gandhi herself, since she is the final authority for the Indian Atomic Energy Commission. (In an interview with this author in August 1977, Mrs. Gandhi had lamented Prime Minister Desai's near "dismantling of the Indian nuclear program" and his susceptibility to Carter's nonproliferation policies.) The response of Senator Glenn and others to Indian threats was summed up in the following words: "So much for appeasement. The United States has continued to send India additional nuclear fuels precisely to head off the threatened reprocessing of previously supplied fuel. If every shipment is eventually followed by a threat of blackmail, why keep tossing good fuel after bad?"[105] General Zia commented after his October 1980 visit to Carter that the entire treatment of Tarapur had put the Pakistani nuclear case "on a higher plane!"

OBSERVATIONS

There were problems of style as well as substance in Washington's handling of the nuclear issue, which it considered to be one of utmost importance to U.S. foreign policy. Disagreements with Pakistan arose immediately after the signing of the fuel reprocessing plant deal with France in March 1976 and escalated rapidly thereafter. The U.S. was fully aware that the Indian test in 1974 had provided a basic rationale for the Pakistani nuclear program. Washington's suspicions that a strong correlation existed between the Indian and Pakistani programs were aroused even earlier when Pakistan followed India's lead in rejecting the NPT. On this, as in so many other issues, the Gordian Knot between India and Pakistan could not be easily cut.

The basic incentive for the Pakistani program remained its perceptions of insecurity in the face of overwhelming Indian conventional superiority. It was essentially similar to the corresponding factor that has motivated the West and the U.S. to join together in the NATO alliance against massive Soviet preponderance in conventional forces in Europe.

A second incentive was the desire to achieve near-autonomy in an important area, i.e., nuclear energy. The prestige issue, while not being totally irrelevant, was neither basic nor important as a factor. However, on this score, Washington labored under considerable misapprehension. Indeed, much of the focus of the U.S. response, particularly under Carter, was based on this false premise. There was also another, equally transparent but mischievous notion that got injected into this issue. This notion is best described by its catchy label: the Islamic Bomb. Washington's inability to comprehend the basic insecurity that Pakistan felt toward its powerful neighbor, India, was reflected in its search for trivial jingles. Accordingly, this phrase was coined to offer a substitute rationale for the Pakistani nuclear effort. Washington's self-delusion that Pakistan's quest for nuclear technology was fueled by the desire of rich, but technologically underdeveloped, Arab countries to acquire nuclear explosives through a surrogate, and its identification of the Pakistani effort with the "Islamic Bomb," contributed significantly to solidifying support for the nuclear program in Pakistan (which, not unlike most other Southwest

Asian countries, is going through a period of religious re-awakening). It was another example of myopia, nay blindness, on the part of Carter's foreign policy apparatus, which injected religious fervor into a totally secular issue. Of course, once the train of thought was set in motion in Washington, it was caught on by the media, both in the U.S. and in Europe, which often finds it easier to sell catchy sensationalism than dull substance to the masses.

Carter's perceptions differed from those in Pakistan as he made nonproliferation one of the central programs of his administration. In Carter's words, these issues were "one of the greatest challenges we are to face in the next quarter of a century."[106] Accordingly, it was the duty of nuclear states to curb their exports of sensitive nuclear technology to nonnuclear states and thus limit membership of the "terrible club" and prevent the threat of a nuclear disaster. The Carter view affirmed that it was the *possession* of nuclear technology that created the inherent threat by de-stabilizing the situation as it made every conflict potentially a nuclear one.

Pakistani perceptions differed. Islamabad felt that it was not the possession of the technology itself that threatened international order. Rather, it was the underlying problem of national security that forced a nation to allocate a disproportionate share of its resources in pursuit of a nuclear option. More specifically, according to the Pakistani view, the United States, an ally of Pakistan, needed carefully to examine the entire context of Pakistani security problems, before it took any initiative in regard to its nuclear effort.

Given these markedly diverging perceptions, the U.S. was bound to run into difficulties in exercising any influence on Pakistani nuclear policy. As stated by a prominent Republican, now a senior member of the Reagan cabinet, "The Carter administration, rather than understanding Pakistan's perceptions of threats to its security and then dealing with the underlying causes of the problem, simply zeroed in· on the symptom, i.e., nuclear proliferation."[107] In this context, it is important to note that in Pakistan it is an almost universal article of belief that the acquisition of a nuclear option would enhance Pakistani security and not, as Carter viewed, de-stabilize the situation further by ensuring a nuclear race with India.

U.S. attempts to influence Pakistan, because they continued to be largely unsophisticated and heavy-handed, gave both Bhutto, and, indeed, Zia, a domestic *cause célèbre*. The former constantly played up his stature as a "true nationalist," while the latter took credit for his ability to withstand "unprecedented foreign pressures" during the 1977–79 period to give up the nuclear program. Zia stated that he was "grateful to the

Almighty for giving him strength and confidence to withstand foreign pressures and thus sustain the nuclear program."[108] Thus, it was poetic justice that Zia should take credit for continuing a policy that had caused his predecessor, Bhutto, much discomfort at the hands of the nonproliferators in Washington and to which, according to their estimates, Zia was much "less wedded."

The public nature of the U.S.-Pakistani debate on the nuclear issue (a trend set by Kissinger because of Ford's vulnerability in an election year), did not serve U.S. interests because it made it extremely difficult to shift attitudes in Islamabad without seeming to give in on a matter that was perceived to be of vital national interest. While it is not clear, given the national security perception of the nuclear option, that Washington could have made concrete positive gains (unless it was prepared to deal with Pakistan's basic military insecurities), frequent and public references to the problem further poisoned the atmosphere for relations.

Thus it is eminently reasonable to conclude that the U.S. failed to influence the nuclear policy of Pakistan. Indeed, by declaring repeatedly that Pakistan was the test case for its nonproliferation policy, Washington made a further faux pas that entailed admitting that the entire policy had floundered! It may indeed have been better for Washington to separate Pakistan's particular insecurities from the peculiarities of its rather skimpy nuclear program.

NOTES

1. Onkar Marwah and Ann Schulz, eds., *Nuclear Proliferation and the Near Nuclear Countries*, Cambridge, Mass.: Ballinger, 1975, p. 2.
2. Shirin Tahir-Kheli, "Nuclear Energy Decision-Making in Pakistan," in James Katz and Onkar Marwah, eds., *Nuclear Energy Decision-Making in Developing Countries*, Heath-Lexington, 1981.
3. Interview with Director, ACDA, Fred C. Ikle; *U.S. News and World Report*, November 8, 1976, pp. 69–70.
4. News Review on South Asia, *Institute for Defense Studies and Analysis*, December 1972, p. 137.
5. The IAEA "Optimum" energy solution for Pakistan recommended one reactor in 1982, another in 1987, and one in 1988. *Market Survey for Nuclear Power in the Developing Countries*, Vienna: International Atomic Energy Agency, 1974.
6. *Pakistan: Economic Survey, 1979–80*, Islamabad, Government of Pakistan, pp. 183–85.
7. Energy potential and requirement are presented in National Science Council, *Proceedings of the Workshop on Planning and Implementation of National Science and Technology Policy*, Vol. I, Islamabad, Government of Pakistan, 1977.
8. Interview, Islamabad, 1979.
9. *Foreign Affairs Records*, New Delhi: Ministry of Foreign Affairs, Vol. XX, No. 6, (June 1974), p. 195.

10. Joseph I. Coffey, "Threat, Reassurance, and Nuclear Proliferation" in Bennett Boskey and Mason Willrich, eds., *Nuclear Proliferation: Prospects for Control*, American Society of International Law., N.Y.: Dunellen, 1970, p. 120.
11. Ashok Kapur, "A Nuclearizing Pakistan: Some Hypotheses," *Asian Survey*, Vol. XX, No. 5 (May 1980), p. 503.
12. *Ibid.*
13. *Ibid.*
14. The NPT was signed on July 1, 1968, and became effective as of March 5, 1970 upon ratification by the U.S., USSR, Britain, and forty other states. Signatories to the treaty pledged nontransfer of nuclear weapons by nuclear states, nonacquisition of nuclear weapons by nonnuclear states, and strict safeguards on nuclear facilities under the aegis of the IAEA.
15. Pervaiz Iqbal Cheema, "Pakistan's Quest for Nuclear Technology," *Australian Outlook*, Vol. 34. No. 1 (August 1980), p. 188.
16. *Ibid.*
17. William Epstein, "Why States Go- and Don't Go-Nuclear," *Annals* (Special Issue on Nuclear Proliferation: Prospects, Problems, and Proposals), Vol. 43 (March 1977), pp. 16–28.
18. Ravi Kaul, India's Strategic Spectrum, New Delhi: Chanakya Publishing House, 1969, p. 200, cited in Robert M. Lawrence, "The Nonproliferation Treaty and the Nuclear Aspirants: The Strategic Context of the Indian Ocean," in Marwah and Schulz, *op. cit.*, p. 65.
19. Stephen P. Cohen, "Security Issues in South Asia," *Asian Survey*, Vol. XV, No. 3 (March 1975), p. 204.
20. For a discussion of the chain effects of nuclear proliferation, as well as the incentives and constraints, see Lewis A. Dunn and William H. Overholt, "The Next Phase in Nuclear Proliferation Research," *Orbis*, Vol. 20, No. 2 (Summer 1976), pp. 497–524.
21. *Pakistan Times*, February 7, 1975.
22. Lawrence, *op. cit.*, p. 74.
23. For example, in Iran alone Kraftwerke Union signed an agreement for $1.5 billion for each of the two 1,200 megawatt reactors it was to build. In addition, Framatome signed an agreement for two 900-megawatt reactors. While the contracts were cancelled by the revolutionary government of Iran and litigation is pending, they were considered real plans at the time the agreements were made under the shah.
24. Edward Wonder, "Nuclear Commerce and Nuclear Proliferation: Germany and Brazil, 1975." *Orbis*, Vol. 21, No. 2 (Summer 1977), p. 298.
25. Set up by the Nixon administration after the Indian nuclear explosion. The original members were the U.S., the USSR, France, West Germany, Canada, Britain, and Japan. In 1976 membership was expanded to include other nuclear threshold powers: Switzerland, Sweden, Italy, the Netherlands, Belgium, Czechoslovakia, East Germany, and Poland.
26. Wonder, *op. cit.*, p. 303.
27. Cited later when Carter did the same, in *Wall Street Journal*, January 11, 1978.
28. Technical problems and fuel shortages prevented KANUPP from operating at its full capacity. Even in 1974 it was out of operation for 60 days because of heavy water leakage. *Dawn*, August 4, 1976.
29. Zalmay Khalilzad, "Pakistan: The Making of a Nuclear Power," Asian Survey, Vol. XVI, No. 6, (June 1976), p. 587; and "Pakistan and the Bomb," *Bulletin of the Atomic Scientist*, Vol. 36, No. 1 (January 1980), p. 13.
30. The actual reserves are presently not known, *Pakistan Economist*, No. 31, August 4–10 1979, p. 22.
31. *Asian Recorder*, February 5–16, 1974.

32. Ashok Kapur, "A Nuclearizing Pakistan: Some Hypotheses," *Asian Survey*, Vol. XX, No. 5 (May 1980), p. 509.

33. Interveiws conducted in Pakistan with relevant officials in 1976, 1977, and 1979 clearly enhanced this view.

34. Kissinger called Bhutto "elegant, eloquent, subtle . . . a representative who would be able to compete with the Indian leaders for public attention . . . . Brilliant, charming, of global stature." *The White House Years*, Boston: Little Brown, 1979, p. 907.

35. Zulfikar Ali Bhutto, *If I Am Assassinated*, New Delhi: Vikas, 1979, p. 138. Bhutto called Kissinger: "a brilliant mind." *Ibid.*

36. For an analysis of Pakistan's case, see Shirin Tahir-Kheli, "Pakistan's Nuclear Option and U.S. Policy, *Orbis*, Vol. 22, No. 2, (Summer 1978), pp. 357–74; and Richard Betts, Incentives for Nuclear Weapons: India, Pakistan, Iran," *Asian Survey*, Vol. XIX, No. 11 (November 1979), pp. 1033–72.

37. K. Subrahmanyam, "India's Nuclear Policy," in Marwah and Schulz, *op. cit.*, pp. 136–37.

38. Anne Hessing Cahn, "Determinants of the Nuclear Option: The Case of Iran," in Marwah and Schulz, *op. cit.*, p. 202.

39. For an analysis of French nuclear policy under Giscard, see Pierre Lellouche, "France in the International Nuclear Energy Controversy: A New Policy Under Giscard d'Estaing," *Orbis*, Vol. 22, No. 4 (Winter 1979), pp. 951–65.

40. Apart from the $150 million reprocessing plant agreement with Pakistan, French nuclear contracts with Iran and South Africa were for $3 billion and $1.1 billion, respectively.

41. *Pakistan Times*, August 7, 1976.

42. Example, *L'Express*, August 16, 1976.

43. *New York Times*, October 15, 1976.

44. Lellouch, *op. cit.*, p. 959.

45. *La Lettre de la Nation*, December 17, 1976.

46. *Interview*, Islamabad, July 1977.

47. Stephen P. Cohen, "Nuclear Issues and Security Policy in Pakistan," paper presented at the Annual Meeting of the Association for Asian Studies, March 21–23, 1980, p. 8.

48. *Pakistan Times*, June 29, 1978.

49. *Pakistan Times*, August 3, 1978.

50. Lellouche, *op. cit.*, p. 960.

51. *Pakistan Times*, November 4, 1978.

52. *Bhutto*, op. cit., p. 136.

53. Knowledgeable Pakistanis found it "incomprehensible" as policy and took it simply as yet another example of Washington's tilt in India's favor.

54. This amendment went into effect on September 28, 1978.

55. Committee on Foreign Relations and Committee on Foreign Affairs, *Legislation on Foreign Relations Through 1978*, Vol. 1, Joint Committee, U.S. Congress, Washington, D.C.: U.S. Government Printing Office, 1979, p. 146.

56. Joseph S. Nye, *The International Nonproliferation Regime*, Occasional Paper 23, The Stanley Foundation, July 1980, p. 6.

57. Pakistani officials used the subterfuge of purchasing parts for a "textile plant." Several of the key components could have application for such a plant.

58. *Washington Star*, December 21, 1979. The design for the enrichment plant was stolen from a Dutch consortium engaged in the development of a joint project for the Netherlands, Britain and Germany.

59. "Pakistan: The Islamic Bomb: How another country is joining the nuclear club," *Time*, July 9, 1979, pp. 40–41; and Edgar O'Ballance, "The Islamic Bomb," *National Defense*, December 1980, pp. 50–55.

60. Most recently, the Swiss have obliged, albeit somewhat resentfully. A Swiss diplomat

was reported to have been bitter at U.S. insistence and felt that Washington had singled out Swiss companies for adverse publicity and pressure. *Washington Star*, December 21, 1979; *Washington Post*, September 21, 1980.
61. *Pakistan Times*, August 5, 1978.
62. *Pakistan Times*, July 13, 1979.
63. *Pakistan Times*, August 1, 1979.
64. Washington, November 1979.
65. Address to the nation, *The Muslim*, July 28, 1979.
66. *Time*, July 9, 1979, p. 40.
67. Interview with Pakistani correspondent (PPI), *The Muslim* and *Pakistan Times*, August 4, 1979.
68. *Nawai Waqt*, August 7, 1979.
69. For a listing of the position of the 137 members of the United Nations with respect to the NPT, see John Maddox, *Prospects for Nuclear Proliferation*, Adelphia Papers #113, London: The International Institute for Strategic Studies, p. 34.
70. Thomas C. Schelling, "Who Will Have the Bomb?" in Augustus R. Norton and Martin H. Greenberg, *Studies in Nuclear Terrorism*, Boston: G. K. Hall, 1979, pp. 42–43; and *Nonproliferation Treaty*, Hearings Before the Committee on Foreign Relations, U.S. Senate, 90th Congress, July 10–17, 1968, Washington, D.C.: GPO, 1968.
71. Maddox, *op. cit.*, p. 2.
72. SIPRI, *Postures for Nonproliferation: Arms Limitation and Security Policies to Minimize Nuclear Proliferation*, London: Taylor and Francis, 1979, p. 10.
73. SIPRI, *Nuclear Proliferation Problems*, London: The MIT Press, 1974, p. 301.
74. Richard Betts, "Nuclear Proliferation and Regional Rivalry, Speculations on South Asia," *Orbis*, Vol. 23, No. 1 (Spring 1979), p. 170.
75. For an explanation of military security as the motivating force behind the acquisition of nuclear weapons, see Epstein, *op. cit.*, pp. 16–28.
76. Interviews, Islamabad, 1977, 1979.
77. It was announced by Islamabad on August 31, 1980, by Munir Khan, chairman PAEC, that Pakistan had joined the ranks of 12 technologically advanced nations by achieving self-reliance in the production of nuclear fuel from natural uranium. The fuel fabrication plant set up at Chashma has begun to supply KANUPP helping it slowly to reach the 80/90 megawatt capacity (137 being the maximum capacity). KANUPP was shut down for over a year for major overhauling. *Overseas Weekly Dawn*, September 6–12, 1980.
78. Shireen M. Mazari, "India's Nuclear Development: An Appraisal," *Strategic Studies*, Vol. II, No. 4 (Summer 1979), Islamabad, p. 57.
79. Statement by Foreign Affairs adviser Agha Shahi, The *Times*, London, March 8, 1980.
80. Maddox, *op. cit.*, pp. 6–7.
81. Richard K. Betts, "Incentives for Nuclear Weapons," in Joseph A. Yager, *Nonproliferation and U.S. Foreign Policy*, Washington, D.C.: The Brookings Institution, 1981, p. 117.
82. *Ibid.*
83. *Ibid.*, p. 130.
84. Interview, 1981.
85. For a transcript of the President's broadcast, see *The New York Times*, January 5, 1980.
86. *Ibid.*
87. CBS, *Face the Nation*, January 6, 1980.
88. NBC, *Meet the Press*, January 6, 1980.
89. *India-Pakistan Nuclear Issues*, Hearing Before the Committee on Foreign Relations, U.S. Senate, 96th Congress, March 18, 1960, Washington, D.C.: GPO, 1980, p. 1.

90. *Ibid.*, p. 3.
91. *Ibid.*, p. 4.
92. *Ibid.*, p. 5.
93. Interview, Washington, January 1980.
94. Harold Brown, Secretary of Defense, *FY 1981, DOD Report*, p. 227.
95. *Congressional Presentation: Security Assistance Program, FY 1981*, p. 145.
96. For example, Christopher Van Hollen, former deputy assistant secretary, NEA, "Leaning on Pakistan," *Foreign Policy*, No. 38 (Spring 1980), pp. 35–50.
97. *Nuclear Proliferation: The Situation in Pakistan and India*, Hearing Before the Subcommittee on Energy, Nuclear Proliferation and Federal Services of the Committee on Governmental Affairs, U.S. Senate, 96th Congress, May 1, 1979, Washington, D.C.: 1979, p. 17.
98. *Financial Times*, London, May 17, 1980.
99. GIST, Bureau of Public Affairs, *Department of State*, Washington, D.C., July 1980.
100. News Conference, September 15, 1980, Bureau of Public Affairs, *Department of State*, Washington, D.C., Current Policy No. 218.
101. GIST, *op. cit.*
102. *The New York Times*, September 25, 1980.
103. *Washington Post*, September 22, 1980.
104. *The New York Times*, September 25, 1980.
105. Editorial, *The New York Times*, February 9, 1981.
106. Address to the UN General Assembly, October 4, 1977.
107. Interview, 1979.
108. Quoted in *Pakistan Affairs*, Vol. XXXII, October 1, 1979, Washington, D.C. Embassy of Pakistan.

$$6$$

THE EVOLUTION AND
INTENSITY OF INFLUENCE

NATURE OF ALLIANCES

The ability of two countries to influence each other depends to some extent on their mutual beliefs and the contribution that each makes to the common enterprise. The relationship stems neither from love nor hate but rather from the joint fear shared by the countries concerned. In the case of the United States and Pakistan, there was a general absence of shared perceptions of a common threat. Even though both countries became entwined in a joint policy for defense, the fear felt by each was not identical with that perceived by the other. Thus, the manifestation of mutual influence was bound to be somewhat unusual.

Even the halcyon days of United States relations with Pakistan were marked by a divergence in focus. The threat of communist gains world-wide lured Washington into alliances with willing nations. Pakistan's location recommended itself greatly in the 1950s to U.S. plans for the containment of the Soviet Union and China. There was no doubt, as far as the United States was concerned, that the "free world's" primary fear stemmed from the potential of a communist onslaught carried out by its two major proponents: "Soviet Russia" and "Red" China.

While the U.S. focus was worldwide, Pakistan's primary focus remained regional. The war for the succession of the British Raj raged not only on the battlefield but also encompassed the political and diplomatic realms. India was the motivating factor for the Pakistanis, and United States' attempts to deny the centrality of the Indian problem meant that its

151

alliance with Pakistan was basically in trouble. The fundamental threat from India that conditioned all Pakistani responses rapidly transformed the South Asian system into a competitive arena for the United States and forced Washington to constantly balance its policy between the two regional rivals. It was indeed unfortunate that the need to please both countries made it extremely difficult, not to mention costly, for the United States to operate in a sustained fashion in pursuit of its interests and to mold Pakistani behavior so that it would redound to U.S. advantage.

The absence of joint interests detracted from the common enterprise. Despite the preponderance of power and asymmetry in its favor, the United States soon found that its range of options in Pakistan was limited, and the latter succeeded in circumventing the pursuit and exercise of influence by the former in a number of ways. First, by refusing to fall in step with U.S. threat perceptions, Pakistan ensured that the Unied States was not a major determinant in Pakistani decisions on key security issues. Second, Pakistan was helped by the fact that its need for the United States was balanced by the perceived U.S. need for Pakistan. The reciprocity of the need made it difficult for Washington to push hard for gains in influence for fear that such pressure would jeopardize its access as well as its presence. Third, because of the competitive nature of the international system, the United States found it more difficult to influence Pakistan than might otherwise have been the case. In the 1950s the Soviet Union was an alternate (even though uncultivated) source for potential help to Pakistan. China emerged in the 1960s and the 1970s, while the late 1970s and early 1980s were the decades of Arab sources of assistance. Had the situation remained one of monopolistic opportunity, the United States might have succeeded in receiving more tangible benefits.

HOW DO WE KNOW?

The evolution and nature of influence is examined in the U.S.-Pakistani relationship through a detailed study of the data covering their interaction. Familiarity with the political systems and key actors on both sides provides an absolutely crucial and salient index of the intensity of the influence attempts and successes or failures. Coupled with interviews with key decision makers, whose access to records is important in weighing the fluctuating events, the above technique is helpful in arriving at the picture in its entirety. Juxtaposed against known goals of both sides, policy outcomes serve as a measure of influence. Where outcomes are no guide to policy, knowledge of domestic constraints of a decision, or nondecision, can tell as much.

Influence is manifested in key issue areas and it can be studied and explained by a detailed examination of the same. The issues of arms sales and pursuit of the nuclear option demonstrate the presence or absence of influence in the United States–Pakistani relationship by identifying the goals of each side, the availability of options, and the fluctuations in policy as well as the intensity of interaction. Because these issues are of fundamental importance to the relationship, their outcomes provide important material for evaluating influence.

A superpower's capacity to influence is constrained by its unwillingness and inability to act beyond certain bounds. This study demonstrates that given the United States' proclivity to generally maintain the status quo, particularly in an unstable but important area of the world, it could not really press Pakistan to the point where its very existence would be in jeopardy. Events following the Soviet invasion of Afghanistan are particularly illustrative of this phenomenon. Despite deep commitment to nuclear nonproliferation and human rights issues, the Carter administration moved overnight to forget about previous pressures on Pakistan and did not, as could have been expected, use the precarious security situation created by a Soviet presence directly on Pakistani borders in order to force concessions.

The pursuit and even the exercise of influence is not unidirectional. In A's attempts to influence B, A is also affected, and it becomes an interactive phenomemon. This study demonstrates the many instances where the U.S.-Pakistani relationship involved not only A's (U.S.) impact on B (Pakistan) and vice versa, but was amply affected by C (India), D (Soviet Union), and E (PRC). In the post-1973 period, Iran and Saudi Arabia also have to be factored in. Part of the complexity involving influence stems from the fact that myriad relationships exist within and amongst nations that multiply the options for B and also constrain the decisions of A.

Influence that is institutionalized is a more lasting and therefore more desirable goal, at least as far as the source of the influence attempt is concerned. The United States–Pakistani relationship has suffered from the absence of interaction between institutional channels within each country, considering that relations ranged from periods of great receptivity (when key personalities in each were friendly) to periods of marked indifference or open dislike (when they were not). The United States entrée to the Pakistani military suffered particularly after 1965 because of the arms embargoes, the closing down of MAAG, restrictive arms sales policies, and the ending of the IMET programs.

Issue-specific aspects of influence are corroborated in this study. Pakistani success in getting the arms embargo lifted in 1975 is illustrative of the fruition of the influence attempt geared up for that specific purpose. Similar in spirit, though different in detail, were the results of U.S. efforts, that were directed at achieving specific behavior patterns on the part of Pakistan. While these attempts at influence were broad-gauged in terms of their time frame, they were only successful whenever they did not run counter to issues that were perceived to impinge on Pakistan's national security.

THE UNWORKING OF INFLUENCE

The study of the United States–Pakistani relationship is illustrative of the following points regarding influence. First, the lack of unity of view regarding the threat led to divergent behavior because of the U.S. attempts to sidestep the issue of the legitimacy of Pakistani perceptions, leaving an air of uncertainty regarding the entire proposition. Pakistani attempts to assure the legitimacy of its perceived threat moved it in directions bound to be contrary to those preferred by the U.S. Therefore, it is no wonder that access did not equal influence. While increase in United States access did not lead to increase in influence in the overall sense, it did increase Pakistani receptivity to the United States generally, which impinged on Islamabad's willingness to be influenced on some issues. Furthermore, the United States access to Pakistan remained a fact long after basic U.S. policy decisions (for example, arms to India in 1962 or the arms embargoes of 1965 and 1971) had vitiated any previous influence the United States may have had. The access was conditioned by the inherent Western orientation of the Pakistani elite. It provided a natural rapport between them and the U.S. in general, which was particularly pronounced in the military and civil service bureaucracy and accounted for the "like-mindedness" that had made Dulles sensitive to Pakistan in the first place. However, over the years, the lowered profile of the United States in Pakistan that resulted from declining aid and fewer military contacts dramatically affected this equation. A new generation of Pakistanis grew up without the exposure to the United States that had made previous groups more receptive.

Second, this study finds that levels of presence and influence are not correlated. Although the United States military succeeded in establishing a major presence in Pakistan fairly early in the relationship, it did not enjoy influence over Pakistani counterparts; thus it was not successful in reorienting the focus of the Pakistani military from India to the "Northern Tier." While the base at Peshawar guaranteed a presence in the area, it did not give the United States any veto powers or political concessions. And even though on certain occasions the presence of key officials (for example, Charles Burton Marshall as adviser to Suhrawardy) kept Pakistani policy in line on some East-West issues (and gave the United States limited influence), it still did not lead to a sustained U.S. ability to influence all aspects of Pakistani policy.

Third, the hypothesis that the greater B's economic dependence on A, the greater A's influence on B, is not confirmed. The nature of influence is such that it eludes even those countries who sit in a very powerful position vis-à-vis seemingly powerless and dependent ones. In the case of the U.S.-Pakistani relationship, the above phenomenon is amply demonstrated. The economic and military picture in Pakistan was particularly bleak at the time that contacts were originally made with the United States. The period spanning the early to mid-1950s was one of unparalleled power for the United States. Yet, despite the discrepancy in capabilities, Washington was not fully able to influence Pakistan into falling in line with the two main aims of its policy, namely, regional defense, and containment of the Soviet Union. Dulles' expectations of Pakistani manpower for U.S. enterprises went unrealized, and his concern for internal stability in Pakistan (a third U.S. goal) made him unwilling to push "like-minded" Pakistanis too hard.

Fourth, the hypothesis that the greater A's aid to B, the greater A's influence in B, is disproven. While absence of aid may deny any opportunities to influence, there is no necessary correlation between the act of giving aid and reaping influence benefits; this follows from all the arguments already put forward in the case of the third hypothesis. In addition, aid did not lead to influence because of the relative perception of the aid, i.e., in Pakistani eyes, U.S. aid fell short (despite Pakistan's allied status) of aid to India. Though Pakistan received 2.5 billion between 1955–65, India received $10.5 billion during the same period. In a comparative sense, Pakistan felt itself outmaneuvered by India, which detracted from the United States' ability to influence. Since the United States had always been concerned with the impact on India of its aid program for Pakistan, it was never able to up the ante sufficiently so as to be able to deal with Pakistani sensitivity. Overall, A's (U.S.) aid to B (Pakistan) was unable to buy influence because C (India) impinged on A's ability to give and B's perceptions of its relative value as reflected by greater aid by A to C.

Fifth, military aid is indeed more effective than economic aid in providing influence (even limited) for A over B. Pakistan's special need for the United States stemmed from its overriding concern with the rapid development of its military. All other problems dimmed in comparison because of the perception by its elite that without military strength the country faced defeat and annexation. In this context, the United States commitment to establishing and equipping five divisions for the Pakistani Army satisfied a critical need. When Ayub pushed for economic aid for Pakistan, he did so in the context of defense support. Conversely, when the United States cut off its military aid in 1965 but continued economic assistance, it failed to resuscitate its relationship with Pakistan. Furthermore, when the nature of United States security assistance changed as grants were terminated and sales became the pattern, Washington's ability to influence further diminished because it not only forced the Pakistanis to look for other and more reliable sources of supply, but it also led to a Pakistani refusal to accept the quality of aid that a United States sensitized to Indian concerns was willing to offer.

Sixth, this study confirms that the political use of economic aid diminishes over time. Because of the focus on military aid, United States ability to influence Pakistan declined sharply after the exclusive nature of military aid (i.e., concentration on *economic* aid for India) was ended following the U.S. response to the Sino-Indian clash in 1962. Since India always figured more prominently in Washington's calculations of economic aid, it restricted United States ability to call in IOU's from Pakistan. It is indeed easier to continue than to stop aid in most instances as was true of the U.S. in its dealings with Pakistan in the late 1950s when Washington had already begun to reassess its relationship but did not really curtail its aid substantially. However, because of the immediate pay-off in improved relations with India that some in the United States, particularly the State Department, believed would occur from a cut-off in aid to Pakistan, the United States was not as hesitant as it might otherwise have been in ending its assistance. Other terminations of U.S. aid, particularly military, reflected an admission of its lack of influence over the direction of Pakistani policy.

Finally, that influence is more likely to result from a higher degree of sophistication in the weaponry sent by A to B can be inferred from the U.S.-Pakistani relationship. The majority of weapons sent to Pakistan were, by and large, obsolete even at the time of delivery. While United States military aid promoted interaction with technical personnel, offered the United States a chance to bring Pakistani military for training to the United States (a potential target for influence), and allowed the MAAG to operate in Pakistan, there was never really a chance to permeate the Pakistani system because of the uncertainty of U.S. supply lines after 1965. Washington's unwillingness to sell Pakistan sophisticated weapons, based on fears of the effect of such a move on India, made Pakistan extremely resentful and unreceptive to United States overtures and influence.

TWO INSTANCES OF U.S. SUCCESS

Despite the accoutrements of power, instances of superpower influence are limited. This is demonstrated in the U.S.-Pakistani relationship as only two issues emerged in the entire period of interaction where the United States can be said to have had a modicum of influence over Pakistan. The first issue was the nondiversification of aid. The U.S. commitment to Pakistan was quite genuine in the 1953–57 period, but it was by necessity a limited one because of U.S. concern with India At first, even as they pressed for higher outlays, Pakistani leaders were happy to accept the U.S. aid package. By 1955, Ayub was distinctly uncomfortable with the slow pace of U.S-assisted military modernization program. While he made known his unhappiness, neither he nor any of the others made any serious attempt to seek assistance elsewhere. Soothing words from Dulles and Radford were sufficient to placate Pakistanis.

The second instance of influence in the 1953–57 period was reflected in Washington's ability to line up Pakistani policy on its side on international issues. This was the case even though it hurt relations with Arab regimes—despite the fact that pro-Arab sentiment ran strong in Pakistan. Some of this interaction stemmed from expectations of appropriate alliance behavior. However, it can also be tied to the overriding need for U.S. arms to buttress military strength against India, a matter of national security and an interest that demanded the necessary sacrifices, albeit painful ones. Suhrawardy's celebrated remark about the inadvisability of a Muslim connection for Pakistan because "zero plus zero still equals zero" has to be taken in the above context.

THE DOMESTIC FACTOR

A number of other conclusions about the nature of influence can also be drawn from this study. Linkage between a nation's domestic and foreign policy was demonstrated in both the United States as well as in Pakistan as domestic capabilities and needs were reflected in foreign policy responses. For example, the pro-Western perceptions of key members of the Pakistani elites led them, in the first place, to look to the United States for support. Later on, even when the ties between the two nations had been considerably weakened, Bhutto tried to revive them because of the domestic pay-off of renewed U.S. support in 1974–75. Similarly, the perceptions of key American decision makers, who were after all products of their own domestic environment, led them into an alliance with Pakistan. In 1971 as well as after 1976, U.S. domestic considerations compelled criticism of Pakistan and finally led to aid cut-offs because the price for sustaining the relationship was no longer commensurate with high political costs at home. Furthermore, in periods of (limited) United States influence in Pakistan (i.e., 1953–57) there were visible manifestations of U.S. influence in the Pakistani political system as epitomized in the person of Charles Burton Marshall who was the U.S. adviser to Mirza and Suhrawardy. In the case of Pakistani infuence, it was never as directly manifested because Pakistan was only one of many U.S. concerns. However, even so, at some key moments, for example in 1971, Pakistan's case was helped at critical points within the U.S. system because of Nixon and Kissinger.

In terms of actual changes in the domestic environment, the United States influence is often credited with the rapid growth in the power of the Pakistani military vis-à-vis the political system. While there may be an element of truth to this theory, it is nonetheless vastly exaggerated. The importance of the military in Pakistan stemmed from the conditions that surrounded the country's formation. Given the extremely painful (in blood and dislocation) nature of partition, there was very little chance for a balanced set of relationships between India and Pakistan. The over-reaction of Indian leaders to the formation of Pakistan and the over-sensitivity of their Pakistani counterparts ensured a continuous state of hostility that *both* expected would result in armed conflict at one time or another. In such a situation, the military was already a priority institution and would in any case have emerged as a key element given the preponderance of Indian power and the newness of the Pakistani political system. One sees the same pattern in Bangladesh (again having been born under traumatic conditions), where the military emerged at the top despite desperate economic conditions and the absence of direct super-power involvement.

WHITHER U.S.-PAKISTAN?

The inability of the United States and Pakistan to influence each other in the past stemmed from their differences in perceptions of the threat facing the two countries. The lack of convergence of interest resulted from the differing perceptions and made it difficult for either party to influence the policy of the other, except for brief periods and on limited issues. In order for the presently revived relationship to show demonstrably better results, Washington and Islamabad would need to arrive at some consensus on the threat, and attain some commonality of goals. How possible is that today?

There is a basic difference in Pakistani perceptions of 1982 from those prevailing in 1954. In contrast to earlier times, Pakistan today accepts the reality of a Soviet threat. The invasion of Afghanistan has put Moscow's troops directly on the Pakistani border. Pakistan's actions and sympathies—which have been with the Afghan Freedom Fighters, *Mujahadeen*, and against the Soviet-controlled regime of Babrak Karmal—

and the fact of the presence of two and a half million Afghan refugees in Pakistan, have displeased the USSR, whose daily calls to the Pakistani government to behave itself are a constant reminder of the threat Pakistan currently faces via Afghanistan.

Continued Indo-Pakistani problems also factor India into Pakistani calculations. However, there are differences between today and the mid–1950s because Pakistan now seemingly accepts Indian predominance. Furthermore, in 1982 Pakistan does not distinguish too greatly between the Indian and Soviet threats because it sees the 1971 Indo-Soviet treaty as having important military clauses that tie the Soviets directly into Indian policies. Therefore, the Indian treaty with the Soviet Union and subsequent Soviet occupation of Afghanistan have brought a commonality between the perspectives of Pakistan and the United States and removed the exclusively regional versus global focus that each respectively held. The regional threat of Soviet or Soviet-backed moves into Southwest Asia is seen as being the foremost cause for worry, not only in Islamabad but also in Washington; for example, the latest manifestation of a global policy to shift the "correlation of forces" in favor of the Soviet Union worries both the U.S. and Pakistan.

The United States has spelled out in no uncertain terms that its vital interests are involved in Southwest Asia. The threat to these interests is seen as coming from the USSR and in this context the following statement reflects the seriousness of the commitment:

> The Soviets must be continually faced with the certain prospect that a military move against the U.S. or allied interests risks a conflict that could be wider in geography, scope, or violence than they are prepared to deal with. *In particular, they must be convinced that an infringement on our vital interests in Southwest Asia would trigger a confrontation with the United States that would not be confined to that region.* (emphasis added)[1]

Renewed interest in Pakistan falls within the framework of the larger commitment to Southwest Asia that allows a new range of possibilities even as it also carries certain risks. Since the United States recognizes that its task of maintaining a favorable security posture requires a degree of cooperation from regional countries with sufficient support capabilities to enhance the U.S. effort, Pakistan becomes a useful ally. Not only does it have port facilities that could be opened to United States needs, but it also has an evolving military relationship with the country of major concern to Washington's policy, Saudi Arabia. Furthermore, Pakistan's importance is enhanced because denial of the same facilities to the Soviet Union is in the United States' interest. U.S. decision makers privately also count on the well-disciplined, though poorly equipped Pakistani army as one of the few effective regional fighting forces. They count on years of MAP/IMET interaction as having enhanced Pakistani receptivity to United States overtures and a resultant willingness to fight, if necessary, alongside U.S. forces.

Saudi Arabia's interest in exploring even a tentative military relationship with Pakistan seems to have Washington's blessing. The statement made by Prince Fahd while on a visit to Pakistan that: "Any interference in the internal affairs of Pakistan would be considered interference or injury to the Kingdom of Saudi Arabia,"[2] was welcomed by Washington. The United States saw in the relationship an immediate chance to augment Saudi defense (since the Saudis have only 50,000 regular troops and about 30,000 members of the National Guard), which is in the U.S. interest. Additionally, the move has two other advantages in Washington's perceptions. First, it sidesteps the issue of maintaining a U.S. physical presence at this time in Saudi Arabia, which is made more difficult because of the Saudi ruling family's sensitivity to such a presence. The second advantage to the United States of closer Saudi-Pakistani collaboration stems from the chance it offers of putting the U.S. relationship with Pakistan on a new footing, i.e., taking it out of the subcontinent where India has been, and is likely to remain a major concern, and moving it to Southwest Asia, i.e., placing it in the Saudi context. If this shift could be achieved, then official Washington will be free to offer a measure of U.S. political and military support to Pakistan whose borders with Afghanistan and Iran have become alive with serious potential for trouble.

There are a number of problems with this scenario that can be avoided only if Washington recognizes their existence. First, any attempts by Washington to explain to the Indians that because Pakistan has become a "front-line" state it needs U.S. support, and that this support also serves Indian interests, will not necessarily be welcomed by Mrs. Gandhi. Her inability to appreciate the presence of any Soviet threat makes it impossible for her to accept the very basis on which U.S. policy in Southwest Asia is built. If Indian concurrence is to be the prerequisite of a sustained dialogue with Pakistan, there are bound to be difficulties.

Second, whenever the United States aid program for Pakistan is fashioned primarily with India in mind, it is unworkable. At this juncture, Washington has to face the fact that Pakistan will not live with a package that seemingly gives India an overriding veto. If India is to remain the primary focus, it would have been indeed preferable not to have proposed any aid. The Reagan administration's handling of the F-16 package will be seen in Islamabad as an important index of the United States commitment.

Third, Washington must recognize that the Soviet invasion of Afghanistan and turmoil in Iran require a long-range response and not trivial pin-prick fixes. In the past, United States policy has often alienated friends and raised questions regarding its reliability. Dealing with this problem requires not only a military presence, but also a psychological buildup of the relationships, a high level of dialogue, and a certain amount of hand-holding of regional countries. This can be achieved in the U.S.-Pakistani relationship only if the United States considers Pakistani integrity to be of vital importance to its overall policy in Southwest Asia. A careful reassessment of this commitment, affirmed in 1973, 1975, and 1979, has to be made by Washington since it is even more appropriate today then it was in the past.

Fourth, if Pakistan's integrity is considered by Washington as being vital, then it would be in the United States interest to make Pakistan part and parcel of its Southwest Asia strategy. Such a move makes geographical sense and offers the possiblity of disengaging U.S. policy toward Pakistan from its baleful Indian context. The difficulties of constantly balancing the two, which have plagued past U.S. policy, can thus be avoided. Zia said in his interview that a factor in turning down the U.S. aid package was Brzezinski's unwillingness to include Pakistan in the same sphere of United States interest as the rest of Southwest Asia. Thus, any separation of Pakistan from Southwest Asia would be construed by the former as signalling a lower priority, which would make it difficult for Washington to obtain any closer cooperation for its policy goals.

Fifth, if terrorism has replaced human rights as the primary issue of concern for the Reagan administration, then some thought needs to be given by long-range planners in the State Department as to how this development will impinge on internal terrorism in Pakistan, i.e., covert external assistance to Baluchistan or overt external terrorism either by Afghanistan and the Soviet Union in concert with India or by India alone.

Sixth, the United States will have to be aware that efforts to press nuclear nonproliferation have had little success with Pakistan. In the past, Pakistan's nuclear option was erroneously linked by State Department and ACDA with support from Qaddafi and therefore was anathema to them. In the future, if the Saudi-Pakistani relationship evolves satisfactorily, Pakistan's nuclear option may possibly be considered by the Saudis to be a positive factor enhancing their security. If that were to happen, how will it affect U.S. concerns on the nuclear issue?

Finally, the United States should carefully weigh its options and policies before getting involved in Pakistan. To do so otherwise serves neither country. There should be some awareness in Washington that the return of the PPP to power in Pakistan could create serious problems for United States policy because of the ingrained anti-U.S. bias of the Bhutto women who lead the party. It is easy to recall that in 1971 the State Department fully opposed Pakistan, thus favoring the formation of Bangladesh. However, this policy did not translate into continued concern for Bangladesh after its formation. From 1976 to 1980, both the State Department and the White House worked against Pakistan on the nulcear issue and yet they dropped the opposition promptly when the Soviets invaded neighboring Afghanistan. Consistency may be "the hobgoblin of small minds," but it looms large in diplomacy and bestows its own rewards. In the final analysis, both countries need to recognize that their obligations toward each other must "reflect a shared conviction of common interest."[3]

Limitations of existing structures for U.S.-Pakistani relations are obvious in their present form. On the Pakistani side, decisions are made by very few and implemented by a core of professionals. In the United States, decisions on Pakistan impinge not only on the White House, the Pentagon, and the State Department, but also on Capitol Hill. Within the State Department alone, at least seven key bureaus get directly involved with major decisions on Pakistan, not counting the Office of the Secretary of State. Given this wide diversification, views get lost, sidetracked, or altered. Even where there is consensus at the top, it is difficult to control the decision as it filters down through the bureaucracy. The inertia generated by the bureaucracy often overwhelms the desires of the administration appointees who are at the top. Only an even and sustained relationship has some chance of nuturing the institutional ties that are necessary guarantors of much-needed continuity in United States' relations with Pakistan.

NOTES

1. General David C. Jones, chairman, Joint Chiefs of Staff, *United States Military Posture for FY 1982: An Overview*, p. vi.
2. *The New York Times*, December 11, 1980.
3. Henry Kisinger quoted in *The London Times*, July 30, 1981.

BIBLIOGRAPHY

Ayub Khan, Mohammad. *Friends Not Masters*. Lahore: Oxford University Press, 1967

Bhutto, Zulfikar Ali. *The Myth of Independence*. Lahore: Oxford University Press, 1969.

Burke, S. M. *Mainsprings of Indian and Pakistani Foreign Policies*. Minneapolis, Minn.: University of Minnesota Press, 1979.

Burki, Shahid Javed. *Pakistan Under Bhutto 1971–1977*. New York: St. Martin's Press, 1980.

Cheema, Pervaiz Iqbal. "Pakistan's Quest for Nuclear Technology," *Australian Outlook*, Vol. 34, No. 1 (August 1980).

Choudhury, G. W. *India, Pakistan, Bangladesh and the Major Powers: Politics of a Divided Subcontinent*. New York: The Free Press, 1975.

Feldman, Herbert. *From Crisis to Crisis: Pakistani 1962–1969*. London: Oxford University Press, 1972.

Griffith, William E. "Superpower Relations After Afghanistan," *Survival* (July-August 1980), pp. 146–51.

Hasan, Masuma. *Pakistan in a Changing World*. Karachi: Pakistan Institute of International Affairs, 1978.

Haendel Dan. *The Process of Priority Formulation: U.S. Foreign Policy in the Indo-Pakistani War of 1971*. Boulder: Westview Press, 1977.

Heeger, Gerald A. "Socialism in Pakistan," in Helen Desfosses and Jacques Levesque (eds.), *Socialism in the Third World*. New York: Praeger, 1975.

Fukuyama, Francis. "The Security of Pakistan: A Trip Report," *Rand*, N-1584-RC, September, 1980.

Kaushik, Brij Mohan and O. N. Mehrotra. *Pakistan's Nuclear Bomb*. New Delhi: Sopan, 1980.

Khan, Sultan Mohammad. "Pakistani Geopolitics: The Diplomatic Perspective," *International Security*, Vol. 5, No. 1 (Summer, 1980), pp. 26–36.

Kissinger, Henry A. *The White House Years*. Boston: Little, Brown and Co., 1979.

Rizvi, Hasan Askari. *The Military and Politics in Pakistan*. Lahore: Progressive Publishers, 1976.

Sen Gupta, Bhabani. *Soviet-Asian Relations in the 1970s and Beyond: An Inter-perceptional Study*. New York: Praeger, 1976.

Taseer, Salmaan. *Bhutto: A Political Biography*. London: Ithaca, 1979. *U.S. Security Interests and Policies in Southwest Asia*, Hearings, Senate Foreign Relations Committee, 96th Congress, Washington, D.C., US GPO, 1980.

Weinbaum, Marvin. "The 1977 Elections in Pakistan: Where Everybody Lost," *Asian Survey*, Vol. 17, No. 7 (July 1977), pp. 599–618.

Wohlstetter, Albert. "Meeting the Threat in the Persian Gulf," *Survey*, Vol. 25, No. 2 (Spring, 1980), pp. 128–88.

Yager, Joseph A. *Nonproliferation and U.S. Foreign Policy*. Washington, D.C.: The Brookings Institution, 1981.

INDEX

A-7, 70, 71, 77, 90, 91, 92, 93, 96, 100, 109
ACDA, 94
Ahmad, Nazir, 118
Ahmed, Aziz, 62
AID, 34
Arms Embargo, 22, 23, 24, 30, 57, 58, 60, 61, 77, 81–82, 86–89, 108
Arms Export Control Act, 91–97
Awami League, 34

Bhutto, Zulfikar Ali, 23, 29, 34, 49, 53–72, 74, 76, 87, 88, 89, 118, 120
Baluchistan, 42, 88
Bangladesh, 43, 47
Basic Democracy, 29
Benson, Lucy, 96
"Bilateral Trilateralism", 64
Blood, Archer, 34, 36
Bogra, Mohammad Ali, 5, 11
Brown, Harold, 101
Brzezinski, Zbigniew, 76, 102, 103, 109
Buckley, James, 104
Bulganin, Nikolai, 14
Bush, George, 43

Carter administration, 66, 72, 109, 131, 138
Carter, Jimmy, 70, 104, 127–131
CENTO, 12, 13, 25, 55 56
Chirac, Jacques, 128, 130
Christopher, Warren, 73, 102
CIA, 19
Council of Foreign Nuclear Policy, (CPNE), 128
Coup d'etat, 67–68

Diego Garcia, 56, 57
Desai, Morarji, 73, 135

Dobrynin, Anatoly, 41
Dulles, John Foster, 2, 5, 7, 12, 25

Eisenhower, Dwight D., 2, 12, 25
Elections-1976, 66–67
Energy Alternatives, 116–117
Enterprise, 44, 56

F-5, 93, 96, 104
F-15, 96
F-16, 104, 105
F-18, 92
Foreign Military Sales, 99
FMS, 84
Farland, Joseph, 34
Federal Security Force, 59, 68–69
Ford administration, 68
Ford, Gerald, 70, 88

Gandhi, Indira, 37, 38, 40, 45
Giscard d'Estaing, 128
Glenn, John, 135
Gromyko, Andrei, 38

Haig, Alexander, 105
Hasan, Mubashir, 60, 66
Hua, Huang, 43
Human Rights, 72, 73–74

Indian Army, 43
Indian Atomic Energy Commission, 62
Indian Civil Service, (ICS), 121
Indian Nuclear Bomb, 119
Indo-Pakistani War, of 1971, 34, 54
Indo-Soviet Treaty, 38–41
International Atomic Energy Agency, IAEA, 94, 116, 129
International Military Education and Training Program, IMET, 110
Islamic Conference, 64

Islamic Summit, 64
Israel, 64

Karachi Nuclear Power Plant,
  (KANUPP), 116–117, 123
Karachi Steel Mill, 32
Kashmir, 12–19, 33
Keating, Kenneth, 36
Kennedy, Edward, 37
Kennedy, John F., 9–10, 15, 23, 26
Khan, Liaquat Ali, 2
Khan, Mohammad Ayub, 2, 3, 4, 8, 9,
  10, 15–24, 29–30, 31–32, 42, 58
Khan, Munir Ahmad, 121
Khrushchev, Nikita, 14
King Faisal, 61, 63, 64
Kissinger, Henry, 37–38, 40, 42, 83,
  126, 128
Kosygin, Alexei, 31

Legal Framework Order, (LFO), 34
London Suppliers Group, 128

Marshall, Charles Burton, 6
Meer, Khurshid Hassan, 60
Military Assistance Advisory Group,
  MAAG, 6, 25, 58, 94
Military Assistance Program, MAP, 8
Military Rule, 30
Mirza, Iskander, 4–5, 12, 15
Mutual Defense Agreement, 4, 7, 11

Nehru, Jawahar-Lal, 13
Nixon, Richard, 31, 32, 37, 42, 53, 81,
  83
Nixon Doctrine, 2, 138
Nonproliferation Treaty, NPT, 122,
  124, 136
"Northern Tier of Defense", 2, 6
Nuclear Regulatory Commission
  (NRC), 142

"One unit", 33
"One Time Exception", 82, 84
Oil Import Bill, 118
OPEC, 63
Organization of Petroleum Exporting
  Countries (OPEC), 119

Pakistan Air Force (PAF), 43, 83, 89,
  96, 97
Pakistan Army, 30, 69, 83
Pakistan Atomic Energy Commission
  (PAEC), 70, 116, 118, 121
Pakistan Institute of Nuclear Science
  and Technology, (PINSTECH),
  118
Pakistan National Alliance, (PNA), 66–
  68
Pakistan People's Party, (PPP), 30, 35,
  59, 60–61, 66, 130
Percy, Charles, 139
Peshawar base, 8, 9, 10, 12, 32
Pirzada, Abdul Hafeez, 59, 60, 67
Plutonium-239, 125
"Point Four", 2

Qadaffi, al-, Muammar, 64

Radford, Admiral Arthur W., 2–3, 5, 25
Rahim, J.A., 59, 60
Rahman, Mujibur, 34, 35, 48
Ram, Jagjivan, 33
Rapid Deployment Force, (RDF), 98
Reagan administration, 103–106
Reagan, Ronald, 105
Reprocessing Plant, 123–131

Salam, Abdus, 121
SEATO (South East Asia Treaty
  Organization), 12, 13, 15, 55, 58
Shah of Iran, 56, 58, 63, 87, 88, 89
Shahi, Agha, 99, 102, 131
Shanghai Communiques, 85
Shastri, Lal Bahadur, 30
Siddiqi, Raziuddin, 118
Simla Accord, 54
Soviet Invasion of Afghanistan, 97, 99,
  101
Suhrawardy, Hussain Shaheed, 6, 15
Symington-Gleen Ammendment, 70, 139

Task Force-74, 44–47, 48–49
Tashkent, 23, 29
Third World Movement, 65

U-2, 9, 10

UN Security Council, 43
Uranium Enrichment Plant, 133–136

Vance, Cyrus, 103, 104

Washington Special Action Group,
   WSAG, 48, 58

Yahya, Agha Mohammed, 31, 35, 38,
   40, 41, 44, 48, 60, 83, 84
Yaqub, Sahabzada, 75

Zia-ul-Haq, Mohammad, 68, 69, 72–76,
   88, 102, 109, 117, 130, 131

ABOUT THE AUTHOR

Shirin Raziuddin Tahir-Kheli was born in Hyderabad (Deccan), India, and raised in Peshawar, in the Northwest Frontier Province of Pakistan. She came to the United States in 1959 and enrolled at Ohio Wesleyan University. Two years later, at the age of sixteen, she graduated from Ohio Wesleyan with a Bachelor of Arts and returned to Pakistan. In September 1962, two weeks after her marriage, she moved with her husband to Philadelphia and joined the M.A. program in International Relations at the University of Pennsylvania. Once again, she completed a degree in record time, receiving her Masters only nine months later. After a stint at the Foreign Policy Research Institute as a research assistant, Tahir-Kheli was back in Pakistan in the fall of 1964. She returned to Philadelphia two years later with her husband and infant daughter.

In 1967, Tahir-Kheli registered as a part-time student in the Ph.D. program at the University of Pennsylvania. She received her Ph.D. in August 1972. She is an Associate Professor of Political Science at Temple University and a Research Fellow at the Foreign Policy Research Institute in Philadelphia. Dr. Tahir-Kheli spent the 1980–81 academic year as a Visiting Research Professor at the Strategic Studies Institute of the U.S. Army War College.

Dr. Tahir-Kheli has published widely in the field of nuclear non-proliferation and security issues pertaining to Southwest Asia and is currently engaged in a study of Defense Planning in Pakistan (for Stephanie Neuman, ed. *Defense Planning in Less Industrialized States* (D.C. Heath, 1983). She is also editing two books: *U.S. Strategic Interests in Southwest Asia* (Praeger, 1982) and *The Gulf War: Old Conflicts, New Weapons* (Foreign Policy Research Institute, 1982).

DATE DUE